Additional Praise for
SAVE BIG

"Elisabeth Leamy hits the bull's-eye for this new era of thinking before you spend. It is easy to say spend less than you make. It is much harder to know how to do that regardless of income. If you follow Elisabeth's easy steps for how to save on life's big expenses, you will change your life."

—Clark Howard, host of the *Clark Howard Show;*
New York Times best-selling author of *Get Clark Smart* and *Clark's Big Book of Bargains*

"Elisabeth Leamy puts her finger on why so many Americans struggle with money—they're not thinking big enough! It's the big expenses, not the lattes, that will swamp your financial plans. In her lively, engaging style, Leamy shows you exactly where and how to cut costs so that your money finally works for you, rather than against you. Using the suggestions in this book will save you thousands of dollars. It's a great return on your investment."

—Liz Pulliam Weston, *MSN Money* columnist;
best-selling author of *Your Credit Score: Your Money and What's at Stake*

"I'm a lifelong pump-my-chest penny-pincher. I'm a believer in sweating the small stuff to save your way to prosperity. But Elisabeth Leamy's premise in *SAVE BIG* won me over. She reminds us all in an engaging way that it's not just the pennies that count. It's just as important to find big ways to save."

—Michelle Singletary, *The Washington Post;* nationally syndicated "Color of Money" columnist

"*SAVE BIG* takes a fresh and innovative approach to savings. Elisabeth Leamy focuses on big savings that have a lasting effect on our pocketbooks and our lives. Elisabeth takes on everything from healthcare to home purchasing, with clarity and precision. This book is a must read for people of all ages, no matter your financial knowledge."

—Mellody Hobson, President, Ariel Investments

"Elisabeth Leamy takes saving to a whole other level. Combining her savvy and seasoned knowledge of the consumer with common sense and a healthy dose of humor, she finds not only big dollar savings but a smarter path to better health. *SAVE BIG* is good medicine for all of us."

—Marie Savard, MD, ABC News medical contributor; author of *Ask Dr. Marie: Straight Talk and Reassuring Answers to Your Most Private Questions*

"Behavioral economists have found that people tend to take mental shortcuts when they make financial decisions—so they end up spending as much time choosing a mortgage as they do a big-screen TV. Elisabeth Leamy's wise book reminds us that we can save big by investing more time on major purchases—and shows readers step-by-step how to get the best value for their money. This book offers a much-needed road map through the world of 'gotcha capitalism,' junk fees, and dynamic pricing."

—Laura Rowley, Yahoo! Finance columnist; author of *Money & Happiness: A Guide to Living the Good Life*

SAVE
BIG

SAVE BIG

CUT YOUR TOP 5 COSTS AND SAVE THOUSANDS

ELISABETH LEAMY

WILEY

John Wiley & Sons, Inc.

Published by John Wiley & Sons, Inc., Hoboken, New Jersey.
Published simultaneously in Canada.

For general information on our other products and services or for technical support, please contact our Customer Care Department within the United States at (800) 762-2974, outside the United States at (317) 572-3993 or fax (317) 572-4002.

Wiley also publishes its books in a variety of electronic formats. Some content that appears in print may not be available in electronic books. For more information about Wiley products, visit our web site at www.wiley.com.

ISBN 978-0-470-55421-0

Printed in the United States of America

10 9 8 7 6 5 4 3 2 1

For Kelsea.
Mommy can come out of the office now . . .

Contents

PART III

Credit: Loans for Less

PART IV

Groceries: Guerilla Grocery Shopping

PART V

Healthcare: Curing High Costs

Foreword

All of us at *Good Morning America* know that Elisabeth Leamy is the real thing. She is a tireless expert on personal finance and consumer reporting. She identifies what works and what does not. And she wakes up each morning a passionate champion of all consumers.

And now she's written a book to help all of us tackle and tame the daunting financial problems in daily life: how to cut the cost of favorite groceries in half; why she would never buy a new car; and the best advice on health insurance she ever got (it came from her dad).

Like Eli, the advice is practical. It takes the fear and anxiety out of saving money. We know she practices it in her own life. She even makes it fun to be smart and in control.

All of us at *GMA* can turn to Eli any day of the week to guide us through our financial and consumer questions.

We are so glad that now our smart and compassionate friend, through her book *SAVE BIG*, will be your guide, too.

ROBIN ROBERTS AND DIANE SAWYER
ABC NEWS
NEW YORK, NEW YORK

Acknowledgments

Several people saved *me* as I was trying to help *you* SAVE BIG.

First and foremost: Big, warm, mushy thanks to my husband Kris and daughter Kelsea, for their love, support, and patience during the writing process. My parents, Patrick and Jeanne, and mother-in-law, Joan, also played an important part in enabling me to write this book in a short three months.

I am still overwhelmed that my wonderful colleagues Robin Roberts and Diane Sawyer wrote a foreword for *SAVE BIG*. They are simply the best.

None of this would have happened without agents Henry Reisch, who pushed me to write another book, and Mel Berger, who sealed the deal with the fine folks at Wiley.

Neighbors Roxanne, Kris, and Kyle Haltmeyer fed me, educated me, and even contributed a SAVE BIG story to the book. Neighbor Sam Serebin actually responded to 2:00 A.M. e-mails asking for graphic design advice.

Thanks to Kathy Sullivan, "the most frugal mom in America," for saying the words that cemented my BIG philosophy.

Jim Murphy of *Good Morning America* gave me his blessing. David Peterkin was so efficient and encouraging. Ida Astute, Donna Svennevik, Brett Oronzio, and Michelle Cutler made me look glam.

Candy Butcher, Michelle Katz, Todd Mark, Stephanie Nelson, Chrissy Pate, Marie Savard, and Carolyn Warren lent me their expert knowledge.

I was lucky to have Lauren Appelbaum as my thorough, thoughtful researcher just long enough to fill in all the blanks.

And finally, thanks to all the friends and family whose names I borrowed. You know who you are. Or you will, when you read the book!

ELISABETH LEAMY

Introduction

My savings sage—the one who crystallized everything I had ever thought about saving money—was a bleached-blonde mom wearing orange mood lipstick and towering, clear plastic high heels. She had this skittish way of laughing after she made an important point. You would think some imposing, paunchy, appropriately graying guy would have been my guru. But no . . .

Good Morning America had dispatched me to the Chicago area for a story about "The Most Frugal Moms in America." I admit I went with a resigned, well-at-least-I've-got-this-down-to-a-science kind of dread, expecting an interview about creative ways to reuse cottage cheese containers and old pantyhose.

But then I met this savvy single mom who had paid off her mortgage in five years. Twice. On two different homes. She had even gotten laid off and managed to stay home with her kids for two years—without a job—because she kept her expenses so low.

"How do you do it?" I asked, with awe.

"I try to focus on the big stuff," she replied.

Then she let out that cute, kooky laugh. But I didn't really hear it this time because I was having my own little epiphany. Of course! I had never put my philosophy into words before, but there it was. I've always preferred to save a *lot* of money on a *few* things rather than a *little* bit of money on a *bunch* of things. I like to SAVE BIG. Not small.

I've never read a book that sees it my way. They all list a litany of what I call Small Stuff Savings on the premise that "every bit counts." Switch to low-flow showerheads, save $5. Inflate your tires properly, save $9. Use your own bank's ATM, save $3. Pack your lunch, save $7. And the all-time favorite target: Skip your morning latte, save $4.

Brace yourself, now, because my advice is to go for it! *Have the latte!*

No, the Coffee Council is not paying me off. No, I'm not caffeine-addled. I don't even drink coffee! The point is, why give up life's little pleasures and conveniences when you can save money by attacking a few BIG expenses instead? In fact, you can save *more* money my way. You can SAVE BIG. The key is to identify the areas where you *spend* the most money, because that's where you can *save* the most money.

The five things we spend the most money on are:

1. Houses
2. Cars
3. Credit
4. Groceries
5. Healthcare

I'm going to show you how to save tens of thousands of dollars in these five parts of your financial life. For example, refinance into a shorter mortgage and you can save $103,536. Find out about a secret warranty where the manufacturer fixes your car for free and save $1,200. Raise your credit score just 100 points and save $93,600. Stockpile groceries when they're on sale instead of when you need them and save $5,772. And pick and choose your prescriptions to save $6,350.

As you can see, I don't believe in pinching pennies. I like to pinch $1,000 bills! In fact, every tip in this book has the potential to save you at least $1,000. Anything less than that didn't make the cut. This book contains $1,176,916 worth of savings in all. You would have to deny yourself 294,229 lattes to save that much money!

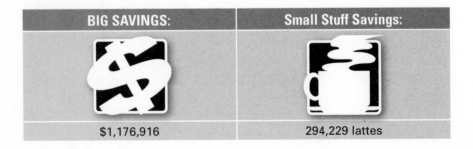

BIG SAVINGS:	Small Stuff Savings:
$1,176,916	294,229 lattes

These savings are possible for anybody who lives somewhere, drives places, charges stuff, eats food, or gets sick sometimes—and wants to do it all for thousands less. In the wake of the tumultuous economic times that began in 2008, there's renewed interest in saving money. My message is that it doesn't have to be a drag.

SAVE BIG (not small) and I think you will find that you save something even more precious than money: time. The puny savings ideas other authors tout take a lot of time. They need constant maintenance. They require willpower. In the face of a zillion different daily deprivations, most people fail. I find it much easier to channel my energy into a few BIG cost-savers that I only have to tackle every once in a while.

That's why most of the savings strategies in this book are things you only have to do every few years. The precise rankings of our top five costs don't really matter. The point is that they are BIG. In each Part of the book, I add up the BIG SAVINGS I'm about to show, then make a Small Stuff Savings comparison, just like I did with the lattes. You won't achieve these savings all at once, but each time you try one of my ideas you will SAVE BIG.

But wait! There's more! I've scattered BIG SECRETS throughout the chapters—insider information that will help you keep *your* money in *your* wallet. Then I summarize each chapter with my list of BIG TIPS, your action plan to get started saving.

My website, www.ElisabethLeamy.com, is a companion to the book, organized chapter by chapter. Every time you see a website or calculator mentioned in *SAVE BIG*, you can go to my site and I will link you to the precise page that you need, so you don't have to hunt for it. I've also included recommended reading and other resources on my site.

You can read this book cover to cover and become one super saver. Or read the house, car, credit, grocery, and healthcare sections when you need them as you go about your life. Each Part of *SAVE BIG* is broken down into bite-size chapters that you can get through in the time it takes . . . to enjoy your latte. Remember, you've got 294,229 lattes to look forward to, because I show you how to save $1,176,916 in the pages of *SAVE BIG*!

P A R T

HOUSES

Home of Savings

If you want to SAVE BIG, you have to figure out the areas where you *spend* the most money, because that's where you can *save* the most money. You might be sitting inside your number one expense right now: your home. According to the Bureau of Labor Statistics, we spend an average of $19,199 on our homes every year and those costs eat up 39 percent of our incomes.

I'll tell you right now that the way to cut those costs is *not* to install low-flow shower heads, yet that's one of the most common tips for saving money around the house. If you do it to save the environment, fine. But to save money? Please. That's Small Stuff Savings: five dollars a month at most. Peanuts. Pennies. Pathetic.

Instead, you can turn your number one expense into your number one savings. I will prove it in the coming pages. I'm going to show you how to attack the dumb, dull expenses that come with every home. The House section of this book contains $781,877 worth of BIG SAVINGS! You would have to install low-flow showerheads in 200 houses and bathe for 65 years to save that much money!

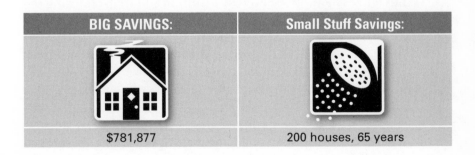

BIG SAVINGS:	Small Stuff Savings:
$781,877	200 houses, 65 years

Homes can be *pigs* that gobble up massive, messy chunks of our paychecks. But they can also be *piggy banks* where we stash a little cash for later in life.

Amazed that you can save that much on your house? It makes sense because what other undertaking has so many side costs associated with it that are in the thousands of dollars? Homes can be *pigs* that gobble up massive, messy chunks of our paychecks. But they can also be *piggy banks* where we stash a little cash for later in life. I can help you keep your home from being a hog.

Chapters in Part I are arranged chronologically, in the order you are most likely to encounter these adventures on the journey of home ownership, from buying a home to maintaining it and then selling it again and starting over.

- **Chapter 1:** In the opening chapters we tackle buying a home. I lay out why you should buy a house ASAP because *spending* money on this giant purchase is actually your number one way to *save* money.
- **Chapter 2:** Here I argue that your mortgage payment should equal your rent as part of my painless plan for affording a house and paying it off early to SAVE BIG. We talk about why you should stoop—not stretch—for a house.
- **Chapter 3:** In this chapter, it's time to make an offer. By negotiating with your realtor before she negotiates for your house, you can SAVE BIG. When it *is* time to negotiate, I tell you how to do the deal in a way that saves you thousands.
- **Chapter 4:** These next chapters are about mortgages. Choosing the right loan might be even more important than choosing the right house because it can save you $100,000 or more! We go over the pros and cons of the different types.
- **Chapter 5:** Next up, choosing a mortgage professional. I'll teach you the tricks bankers and brokers use to make money off of you and how to beat them at their own game and get a fair deal.
- **Chapter 6:** Then we conquer closing costs, the fees you pay in order to complete your loan. Fight junk fees and you can save another couple thousand dollars.

- **Chapter 7:** Once you are in the home, there are more ways to save. Have you ever thought of fighting your property tax assessment? Only 2 percent of people do and it's a way to SAVE BIG.
- **Chapter 8:** Refinancing is one of the truly unique opportunities to cut costs, but how do you know if the time is right? My simple Rule of 5s will help you decide.
- **Chapter 9:** Pay your mortgage off early and you can cut thousands of dollars and several years off of your loan. I'll show you where to find free money to do this.
- **Chapter 10:** Finally, when it's time to move on, consider selling your house yourself without an agent. Do this with even one of the homes you will own in your lifetime and you will SAVE BIG.

Ready to learn how to save $781,877? If you do that, it really *will* be a home sweet home. Let's get started.

Buy a House ASAP

You should buy a house as soon as possible, because it's the one investment you can make with money you have to spend anyway. After all, you have to pay money to live *somewhere*. If you currently rent, it's your biggest expense, but you can make that money serve *two* purposes by buying a place instead. You get a nest *and* a nest egg. By contrast, you can't sleep in a stock, and bonds don't keep you warm in the winter. Besides, many people can't *afford* to pay their rent *and* buy stocks and bonds, and others aren't disciplined enough to be reliable investors.

According to the Federal Reserve, the median net worth of homeowners is $234,000, while for renters it's $5,100. Buying a house is a forced savings plan where you can shelter your money *and* shelter your family. Go for it and you will SAVE BIG.

In this chapter, learn to SAVE BIG by:

- Making your housing payment serve two purposes: shelter and savings.
- Buying a house using somebody else's money—but keeping any gains.
- Locking in a monthly payment instead of paying increased rent every year.
- Making money tax-free in the form of real estate appreciation.

Why You Should Buy

In the post–housing bubble years, it's fashionable for naysayers to contend that houses are not good investments and that you should rent instead. They say that real estate doesn't appreciate as fast as the stock market. They babble that it's not a good idea to put all your eggs in one investment basket. They moan that houses are not liquid investments, so your money is stuck.

Guess what? It's all true.

But they're still wrong!

Let's explore why, by looking at the fabulous financial fringe benefits that home ownership brings—from the opportunity to profit, to fat tax deductions, to locking in a steady housing payment you can count on.

Probable Profits

The best part of buying a house is this: What other investment enables you to use somebody *else's* money to *make* money? That's exactly what happens when your house appreciates in value and you sell it for a profit. Even though you still owe money on your mortgage, the people at the mortgage company don't make you share the proceeds with them, now do they? What a deal! And to make this profit, you don't have to overhear a brilliant stock tip or try to comprehend bond rates. All you have to do is pay your mortgage.

According to the U.S. Census Bureau, the average purchase price of a home in the United States right now is about $250,000. (I've rounded for easy math.) According to the National Association of Realtors, property values have gone up an average of 6 percent a year since 1968. I believe in making a full 20 percent down payment, which is $50,000 on that average $250,000 house. So let's put those three factors together and see how we can profit:

 Making Money Using Somebody Else's Money

Cost of house	$250,000
Down payment	$ 50,000
Appreciation	$ 15,000
BIG RETURN =	**30%**

In this scenario, our home's value has gone up 6 percent, which is $15,000, but your return on investment is much greater. Why? Because you only put down $50,000 of your own money. A $15,000 profit on your $50,000 down payment is a whopping 30 percent return! If you made that kind of gain as a stock broker, you'd put out a press release!

Tax Benefits

But wait, there's more! Home ownership comes with lucrative tax benefits. The first benefit starts the moment you move in. The IRS allows you to deduct the interest you pay on your mortgage from your federal income taxes. It's the government's way of supporting home ownership and it will help you SAVE BIG.

Let's say you have a $200,000 mortgage with a 6.25 percent interest rate and you're in the 25 percent federal income tax bracket. Here's the average amount you will save in taxes every year:

 Mortgage Interest Tax Deduction

Annual mortgage cost before tax deduction	$ 14,777
Annual mortgage cost after tax deduction	12,242
BIG SAVINGS =	**$ 2,535**

That's $2,535 in tax relief that renters don't receive! I have a plan to use that "free money" to save even more money. You'll see how in Chapter 9.

Here's another tax treat courtesy of Uncle Sam. If you make money on a business or a bond, you have to pay capital gains taxes on the profit. But if you sell your *house* at a profit, the gain is tax-free up to $250,000 for individuals and $500,000 for couples.

Rent Goes Up, Mortgages Stay Steady

And finally, by buying a house you are locking in your monthly housing payment. By contrast, rent is almost guaranteed to go up. Since 1990, rents have risen more than 3 percent a year, according to Reis, Inc., a real estate forecasting firm. If you buy a house and choose a 30-year fixed-rate mortgage, your housing payment is set for decades. Even an adjustable rate mortgage payment can stay steady for up to 10 years. By buying instead of renting you are beating inflation at its own game by guaranteeing your payment.

Let's do some math to see how you can SAVE BIG by buying over renting. Say you have $1,000 a month to spend on either rent or a mortgage. Since rents go up 3 percent every year, but mortgage payments stay steady, you can SAVE BIG by buying. Check it out:

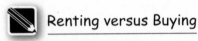 Renting versus Buying

Rent cost over 10 years	$137,566
Mortgage cost over 10 years	120,000
BIG SAVINGS =	**$ 17,566**

You save $17,566 over the course of 10 years! *That's* what I mean when I say SAVE BIG. Better yet, this math problem doesn't even take into account the fact that renters are giving money away to a landlord while buyers are paying *themselves* by investing in a home. If the home goes up in value by just the same amount that the rent went up in price—3 percent a year—the homeowner will have gained $83,287 on a $165,000 home!

There's one last benefit: When you own instead of rent, you can paint the whole place pink and blast your Bryan Adams albums if you want—and *that* is priceless.

Don't Rent, But If You Do, Negotiate

You may be able to wrangle a lower rent payment. Most people never think to ask, but at times when there are a lot of rentals on the market and not many qualified renters, you should. Do your homework. Know local rent prices; know how much your landlord is charging brand-new tenants and any specials being offered. Finally, know whether your landlord is struggling financially. Then make your case. It works especially well if you are a reliable tenant who pays on time and doesn't cause trouble. Use the money you save to start a house-buying fund!

Roll the Dice

Of course, home ownership is not Pollyanna perfect. Things can go wrong. For one thing, your home's value could go down instead of up in turbulent times. But think of it this way: A house is the *only* product we buy that even has the *potential* to rise in value. No car, TV, or computer will do that for you. Remember, property values have been going up an average of 6 percent a year since 1968.

So, I say, take a gamble on a *possible* gain. What's the worst that could happen? You *might* lose money? Well, if you keep paying rent, you will *definitely* lose money. Go for the *potential* earnings instead of the *sure* loss. (You will hear me say things like this throughout the book.)

There's always a chance your home's value will drop right when you need to sell, making it hard to get your money out. Yes, houses are nonliquid investments. But so what? I'd rather have a nonliquid investment than *no* investment. Later, I'll talk about the importance of buying for the long haul and buying below your means, which are both good ways to avoid this sort of scenario.

When to Buy

We've tackled whether and why to buy a house. Now it's time to talk about when. The answer is so simple: Buy a house when you are ready to settle down and your finances are secure. The two S's: settled and secure. Let's take *settled* first.

Settled

To figure out if you're ready to buy, ask yourself: Are you at a point in your career (and love life!) that you can commit to a location? You want to make sure you are prepared to settle down for enough time to recoup the closing costs you have to pay to get a mortgage.

The old advice was not to buy a home unless you planned to stay put for at least three years. Today, longer is better, because in the aftermath of the housing bubble, values are less certain. So I'd suggest that you aim to stay in your home for at least five years.

In fact, try to stay as long as possible. Don't be in a huge rush to trade up to a swankier place. My husband and I lived below our means in a modest condo for the first seven years of our marriage. Our monthly mortgage payment was ridiculously low, well below most rental prices in the Washington, D.C., area. Real estate was hot and friends kept asking, "Why don't you buy a *real* house?" The truth is, we loved those carefree years with no financial pressure, no yard work, and fun neighbors close by. And the condo tripled in value in that time, allowing us to buy a real house later when we were ready to start a family.

Set a Spousal Spending Limit

BIG SECRET

One way to save money is to limit the amount you're allowed to spend without your spouse's approval, and vice versa. Pick a number that works for your family: $50? $100? $500? Then vow that you will not spend more than that without checking in with each other.

Secure

Now for the other S, *secure*. Not only should your career be at a stage where you're fairly certain you won't have to move to another city, it should also be at a point where you make enough money to afford a home comfortably. I know, that's a big "duh." But *secure* refers not only to making money but also to not *owing* money. If you have credit card debt or other loan obligations, stop reading and skip to Part III, which is about credit. No house for you yet. I'll show you how to pay off your debts as fast as possible and *then* you can return to Part I and buy a home.

It's also a good idea to make a habit of maxing out your IRA or 401(k) before you buy a place. You should at least be contributing enough to get the full company match, if your company makes one. Yes, real estate can experience impressive appreciation, but a company 401(k) match is a guaranteed 100 percent return on your investment. Hard to beat!

BIG TIPS

- Use your housing payment for two purposes, nest and nest egg, by buying a home as soon as you can afford it.
- Lock in your housing payment by buying instead of renting.
- Use somebody else's money to make money on real estate.
- Make sure you are settled and secure before you buy.

CHAPTER 2

How Much Should You Spend?

It seems like you buy my argument that you should buy a house, because you're still reading. Excellent! Settled and secure? It's time. Now, how much can you afford to spend on a house? The way the mortgage industry answers this crucial question is with a mathematical formula based on a percentage of your income. I think vague, theoretical formulas like that get people into trouble. I'm going to show you a better way that's rooted in real life.

Want to know how much you can *really* afford to spend? Simple. Spend the same amount on your monthly mortgage payment that you currently spend on your rent payment. You may call me crazy, but you'll see that it's possible once you read my "Four Walls of Home Ownership," a four-part plan for saving, affording, maintaining, and paying your home off early. Once you know how much you can spend, it's time to find a house, and if you buy below your means you will SAVE BIG.

In this chapter, learn to SAVE BIG by:

- Ignoring what the mortgage industry says you can afford.
- Saving up an old-fashioned 20 percent down payment in a special house savings account.
- Making your mortgage payment equal your rent payment.
- Converting your house savings account into a house maintenance account.
- Stooping instead of stretching for a house.

Figuring Out What You Can Afford

When you're trying to figure out what you can afford to spend on a house, don't let a real estate agent or mortgage broker set your budget for you. After all, they are paid on commission, and the more you spend, the more they make. Not that they're dishonest, but they have skin in the game. Plus the entire mortgage industry goes about this the wrong way. They use vague formulas that aren't based on real life. Let's take a look.

The Wrong Way

During the real estate boom, most mortgage lenders were approving people for loans if their debts added up to 40 to 45 percent of their incomes. In their calculation, debt includes housing payment, property taxes, homeowner's insurance, auto financing, student loans, and credit card payments. Income means your monthly pre-tax income, before Uncle Sam takes a cut. This calculation is called *DTI*, your debt to income ratio. And I can tell you right now, 40 to 45 percent is too high. Worse yet, some banks were lending to people who had a DTI of 50 to 55 percent. That's outrageous!

Cancel Cable and Have More Money for Your House!

According to Consumers Union, the average American pays $720 a year for cable. That's way too much. If you're trying to save for a home, pull the plug on cable. You'll still be able to watch your favorite shows. Most broadcast networks offer their shows on their websites soon after they're shown over the airwaves. At www.Hulu.com you can find thousands of episodes of hundreds of shows—all free. And the website www.CancelCable.com has a show-finder tool that helps you find a way to watch your favorite shows some way, somehow.

If your debts are eating up 55 percent of your paycheck and income taxes are eating up another 4 percent or more, you have to wonder what's *left*? Actually, you don't have to wonder. I'll do the math for you.

Let's take a look at the case of Katherine and Calvin D. in Kansas who make a gross income of $50,000 a year, which is $4,166 a month. Here's how their monthly income would look with a 55 percent debt to income ratio and income taxes in line with their tax bracket:

 Irresponsible 55 Percent Debt-to-Income Ratio

Monthly income	$ 4,166
Monthly taxes	164
Monthly debt	2,291
Money left =	**$1,711/month**

By allowing nice people like Katherine and Calvin to take on oversized mortgages, lenders were leaving them just $1,711 a month (or $395 a week) to pay for *everything* else—child care, groceries, gas, parking, vehicle registration, home maintenance, heat, water, telephone, retirement savings, life insurance, clothing, haircuts, entertainment, and so on. That's just $56 a day, obviously not enough money to support a family of four. *That's* why you don't want the modern mortgage industry determining what you can afford to spend on a house.

The 28/36 Rule Back in the old days—the 1990s and before—bankers used a somewhat better formula called the 28/36 rule. It sounds almost quaint now, but here it is. Lenders used to require that your monthly housing-related expenses (mortgage, property taxes, homeowner's insurance) be no more than 28 percent of your monthly pretax income. As an additional safeguard, they also insisted that your total housing costs *plus* long-term debt (car loans, student loans, alimony, credit cards, medical bills) should be no more than 36 percent of your monthly pretax income.

The 28/36 rule is a much healthier one, but I'm still not a fan of formulas. Formulas are cold, hard numbers that just don't take into account all the hot, sticky situations that human beings get themselves into.

Using the 28/36 rule now, here's how much money Katherine and Calvin would have left each month after they pay their mortgage:

 Reasonable 28 Percent Debt-to-Income Ratio

Monthly income	$ 4,166
Monthly taxes	164
Monthly housing	1,166
Money left =	**$ 2,836/month**

That's more like it. By following this more old-fashioned formula, they are left with $2,836 a month to pay living expenses for their family of four.

I suggest you commit even less than 28 percent of your income to your housing costs if possible. I encourage you to take a hard look at whether you have any unique expenses that are not included in these standard formulas. Do you spend money to care for an elderly relative? Does one parent want the flexibility to stay home with the kids someday? Did you attend a prestigious but pricey college, leaving you with high student loan payoffs? The 28/36 rule is inadequate. It's just a starting point. I know a better way. Keep reading!

Dial for Dollars to Save More Money for Your House

BIG SECRET

Most people spend more than they need to on phone services. Craig, Amy, and Linnea S. of Illinois were spending $3,252 a year for three cell phones. They are super savers, so they paid the website www.MyValidas.com $5 to analyze their calling patterns and found they could save $1,936 a year by switching to a plan that fit them better! Many people are ditching their landlines, but if you don't want to rely totally on a cell phone, try Skype. A typical landline phone bill with a traditional phone company is $540 a year. Skype charges about $36 a year!

A Better Way

Here's a better way to figure out what you can afford. My method is based on real life. If you currently pay rent, buy a house with mortgage payments the same size as your rent payments. That's my formula. Complex, huh? If you can afford your rent payments, you will be able to afford your house payments. It's that simple. Don't believe it's possible? I've got a four-part plan to make it happen. I call it "The Four Walls of Home Ownership."

The Four Walls of Home Ownership

Houses need four walls to stand, right? Your financial foundation for home ownership needs to be strong, too. When you have all four of these walls in place, they will be a sound financial structure for the sturdy house you hope to buy.

- **Wall 1: Down payment = 20 percent or more.** For the first wall, you save up a substantial down payment of 20 percent or more in a house savings account. Stretch and strain for this sizable down payment because it's the key to everything.
- **Wall 2: Rent amount = Mortgage amount.** The next wall is making your mortgage payment equal your rent payment. That mortgage payment must include principal, interest, taxes, homeowner's insurance (PITI), and condo fees, if applicable.
- **Wall 3: House savings account = Maintenance account.** Wall number three is converting your house savings account into a house maintenance account to pay for repairs. You're already accustomed to saving this money so it's a painless transition.
- **Wall 4: Tax deduction = Mortgage prepayment fund.** The final wall of your sound financial structure is using the "free money" you get from your mortgage interest tax deduction to prepay your mortgage, saving thousands and paying the loan off years early.

I'm sure you have a lot of questions about how to build your Four Walls of Home Ownership, so allow me to explain in more detail.

Wall 1: Down Payment = 20 Percent or More   I urge you to save up a full 20 percent down payment. Those sudsy zero-down loans they were handing out during the bubble years have dried up.

They were a bad idea anyway. Why 20 percent? Because that's the amount that helps you SAVE BIG. If you don't make at least a 20 percent down payment, you're going to have to pay private mortgage insurance (PMI). PMI is insurance that covers the lender's loss if you stop paying your mortgage. It's not for your benefit at all.

PMI is a big bore and a bad deal. It costs about $150 a month on a $200,000 mortgage. At one time there were creative mortgages you could get to avoid PMI, but they are gone, too. You don't get to stop paying PMI until you have at least 22 percent equity in your home. Let's say that takes 10 years to achieve. Here's how much you can save by avoiding PMI:

 Avoiding Private Mortgage Insurance

Mortgage cost over 10 years with PMI	$161,880
Mortgage cost over 10 years without PMI	143,880
BIG SAVINGS =	**$18,000**

You can save $18,000 by avoiding PMI. *That's* why you want to make a fat 20 percent down payment. There's also a more profound reason: Saving a substantial down payment is how you prove to yourself that you're ready for home ownership. Suze Orman makes this point early and often and she's absolutely right. Here's how she puts it in her *2009 Action Plan* book: "If you can't afford to make a down payment, it's a sign you can't afford a home." How are you going to accumulate the money for it? Read on.

Help for Home Buyers

BIG SECRET

Check out first-time homebuyer assistance programs offered in most every state. They may be able to help you afford a home faster, by helping with your down payment or closing costs or mortgage rate. And the funny thing is *first-time homebuyer* is defined very loosely. If you haven't owned a home in three years, many of these programs consider you a first-timer. Kinda reminds me of a couple I know who vowed not to have sex for six months leading up to their wedding, so they could be "born again virgins." But I digress —*big* time. Whew. Here's a website with information about state first-time homebuyer programs: www.ncsha.org.

When I was a little girl, I desperately wanted a horse. I was so horse crazy that when westerns came on TV, I would go sit on top of the television and try to ride it. My parents made me get a goldfish first. Then doves. Then a dog. I was learning responsibility and all the while saving up for a horse in a special account. Finally, my parents said it was time. We split the $500 cost of a sweet, sway-backed mare named Sheba. I hated waiting, but I have to admit, I was finally ready for the early-morning feedings and other hard work.

Substitute your house for my horse and you get the idea. You don't even have to suffer through cleaning a goldfish bowl. Just open a special house savings account and stash cash in it to prove to yourself that you are ready for home ownership. Have part of your paycheck automatically deposited into this account so your greedy little hands never touch it. Maybe you're more disciplined than me, but I have found direct deposit into a savings account is *the key* technique that helps me save.

If you get a raise, sock that money into the savings account, too. I'm not into suffering. It's all about making changes that feel painless. Since you're not used to having the extra money from your raise, pretend you don't. Put it toward the house. Throughout this chapter there are BIG SECRETS with additional sources of savings you can put into your special house account. It's essential that this account be segregated from all your other bank accounts, because it is uniquely important. Buying a house is your number one way to SAVE BIG.

You may be wondering how you'll know if you've saved enough. When your down payment is big enough that your monthly payments can be the same as your rent payments, you're ready to buy. Read on for more about the monthly payment part of the plan.

Wall 2: Rent Amount = Mortgage Amount   Buying a house at a price point where your monthly mortgage amount can equal your monthly rent amount is the Second Wall of Home Ownership. It may sound unlikely that you can own a place for the same cost as renting one, but remember you've been stashing cash for a down payment as fast and furiously as you can. That is the crux of the entire plan. The higher that *down* payment, the lower your *monthly* payment.

Here's an example. Patrick and Jen M. of Illinois pay $1,000 a month in rent, which is close to the median cost of a rental nationwide, according to the U.S. Census. They also have $36,000 saved up to cover their down payment and closing costs. This young couple has been moving from rental to rental as they wound their way through graduate school—and they're tired of it. Can Patrick and Jen finally afford to buy a home?

Let's find out. If they use $33,000 of their savings as a 20 percent down payment, they can buy a home for $165,000. They will have $3,000 left over to pay their closing costs. Their loan amount will be $132,000 with an interest rate of 5.5 percent, the average rate as I write this, according to www.Bankrate.com.

 How Monthly Rent Can Translate to Monthly Mortgage

Patrick and Jen's Resources			Patrick and Jen's Mortgage	
Down payment	$33,000		Purchase price	$165,000
Closing costs	$ 3,000		Loan amount	$132,000
Monthly rent	$ 1,000	=	Monthly mortgage	$ 1,000

As you can see, Patrick and Jen's monthly mortgage (principal, interest, taxes, and insurance) will equal their monthly rent: $1,000. All because they have diligently saved a healthy, hefty 20 percent down payment, plus extra for closing costs. I'll say it again: The higher your down payment, the lower your monthly payment.

BIG SECRET

New Homes Can Make You Feel Used

It's often riskier to buy a brand-new home than an existing home. It takes a while to work the bugs out of new construction. Other considerations: If you're one of the first buyers in a new subdivision, there's a chance the developer will go under before it completes the neighborhood, leaving you in a half-built wasteland. On the flip side, if you go to sell your house in a couple of years, you may be in competition with brand-new houses the developer is still constructing. Why would buyers choose your house when they can customize a brand-new one to their tastes? Finally, new neighborhoods haven't had time to establish a true value yet. It's easier to determine the appropriate price of an older, existing home so you don't overpay.

You may be thinking that not everybody pays $1,000 in rent each month, so how can this advice be sound? Converting rent amount to mortgage amount works because where rents are higher, home prices are higher, too. For example, rental prices are higher in New York City as are home prices. Purchase prices are lower in North Carolina, but so are rental prices. The two don't move precisely in tandem, but close enough.

Wall 3: House Savings Account = Maintenance Account The Third Wall of Home Ownership is converting your house savings account into a house maintenance account. Remember how you set up a house savings account to save for your down payment? Since you've made your mortgage equal your rent, your monthly out-lay remains the same. That means you will be able to keep putting the same amount of money into this account each month. You will now use that pot of money to pay for maintenance. You're used to setting aside this money, so it should be painless. Painless is my goal.

Everybody always preaches about the importance of having a home maintenance fund. They're right. The most common rule of thumb is that each year you should save 1 percent of your home's purchase price for maintenance. On a $250,000 house that would be $2,500. Since you've been saving so aggressively for your down payment, you are covered. When the furnace goes cold or the air conditioner burns up, you'll be ready.

Wall 4: Tax Deduction = Mortgage Prepayment Fund The Fourth Wall of Home Ownership is using your tax deduction to prepay your mortgage. The IRS allows you to deduct the interest you pay on your mortgage from your federal income taxes. Many people use this windfall to stretch for a more expensive house. Instead, I want you to use it to pay your mortgage off early. Do so and you will SAVE BIG. *Really* BIG. This is such an exciting savings oppor-tunity that I've written an entire chapter about it. You can read the jaw-dropping details in Chapter 9.

So there you have it. My Four Walls of Home Ownership help you save for a house, afford the monthly payments, maintain the place and pay it off early—all so you can SAVE BIG.

Buy a Foreclosed Home

When somebody can't make their mortgage payments and the bank seizes and sells off their house, it's rotten for them but a tremendous financial opportunity for you. According to real estate website www.RealtyTrac.com, foreclosed homes typically sell at a 20 to 40 percent discount. Let's start with the national average home price of $250,000 and see what happens with even the low-end discount of 20 percent:

Benefit of Buying a Foreclosed Home

National average home sales price	$ 250,000
Foreclosed house at 20% discount	200,000
BIG SAVINGS =	**$ 50,000**

Wow, what a bargain! You can save big—$50,000—by buying a foreclosed home. Just be sure to assemble a team of experienced professionals to help you through the headaches involved in purchasing a foreclosed property.

Don't Stretch for a House

If your rent amount translates into less house than you were hoping for, suck it up. Seriously. It's much easier to adjust your housing aspirations to your budget than the other way around. You can choose a cheaper house. You can't necessarily make more money. Perhaps your first home will have to be a modest one. I recommend it. It's less stressful. Buy a condo instead of a townhouse, a townhouse instead of a single family home. If you're gutsy, buy in an emerging neighborhood that is just starting to be rediscovered. You'll probably have even more profit potential.

I'm sure you've heard the advice to stretch for the best house you can afford. You can easily guess that I am against that thinking. Yes, I want you to find a house that will delight you when you come home to it, but I don't want you to come home and cringe when you pass the pile of bills on the front hall table. As far as I'm concerned, the right house is one below your means. Don't stretch for a house. *Stoop* for a house!

In her book *50 Simple Things You Can Do to Improve Your Personal Finances,* syndicated columnist Ilyce Glink puts it this way: "Buy the smallest, cheapest . . . least fixed up house on a very good block in the best school district you can afford." I couldn't agree more. She's making a few great points about the value—and resale value—of your home. So let's go over them piece by piece.

- **Smallest.** McMansions are out. The not-so-big house is in. Don't pay for more square footage than you will use. How many people have formal living rooms they only set foot in once a year?
- **Cheapest.** The message here is to buy a house that is inexpensive compared to the ones around it. If you buy the priciest house on the block, the cheap ones drag its value down. Buy the cheapest, and the others will pull your home's value up.
- **Least fixed up.** If the house is not fixed up, *you* can be the one to bring it up to the level of the ones around it. This is a great way to turn a profit, especially if you are handy enough to do some of the work yourself.
- **Very good block.** By buying on a very good block, you get the enjoyment of living in this great neighborhood, for less than the people around you. And when it's time to sell, the quality of the block will do wonders for your property value.
- **Good school district.** Even if you don't have children, houses in good school districts have a record of going up in value faster. It's all supply and demand. There will be lots of demand for your house when you sell.

BIG TIPS

- Don't rely on the mortgage industry to tell you what you can afford.
- Start a special house account to save up a 20 percent down payment.
- Make your mortgage payment equal your rent payment.
- Turn your house savings account into your house maintenance account.
- Use your mortgage interest tax deduction to prepay your mortgage.
- Buy below your means.

CHAPTER

Doing the Deal

Once you've used the Four Walls of Home Ownership to figure out what you can afford, it's time to look for four physical walls you can move into: your house. A house below your means, of course. Wouldn't it be nice if once you find the perfect one you could save even more by knowing the best way to close the deal? You can.

The first step is to get your realty services for less by negotiating your agent's fee. The next step is to get the actual real estate for less by learning to negotiate, tycoon-like, on the price of the property. Notice, I used the term *real estate* rather than *home* here? At this stage of the game, it helps to think of it as investing in real estate rather than buying a home. Stay a little emotionally detached so you can make a great deal and SAVE BIG!

In this chapter, learn to SAVE BIG by:

- Negotiating with your agent before they negotiate for you.
- Making a winning offer.
- Outnegotiating the seller.

Saving Big on Real Estate Agents' Fees

Traditionally, residential real estate commissions are 6 percent of the purchase price. That commission is split between the seller's agent and the buyer's agent. As we've been discussing, the median home price in the United States is about $250,000. A 6 percent commission on a $250,000 home is $15,000. That's big bucks that people blindly pay. Question is, are the services that your buyer's agent is providing you really worth that much money? Sometimes yes, other times no. I've had one of each in my home-buying background.

When I was searching for my current house, my agent, Julie-Ann K., (a former television producer known for her ferocious work ethic), earned her commission by prescreening 200 houses for me. Yes, 200 houses! Julie-Ann would go see them first to figure out if they were worth my time. Later, her knowledge proved to be absolutely essential when we got into a bidding war with five other families over the house I wanted.

By contrast, when I bought the condo I owned previously, I was already renting in the community where I was looking, so I knew I wanted to live there. Plus, I found the place I wanted by attending a series of open houses on my own. All the agent really did was help me prepare the offer. Offers are important, but in many areas, like Washington, D.C. where I was looking, an offer is just a form that you fill out. Is form-filling worth thousands of dollars? I don't think so.

I know you're thinking, "Why should I care? The seller pays the agents' commissions, not me." Yes and no. True, the commissions come out of the purchase price, but *you* are the one paying that price. It's really your money.

So here's what you do. Assess how many services your agent is really going to provide you and then negotiate the commission accordingly. Many buyer's agents will take 2 percent rather than 3 percent, especially if they recognize that working with you is going to be light duty for them. Let's do the math for that $250,000 average home.

 Bargain with Your Agent and Save

House price	$250,000
3% commission	$ 7,500
2% commission	5,000
BIG SAVINGS =	**$ 2,500**

As you can see, you SAVE BIG if you simply negotiate with your agent before they negotiate for you. By doing so, you could have $2,500 more to put toward your house. It might even be enough to cover your closing costs. One easy way to get the 1 percent back from your agent is to have them credit it to you at closing. Agents are familiar with this simple procedure and will know just what to do if you negotiate such an arrangement. The settlement attorney who closes your loan will simply cut your agent a check for 2 percent instead of 3 percent, and credit the difference to you.

Do You Need an Agent at All?

I know real estate agents are hating me about now, but you may not need an agent to help you buy a house at all. There. I've said it. There's too much money at stake to be polite. Whether or not you need an agent depends on how extensive your search will be and how intensive your negotiations will be. I've done it both ways. (*Selling* a house without an agent is a blockbuster money-saver, too, and I'll discuss that in detail in Chapter 10.)

Remember how I said an agent helped me fill out the offer form for my condo, the first home I ever purchased? Well, there's more to the story. The seller countered my offer and I didn't think the counteroffer was good enough. So I walked away. Disheartened, I stopped my search for a couple of months. The contract I had entered into with my agent expired. I found I was still daydreaming about that perfect condo and it was still on the market.

So I approached the seller directly. Remember, I already lived in the community. We were neighbors. I could see the condo I coveted from the bedroom window of the one I rented. I asked the seller if she'd like to sell it to me on a for-sale-by-owner basis. She wasn't comfortable with that because her agent had done a lot of work marketing the place. We struck a deal to pay her agent 3 percent and discount the price by another 3 percent, since my agent was out of the picture. I saved about $5,000 on the deal. See?

Benefit of Working without a Buyer's Agent

Price paying two agents commission (6%)	$179,000
Price paying one agent commission (3%)	173,630
BIG SAVINGS =	**$ 5,370**

My own story came about in a backwards sort of way, but here's how you could put the idea to use. If, for whatever reason, you don't need much help searching for a home, consider looking on your own. Properties that are for sale by owner could be the best deals of all, because the owners can be more flexible with the price given that *they* don't have to pay an agent. Or you can make an offer on a house that *is* represented by an agent, but ask that he take only his 3 percent commission. Believe it or not, when people don't request this, seller's agents sometimes scoop up the entire 6 percent commission, even though they haven't done any extra work.

If you don't use an agent, you may still want some help writing up the offer. As I said, in many jurisdictions it's just a basic form. But if you're not confident doing it yourself, hire a real estate attorney to help you. We all know lawyer's fees are high, but not as high as real estate agents' commissions. You'll pay by the hour for a couple of hours of work. I bet you'll spend a tenth of what you would on real estate commissions.

The All-Important Offer

Once you've found the right house, it's time to focus on paying the right price. This is exciting stuff because, since it is the single biggest purchase you will make in your lifetime, it could be the single biggest savings. You've already chosen a home in an appropriate price range. Now let's see if you can push the price down even further.

Who's Got the Upper Hand?

Your first step in determining your offer is to figure out who has more power. Is it a buyer's market, where there are more homes for sale than there are buyers? Is it a seller's market, where the opposite is true? Or is it a balanced market with roughly equal supply and demand? The state of the real estate market determines your entire approach.

Don't base your conclusions on what you hear on the national news. Even if real estate nationwide is sluggish, it is possible for local neighborhoods to be hot and vice versa. So you need to focus in on the local data. For instance, a good indicator is the number of days houses are remaining on the market before selling. Agents call this the days on market (DOM). Find out the DOM for the house you are interested in, but also for the entire neighborhood.

If it's a buyer's market, you will be able to make an offer significantly below the asking price. On top of that, you can also request that the seller pay some or all of your closing costs. You even have the upper hand in choosing a closing date that is convenient for you. (But you may want to give the seller the closing date they want in exchange for an even lower price.)

If it's a seller's market, wait until it's a buyer's market. Just kidding. Waiting could save you money, but it might not, because if homes keep appreciating, the entire market will be higher priced when you finally jump in. If you are settled and secure and your family is ready to buy a home, go for it, as long as you plan to live there for at least five years. In a seller's market, the key is to make a *clean* offer, free of messy complications like demands for repairs or waiting for your existing home to sell.

What Are the Seller's Needs?

Even in a seller's market, the seller may have problems or needs that give you power. For example, divorces and deaths can create opportunities for buyers because sellers often want out fast. In addition, vacant homes often mean somebody is making more than one housing payment. Contact the seller's agent to learn about the seller's needs so that you can better plan your offer.

Here are some examples of needs that can spell opportunity for you. Perhaps the seller needs a long escrow period before moving out of the home. Maybe the seller has had previous real estate transactions fall through, and will be comforted by a substantial good-faith deposit and a lender's preapproval letter. You could encounter a seller like my husband, who absolutely hates to deal with home repairs and would lap up an as-is offer.

Skip Home Warranties

If the seller is offering a home warranty, ask for a cash credit toward closing costs instead. Home warranties have so many exclusions and age limits that you're better off using the cash to pad your own home maintenance fund. For 10 years, Jackie H. paid $375 annually for a home warranty. When her air conditioner blew, she figured it was about to pay off. Sure enough, the technician said her AC unit was hopeless and needed to be replaced. But then came the let down. The warranty company refused to cover Jackie's air conditioner because it was 21 years old. The policy only covered appliances up to 20 years old.

If possible, find out how much the sellers paid for the property. If they haven't lived there long, you can guess that they are probably concerned about getting enough money out of the house to recoup their closing costs and pay off their mortgage. If they bought the house decades ago and didn't put any major money into it, you will know that they are looking at a nice potential profit. Perhaps they have more price flexibility.

Finally, find out if there are other offers. It doesn't make sense to make a lowball bid if you have competition. In fact, if you're trying to bag a bargain and there are multiple offers, maybe it doesn't make sense to bid at all.

I believe you should cater to the seller's needs as much as possible, because it's free. These little concessions don't cost you anything. In the end, price is paramount, but if your price is close enough and you've offered the sellers everything else they want, there's a better chance they'll accept.

The Opening Bid

Which brings us to price. If you're working with a real estate agent, don't expect her to tell you how much to offer. Some will, but many decline. Why? For fear you won't get the house and will be mad at them for suggesting too low a price. Or that you *will* get the house—too easily—and will be mad at them for suggesting too high a price. Besides, it's your money and your mortgage payment, so it should be your decision.

The most helpful thing you can do to decide how much to offer is to look at comparable sales in the neighborhood. Appraisers look only at comparable sales that have taken place in the past six months, and you should, too. Be sure they are substantially similar to the

Buy December through February for a Better Price

According to the National Association of Realtors, winter is the slow season for home sales. For one thing, people go Christmas shopping instead of house shopping. For another, many buyers want to wait until summer and move when their kids are out of school. People with homes to sell can get downright desperate. You could use this to your advantage.

home you are interested in. There will always be differences, and the toughest task is to assign dollar amounts to those differences. Then add or subtract those dollar differences from each house.

Finally, take the average of all your adjusted comps and see how that compares to the house you want. Is the asking price above or below the average comparable figure you've come up with? One more number you can look at is the gap between the asking price and the selling price of homes in the neighborhood. If you see a clear pattern—maybe every home sold for about 5 percent less than the asking price—that is very instructive.

Once you've determined the price you want to pay, many experts suggest making your opening offer 10 percent less to leave room for negotiation. I think that's a reasonable rule of thumb. I would always err on the low side, because I'd rather offend the seller than overpay. There's so much money involved that I'm not worried about helping anybody save face.

Asking the Seller to Pay Some Closing Costs

In a slow real estate market, you may very well be able to get the sellers to chip in and help you buy their house. I know, it sounds goofy, but it happens all the time. It's all psychology.

For example, Phil C. and Mary B. of Florida coveted a cute St. Petersburg house with an idyllic deck and luxurious hot tub, but they needed to get the price down. Rather than ask the sellers to lower their price beyond a certain point, they asked them to help pay their closing costs. Phil and Mary recognized that this way, the sellers still got to brag that they sold their house for an impressive price. That price is what would be published in fine print in the local paper and so on. But this savvy couple knew that they had actually paid thousands less than that because the seller contributed to their closing costs.

There are a few different ways to structure this closing cost assistance.

1. In a super-slow market, you can ask the seller to cover all the closing costs.
2. In a balanced market, you may come to a compromise in which the two parties split the closing costs down the middle, even the ones traditionally paid by the buyer.

3. Another option is to have the seller credit you back cash at settlement which can be used for closing costs.

4. And finally, some people ask the seller to pay one or two points (1 or 2 percent of the purchase price) toward closing. The deal is often structured this way if the purchaser wants to use this money to buy down the interest rate. (More on paying points in Chapter 4.)

Never Skip the Home Inspection

Even in a seller's market you don't have to give up your home inspection. During the real estate surge, when prospective buyers were getting into bidding wars, many buyers were waiving their right to a home inspection to make themselves more attractive as buyers. Terrible idea! And unnecessary! Do a pre-inspection instead. Hire a home inspector to check out the property *before* you make an offer on it. That way your offer is not contingent upon a home inspection. Rather, if the inspection uncovers horrible flaws, you won't make an offer at all.

Negotiating the Final Contract

Your offer should give the seller no more than 24 hours to make a decision. Any more than that is torture—for you. The sellers will either accept your offer, reject it, or make a counteroffer. If it's a counteroffer, veteran negotiators suggest raising the price of your next bid by less than the sellers lowered their price. Psychology again, to show you have more resolve about your price than they do.

Whatever happens, many experts suggest you should only offer two prices beyond your initial one. Prolonging negotiations past that point is fruitless, unless the two sides are just going back and forth about logistical details like the closing date and who gets to keep the freezer in the basement. (Hint: You want the freezer, so you can SAVE BIG by stockpiling groceries, as described in Chapter 23!)

BIG TIPS

- Negotiate to pay your agent 2 percent instead of 3 percent.
- Consider buying without the help of an agent.
- Learn the seller's needs and play to them.
- Offer 10 percent less than what you want to pay.
- Ask the seller to pay some closing costs.

CHAPTER 4

Getting a Good Mortgage

Shopping around for a mortgage is just as important—though not as fun—as shopping around for a house. In fact, it's more of a quest, an odyssey. It's that important. Yes, quests and odysseys take some time, but you are going to have this loan for some time, too. At least three years—maybe 30. It doesn't make any sense to pour all this time into finding the right house at the right price and then get the wrong loan. The wrong loan will cost you money.

People in the industry call home loans mortgage *products,* and you should think of them that way, too. As I argue in my little rant at the beginning of Part III, the credit section, credit is a product with a price. A mortgage is the biggest kind of credit you can buy, so it pays to pay attention. Literally. I'll tell you how to choose the right one and SAVE BIG.

In this chapter, learn to SAVE BIG by:

- Understanding different mortgage types and choosing the right one for you.
- Applying for an FHA mortgage that only requires 3.5 percent down.
- Paying points only when it's beneficial.
- Locking in your interest rate at the right time.
- Rejecting prepayment penalties.

Picking the Right Mortgage Product

There are lots of different types of mortgages and there is no one right choice for everybody. It all depends on your circumstances. The trick is to choose the ideal mortgage that helps you cut costs. In this section, I describe each mortgage type and then tell you in what situations that type of mortgage is a good idea.

Fixed-Rate Mortgage

The fixed-rate mortgage is your father's loan, the most traditional, safe type of mortgage available. There was a time when it was the *only* type of mortgage available. With this product, your principal and interest payments remain the same for the life of the loan. That can be comforting. It's nice when your income goes up over the years but your mortgage remains the same. On the other hand, with a fixed-rate mortgage, if interest rates drop significantly, there is no way for you to benefit except by refinancing into another loan.

You Can Get an Energy-Efficient Mortgage

These mortgages are part of a federally recognized program that gives you a larger loan if you purchase an energy-efficient house or agree to make energy-efficient upgrades. It's not that lenders have gone green, necessarily. Rather, they figure that the less money you have to spend on energy, the more green you will have available to send *them* for your mortgage. The federal government estimates that if you would normally qualify for a $133,000 mortgage, you could qualify for a $142,000 energy-efficient mortgage!

Fixed-rate mortgages come in 10-, 15-, 20-, 30-, and 40-year terms. Don't even consider a 40-year mortgage. It stretches out the interest payments far too long, costing you tens of thousands of dollars. A 30-year fixed is by far the most common and it is perfectly respectable. But if you can afford a 10-, 15-, or 20-year loan instead, you will SAVE BIG because they typically come with lower interest rates and you won't be paying that interest for as long since the loan term is years shorter.

To give you an idea of the BIG SAVINGS, let's shop for 15- and 30-year fixed-rate mortgages on a $200,000 loan. As I write this, the 30-year mortgage is available at 6 percent interest, while we can get the 15-year mortgage at 5.85 percent interest. Here's how the lower interest rate and shorter loan term help us SAVE BIG:

Benefit of 15-Year Mortgage

Length of Mortgage	Interest over Life of Loan
30 years	$ 231,676
15 years	100,879
BIG SAVINGS =	**$130,797**

Nice! We'd all love to save nearly $131,000 in interest over the life of our mortgage. Of course, you have to weigh whether you can afford the substantially higher monthly payment that you have to make in order to pay for the 15-year mortgage. The monthly payment on the 30-year loan is $1,199, but the payment on the 15-year is $1,672—$473 dollars more per month. That's pretty hefty.

Let's see if the monthly payment is more manageable on a 20-year fixed-rate mortgage. The interest rates are the same, 6 percent for the 30-year and 5.85 percent for the 20-year, so we're not sacrificing anything if we choose to go with the 20-year mortgage instead of the 15-year. Here's how the savings play out:

Benefit of 20-Year Mortgage

Length of Mortgage	Interest over Life of Loan
30 years	$231,676
20 years	139,746
BIG SAVINGS =	**$ 91,930**

Well, $91,930 is still big savings. And the monthly payment on the 20-year mortgage is $1,416, only $217 more than the monthly payment for the 30-year mortgage, which is $1,199.

I believe in being aggressive, but the 20-year deal might be more manageable for some folks, and that's fine. The point is to explore your options. Ask lenders to run these different scenarios for you or do it yourself using an online mortgage calculator. I like the mortgage payment calculator at www.Bankrate.com and I'll link you right to it from my website, www.ElisabethLeamy.com.

When to Choose a Fixed-Rate Mortgage　Get a fixed-rate mortgage if you plan to stay in the home more than five years and interest rates are low. A fixed-rate mortgage is also the way to go if you are simply unsure of your plans and interest rates are low. Since the year 2000, we have been enjoying relatively low interest rates—historically low at times—so fixed-rate mortgages have been a great deal overall. Of course, that could change, so monitor those rates frequently.

Rural Area Living

If you live in a rural area—or want to—there's a program to help you buy a home. The mortgages are called Section 502 loans or Rural Housing Guaranteed Loans. They are intended for people with low to modest incomes. The program allows you to get a competitive mortgage with no down payment. To learn more, visit the U.S. Department of Agriculture's website at www.rurdev.usda.gov.

Adjustable-Rate Mortgage

The other mortgage product mainstay is the adjustable-rate mortgage (ARM). ARMs start at one interest rate and then adjust to another interest rate after a set period of time, usually changing every year thereafter. When you see an adjustable-rate mortgage described as a "3/1 ARM," the first number means the interest rate is initially fixed for three years and the second number means that it adjusts every year after that.

The most common ARMs are the 3/1 ARM, 5/1 ARM, 7/1 ARM, and 10/1 ARM. Technically, these are *hybrid* ARMs because they are fixed for a while and then adjust. ARMs can sound scary since your future interest rate is unknown. However, the *initial* interest rate is lower than a fixed-rate mortgage, and that can help you SAVE BIG.

How do ARMs help you save? It all depends on your circum-stances. Take Lee Z. of Maine, a successful career woman. Her company just rotated her to a new city, and she knows she will be transferred again in five years. In her case, a five-year ARM is ideal because she will be selling right as it adjusts. Let's put this to the test.

I just checked a mortgage website and saw that the interest rate on a 30-year fixed is 6.5 percent, but the initial interest rate on a 5/1 ARM is 5.5 percent, a full point lower. Here's how that lower interest rate will save Lee on a $200,000 mortgage during the five years she owns the home:

Adjustable-Rate versus Fixed-Rate Mortgage

Loan Type	Interest Owed over Five Years
30-year fixed	$75,840
5/1 ARM	68,160
BIG SAVINGS =	$ 7,680

As you can see, Lee will stockpile a nice $7,680 savings over five years if she chooses the 5/1 ARM over the 30-year fixed-rate mortgage.

When to Choose an Adjustable-Rate Mortgage   Most experts advise that you choose an adjustable-rate mortgage only if your goal is to get out of it before it adjusts. I will add that I would not enter into any adjustable-rate mortgage with an initial term of less than three years. To me, that defeats all its benefits. Having said that, there are multiple reasons to choose an adjustable-rate mortgage.

As you saw, an ARM is a great choice if you know you will be selling the house before the interest rate adjusts. Another shrewd move is to choose an adjustable-rate mortgage if you are planning to pay the loan off before the rate changes. A 10/1 ARM might be best for this, giving you 10 years to pay off your house at the lower opening interest rate you enjoy with an ARM.

A third tactic is to take out an ARM when interest rates are high, in hopes that you will be able to refinance when rates go down. If this is your plan, make sure not to pay a lot of points or fees up front for your ARM, because it's hard to recoup these costs if you refinance quickly. Also study the interest rate caps in the loan contract to make sure your loan won't adjust to a monthly payment you can't afford in the event that you get stuck with it for a while before refinancing.

Banks Are Notorious for Miscalculating Adjustable-Rate Mortgage Interest Rates

When it's time for your ARM to adjust, be sure to look up the index it is pegged to and calculate it yourself. I know, you'd rather eat dirt. But you may be paying too much for your little *piece* of dirt! Don't worry. Thanks to the Internet, you don't have to actually do any math. Just go to www.Bankrate.com and click on the adjustable-rate mortgage calculator.

Interest-Only Mortgage

My name is Elisabeth, and I have an interest-only mortgage.

No, I don't need a 12-step program, because interest-only loans are not always the irresponsible, addictive products they've been made out to be. Interest-only mortgages are loans in which you are only required to pay the interest—no principal—at the beginning. After either 5 or 10 years you start paying the principal, too, and you have to pay a lot more of it per month because you're cramming it into less time. Plus, many interest-only loans are ARMs, so you get a new interest rate at the 5- or 10-year mark. If you actually paid the loan the way it is written, that *would* be irresponsible.

You and Your Credit Are a Commodity

When you apply for a mortgage, the lender pulls your credit report at the big three credit bureaus. No surprise there. But here's the shocker: The credit bureaus then sell the fact that you're shopping for a mortgage to other mortgage lenders. If you start receiving random calls from brokers and bankers, that's why.

When to Choose an Interest-Only Mortgage You should only get an interest-only mortgage if you intend to pay more than just the interest only. Make sense? You *must* know yourself and your finances and be certain that you have the means—and the willpower—to regularly pay extra toward principal. Just remember that, like an ARM, an interest-only loan changes at the 5- or 10-year mark. So if you won't be able to afford the new, higher payment, you need to have a plan to pay down the loan, refinance, or sell the property before that happens.

If you can pull this off, an interest-only loan has real benefits. For example, if your income fluctuates from month to month, perhaps because your salary is commission-based, you have the freedom to pay just the interest in a slow month and then send in a large principal check in a strong month. When you send in that chunky check, the loan reamortizes, which is a fancy industry way of saying it's recalculated. Your future monthly payments immediately drop. With traditional mortgages, paying extra doesn't change your monthly payment.

FHA Loans

As you know, I'd like to see you save 20 percent for your down payment, but I will let you in on a little secret: There is a legitimate way to buy a house with as little as 3.5 percent down. It's not some sleazy back-alley deal, either. You do it by getting your good ol' Uncle Sam to be your cosigner. The Federal Housing Administration (FHA) was founded in 1934 with a single-minded mission: to advance home ownership. The idea is that owning a home makes people care more and strengthens communities.

If you can't otherwise qualify for a mortgage, you may be able to with the help of the FHA. When you take out an FHA loan, the Federal Housing Administration provides mortgage insurance to your lender. In other words, the FHA guarantees that if *you* don't pay your mortgage, *it* will. You pay for this mortgage insurance—about 2 percent of the home's purchase price—when you close on the home. The interest rates on FHA loans are excellent.

FHA Criteria

FHA loans are limited to homes that the buyer intends to live in, not investment properties. These government-backed loans can only be used for relatively affordable houses. The limits change with time, but as I write this, you can get an FHA-insured loan for up to $271,050 in inexpensive areas and for up to $625,500 in pricier places. You can even roll your closing costs into the loan.

Has Your Mortgage Really Been Sold or Is It a Scam?

After you go through all the trouble of choosing the ideal loan and lender, that company could turn around and sell your loan to some other bank. Some consumers have run into problems where the new bank fails to credit their payments in a timely manner—if at all. Worse yet, other mortgage holders have received a letter stating their mortgage has been sold and instructing them to send their payment to a new location, only to discover the letter was a scam and crooks are cashing their checks. When your bank sells your mortgage, you should get two letters, one from your old bank at least 15 days before the transfer and another from the new bank within 15 days after. Call your old bank's customer service center, using the number on your statement, to confirm the switch is legitimate.

There is no minimum income requirement for FHA loans. You do have to demonstrate that you've had a steady income for at least three years, although that income can be from a wide variety of sources, even child support and unemployment compensation. The FHA allows you to go slightly over the 28/36 debt-to-income ratio we discussed earlier. Housing costs can be 29 percent of your gross income and housing plus other long-term debts can be up to 41 percent. In other words, FHA's ratio is 29/41. I'm not saying I agree with it, but there you have it.

Additionally, you don't have to have perfect credit to qualify for an FHA loan, although there are some credit requirements. The Federal Housing Administration will consider approving your loan if you carry a bit of credit card debt, although I don't recommend it. The FHA gives young people without much of a credit history other ways of proving their trustworthiness. You can even have a bankruptcy in your past, as long as the bankruptcy process was completed more than two years ago. The government *really* believes in the positive power of home ownership, huh? If you qualify, you might as well take advantage of it.

I repeat, FHA loans only require a 3.5 percent down payment. Very generous. Nelson J. of Wisconsin was surprised and pleased to learn that there is even one program within FHA that allows you to count sweat equity as part of your down payment. In other words, if you are handy—like Nelson is—and plan to work hard to fix up the place, the value of that work is counted toward your down payment. Nelson knew he could add value to his home and hatched elaborate plans to finish the basement, add a back deck, and remodel the kitchen.

You Can Make up for Weak Credit with a Bigger Down Payment

Some people have an interesting problem: a high income but a low credit score. If that's you, you won't qualify for an FHA loan—not because of your poor credit but because your income is too high. But you may be able to qualify for a conventional loan if you put down a larger-than-conventional down payment. This also works for people who have weak credit but inherit money with which they can make a sizable down payment.

Moving Parts of a Mortgage

No matter which mortgage you choose, there are a few moving parts common to all of them that can make a huge difference in how much your loan ultimately costs. Should you buy down the interest rate by paying points? When should you lock in the rate? And how do you make sure there's no prepayment penalty, so you will be able to pay your mortgage down early and SAVE BIG? Those are the questions. Here are the answers.

Paying Points

First let's talk about what points actually are. As a word nerd, I'm a bit flustered by the fact that the term points is used for several totally different concepts. At its most basic, a point is just 1 percent of the loan amount. Get it? A percentage *point.* The trouble comes in how the term is used and abused from there.

Basically, any fee that is a percentage of the loan amount is referred to as a point these days. This can be the typical 1 percent loan origination fee, which pays for the lender's up-front profit. It can be a mortgage broker's fee, the money paid to the broker for getting you the loan. And it can be the amount the seller will pay toward your closing costs—a point or more.

But the true, original meaning of point is the loan discount point, a fee you pay to obtain a lower interest rate. Yes, a loan *discount.* For whatever reason, that fee is calculated as a percentage of the loan amount. Another way of explaining it is that loan discount points are interest you pay in advance in exchange for paying a little less interest later. That's why they're tax deductible, just as mortgage interest is tax deductible.

Historically, each point the buyer paid lowered the interest rate a quarter of a percent. So if you paid one point, you could lower your rate from, say, 6 percent to 5.75 percent. Lenders sometimes give bigger or smaller discounts, depending on the economy, but that is the most common rule of thumb. So, should you do it? There are a bunch of *ifs* in my answer.

If interest rates are high.

If you plan to keep the loan a long time.

And *if* you have the money.

With the historically low interest rates we have right now—and have had for several years—I see no *point* in paying points. Interest rates in the 4 to 7 percent range are just so affordable that you might want to invest your money elsewhere instead of paying discount points. If interest rates get up into the double digits again someday, points will once again be major players.

For points to be worth it, you have to keep your loan long enough to earn back the fee you paid up front for the point. This is the true trick. Many first-time homebuyers just don't stay in their homes long enough.

Take 20-something sisters Bonnie and Laura M. of California. They are considering buying a house together, but they know it won't last forever because eventually they will start their own families.

Bonnie and Laura are looking to take out a $200,000 mortgage. A point would be $2,000. If they pay a point to lower their rate from 6 percent to 5.75 percent, here's how the math would look:

Paying a Point, Short Term

Interest Rate	Monthly Payment
6%	$1,199
5.75%	1,167
Monthly Savings =	$ 32

As you can see, that $2,000 would only get them $32 worth of savings each month. That means it would take them 62 months— more than five years—to earn back the $2,000 they paid for the point. Not a compelling deal considering that they don't want to live in that home for very long.

However, if neither young woman ever met the man of her dreams (unlikely, as they are both smart, pretty, and fun) and Bonnie and Laura stayed in the house much longer than five years, then the savings would become worthwhile. Let's say they manage to live in the house together the entire 30 years of the loan without killing each other! Here's how their savings would look then:

Paying a Point, Long Term

Interest Rate	Interest Paid over 30 Years
6%	$431,640
5.75%	420,120
BIG SAVINGS =	$ 11,520

If they become spinsters, Bonnie and Laura will be able to save $11,520 over 30 years by paying one point. That is the argument loan officers will make when trying to sell you points. But don't count on staying put long enough for it to be worthwhile, because to pull it off you have to be *complacent* enough to stay in one house for that long and *psychic* enough to know you're going to be that complacent!

Most first-time homebuyers are neither. Besides, many first-time homebuyers don't have the money to pay discount points.

They are relieved just to manage a nice down payment and closing costs. Bottom line: Paying points is not high on my list of recommendations.

Fake Discount Points   Paying fake points is even worse. Some shady brokers and bankers charge people discount points and then don't give them a discount. Uh-huh. A discount point is supposed to give you a discount off of the going market rate that you qualify for, right? But how are *you* to know what rate you really qualify for? It's easy for sneaky mortgage professionals to quote you an inflated rate, then sell you a discount point that brings your rate down but doesn't bring it below market rate as it should.

Shopping around will help you get a feel for what interest rate you qualify for, but you can do more. Ask the lender what the *par rate* is for your loan. That's the base market rate that you qualify for and, by law, the lender should tell you. If you are paying discount points, your rate should be *below* that par rate. If the rate you've been quoted is the same as or higher than the par rate, the loan officer is cheating you.

Locking and Floating

In addition to choosing your loan and your lender, there's one more decision to make: when to lock in your rate. You can either lock in a rate as soon as you sign up with a lender, or you can *float* if you think interest rates are likely to go down. My question is, how in the heck are you supposed to have *any* idea if interest rates will go down? Are you an economist or something? I'm *not*, so what I suggest you do is lock in your rate right away so that at least it can't go any *higher.*

Then, if rates *do* happen to go lower before you close your loan, you can always ask for the lower rate. Some banks advertise "one-way commitments," which are interest rate floats that go down but not up. That sounds pretty snazzy, but the truth is, the lender needs to make you happy or you can take your business elsewhere. Getting a relock should not be a big deal and the bank certainly shouldn't charge you for the privilege. Some ballsy banks have started charging people a few hundred bucks for a float down option—whether you use it or not. That's a rip-off.

When you lock in your rate, get the commitment in writing and hang on to it. This lock-in document should state the interest rate and any points you will be paying. It's critically important because getting the right rate can mean tens of thousands of dollars over the life of the loan.

Beware of Rate Lock Gambling

Mortgage brokers and loan officers have been known to gamble with people's rate locks, either because they genuinely want to get their customers a lower rate, or because they genuinely want to get themselves a fatter commission. It works out all right when rates go down, but when rates go up instead, sleazy operators may try to slip the higher interest rate into your loan without you noticing.

Prepayment Penalties

There's one more moving part you should look out for: the prepayment penalty, a punitive fee for canceling the loan before the term is up. Often there is no prepayment penalty if you sell the house, but a hefty one if you refinance it. You do not want to accept a prepayment penalty of any kind under any circumstances. Why? Because under my Four Walls of Home Ownership you are going to pay your mortgage down early to SAVE BIG. A prepayment penalty would cut into your profits.

Don't take the lender's word for it as to whether there is a prepayment penalty. Look it up yourself. It's easy. When you request Good Faith Estimates from lenders, they are also supposed to provide you with a Truth in Lending form. Ask for it. It's a one-page federal form required by law. On this form, a couple of inches from the bottom, is a line item called "Prepayment." If the box is checked that says you "will not" have to pay a penalty, then, you guessed it, there is no prepayment penalty. But, in true government-ese, if the box is checked that says you "may" have to pay a penalty, it means you *will* have to pay one. If the "may" box is checked, go back to the lender and tell them you "may" just have to take your business elsewhere unless they remove the prepayment penalty!

BIG TIPS

- Spring for a 10-, 15-, or 20-year mortgage if you can afford it.
- Choose the right loan for your situation.
- Ask about FHA loans that only require 3.5 percent down.
- Don't pay points unless you plan to stay put.
- Get your rate lock in writing.
- Never take out a loan with a prepayment penalty.

CHAPTER

Choosing a Mortgage Professional

One way to choose the type of mortgage that is right for you is to get what's called a Good Faith Estimate from a few different lenders. But don't take their advice at face value, because they may make more money on one type of mortgage than another. Instead, compare and contrast the advice you receive from each and consider that advice with a cynical eye.

You see, mortgage brokers and bankers do not have a legal obligation to find you the very best deal. They *may* get you a great deal because they are nice people or are competing hard for your business, but they do not have a fiduciary duty to you. As you work with them, never forget that these are salespeople, paid on commission. If you're naive it will cost you. Knowing how they work—and, more importantly, how they're paid—will help you SAVE BIG.

In this chapter, learn to SAVE BIG by:

- Getting three full-fledged Good Faith Estimates from the right sources.
- Comparing and contrasting not just interest rates but fees, too.
- Understanding how mortgage brokers and bankers make money—so you won't be ripped off.
- Spotting hidden lender fees that can cost you tens of thousands.

Get Three Good Faith Estimates

Once you've settled on a mortgage type, many people think it's time to talk interest rates. Don't make the mistake of choosing a lender based on the interest rate alone. That's a blunder that allows the lender to quote you an enticingly low rate, then hide astronomical fees in your closing costs. So hear this: An interest rate quote is not enough.

What you need are three full-fledged estimates, called Good Faith Estimates (GFEs), from three different types of lenders. More on who the players are in a moment. The Good Faith Estimate includes all the fees and charges you can expect to pay. This allows you to get a complete picture of each lender's loan. Ask all three to base their estimates on paying zero discount points, because that makes it easier to compare them.

The Annual Percentage Rate Is Useless

The annual percentage rate (APR) is another creation of government bumblers. It's your interest rate with fees added in. It's supposed to help you shop and compare among loans, but it doesn't work because every lender calculates it differently. Some include every single fee. Others leave fees out. Ignore the APR.

Ideally, you will ask for all three GFEs the same day. That way you'll know you're comparing and contrasting their actual offers, rather than rate fluctuations that occurred in the marketplace. Lenders are required by law to provide you a Good Faith Estimate within three days of your request. You shouldn't have to pay an application fee to get the GFE. In fact, a new federal rule passed in July 2009 requires lenders to give you an estimate before charging you an application fee or any other fees.

If you provide your credit score (learn how to check your score in Chapter 19) and your loan amount, lenders should be able to work up a GFE. They should include the Truth in Lending form as well, which lists other important factors that we'll discuss shortly.

Who to Get Them From

You should get your Good Faith Estimates from three different sources—one from a banker, one from a broker, and one from a mortgage website. That way you are cross-referencing all three different ways people get mortgages these days. Here are the pros and cons of each.

Banker

Pro	Con
• Works directly for the bank, so fees may be lower because you don't have to pay a third-party broker. • Bank lends you its own money so is less likely to sell your loan to a loan servicer, which can be a headache. • If you have excellent credit and a checking, savings, or investment account there, you may be able to get a discount on the interest rate.	• Offers competitive loans that are better than sleazy brokers, but may not be as good as stellar brokers.

Broker

Pro	Con
• Shops and compares wholesale lenders to find the best mortgage for you. Using a broker is like going to several banks because brokers work with multiple banks. • If you have marginal credit, a good broker can scour the mortgage world to find a lender who will approve you and give you a decent loan.	• Since they are not (usually) lending you their own money, they may have less incentive to build a trustworthy, long-term relationship. • Brokers are middlemen and middlemen must be paid. A broker's compensation may be higher than an in-house banker's.

Website

Pro	Con
• A quick and easy way to get multiple quotes. (Make sure you use a site that quotes rates from multiple banks, not just one.) • Best for refinancing where there are no purchase complications. All you need them to do is provide the money.	• Often unfamiliar with the closing customs and tax laws in your area, so unable to assist when questions arise. • May be just a lead-generating service, which means you will be deluged with annoying, aggressive sales calls.

Refer to Referrals Carefully!

It's always a good sign if a friend had a good experience, but you should not *reveal* the referral until *after* you've gotten the Good Faith Estimate. This counterintuitive advice comes from Carolyn Warren, author of *Mortgage Rip-Offs and Money Savers*. In her book, Carolyn, a former mortgage professional, explains, "Loan officers know that a referred client is a naive client who is not going to compare GFEs . . . you're sealing your fate to pay an extra junk fee and probably a quarter to a half percent more in rate as well." Yikes! Who knew!

Get Some Insider Insight

Author and former mortgage professional Carolyn Warren has been there as a mortgage broker herself. If you want more detail than I can provide about the murky mortgage world, Carolyn's books are your essential source. She is now *my* mortgage guru, and I felt that way even before I found out that *Mortgage Rip-Offs and Money Savers* was published by Wiley, same as my book. (Kiss, kiss!) Carolyn has now written a second book called *Homebuyers Beware: Who's Ripping You Off Now?* It's chock full of the latest information on mortgages and credit. Carolyn Warren is passionate about helping homebuyers and it shows. OK, commercial over, on with the show!

After you've scrutinized your Good Faith Estimate, *then* you can drop your friend's name.

Often real estate agents refer people to mortgage professionals. That's fine. They're in the business and should know good people. But never make your agent's referral your only stop because, although kickbacks are illegal, they are a very real part of the real estate world. And you can guess who ends up paying for that favor: you.

Actually, I obtained my own mortgage through a banker my agent sent me to, but I went to her last. When I was buying my house, at first I thought it would be easier and cheaper to use the same lender that had financed my condo. We had a relationship, right? Ha! The company quoted me a decent rate and when I grilled the loan officer about fees, he swore they were low. But when I got the actual Good Faith Estimate, it included a $5,000 loan origination fee that the loan officer hadn't mentioned despite my intense questioning. Sleazy!

Next, I was offered a better deal by a mortgage broker who I knew and trusted. I would have done fine with that mortgage. But then I decided to get one more GFE. What do you know, the best loan offer of all came from the banker my agent had referred me to. That loan had a lower rate *and* zero origination fee. That's why you want three Good Faith Estimates. You just never know where the best deal will be.

Here's how shopping around among mortgage professionals helped me SAVE BIG:

 Benefit of Getting Three Good Faith Estimates

Fees charged by first lender	$ 6,105
Fees charged by third lender	1,105
BIG SAVINGS =	**$5,000**

How Mortgage Brokers and Bankers Make Money

I remember going on a shoot with a *Good Morning America* producer who was buying her first condo. In between interviews, she was frantically fielding phone calls from her mortgage broker about what type of loan she wanted. Since I'm a consumer reporter—and a buttinski—I started whispering questions for her to ask the guy. The number one thing I wanted her to ask was, "How much do I pay you for arranging this loan for me?" So she asked. The broker acted like she was stupid and answered, "Why, you don't pay me a thing. The bank pays me for bringing in your business." As I will explain, that answer was both the truth—and a total lie.

Trust me, when you take out a mortgage, you pay the mortgage broker or the internal loan officer for their services. That payment is in the form of either a loan origination fee, a broker's fee, a yield spread premium, or a combination of these fees. In this section I explain what each fee is for and when to pay it or avoid it. When I say you should avoid a fee, it just means you will be paying one of the other types of fees instead, because it is more advantageous to your situation. You will be paying at least one of these fees. Nobody works for free.

Loan Origination Fees

Loan origination fees are usually item number 801 on the Good Faith Estimate. A loan origination fee is one portion of the broker's or lender's profit. If you are working with an outside mortgage broker, the loan origination fee is part of their compensation for arranging your loan. If you are working directly with a bank, the loan origination fee may go to your loan officer, or may be absorbed as general profit on your loan.

Loan origination fees are usually charged as a percentage of the loan amount. One percent is a typical loan origination fee paid by people with good credit. The percentage may rise to 1.25 percent if it's a very small loan of less than $100,000, because smaller loans take just as much work and the loan officer wants to make a decent commission. You will also pay more if you have subprime credit, because arranging a loan for you is more difficult. Expect to pay 3 percent for a decent-size loan, as much as 5 percent if the loan is $100,000 or less.

When to Pay a Loan Origination Fee A lot of lenders will brag that they're offering you a loan with no origination fee. But if there's no origination fee, you're still paying the mortgage broker or loan officer for their work, you're just paying some other way. Here's when you should pay—or avoid—a loan origination fee.

Pay It

- If you plan to stay in the house a long time, it's better to pay a loan origination fee, because it's a one-time fee, paid at closing, that doesn't affect your interest rate.
- Loan origination fees are tax deductible, so it is better to pay a loan origination fee than some random fee that doesn't give you a write-off.

Avoid It

- If you know you will not live in the home very long, you should avoid paying a loan origination fee, because the house won't have time to appreciate enough to recover this fee when you sell.

- A loan origination fee is also a bad idea if you are short on cash for closing, because it's yet another payment that is due at the settlement table.

Mortgage Broker's Fees

The mortgage broker's fee is really the same as the origination fee, except that it's for third-party mortgage brokers only, not internal bank loan officers. You will typically see the mortgage broker's fee listed as item number 808 on your Good Faith Estimate. Brokers are supposed to list their fee because they are third-party middle-men. Bankers charge a fee, too, but they don't have to list theirs. At least it's refreshingly plain English: A broker's fee is a fee that goes to the broker.

The most common mortgage broker's fee is 1 percent of the loan amount. Like the origination fee, it is tax deductible. You will see variations on the percentage listed because brokers don't like you to think about how much you're paying them—especially when they're competing with bankers. So they may describe part of their fee as a loan origination fee and part as a broker's fee, or they may not list anything under "Mortgage Broker's Fee" at all, opting instead to list their entire fee as an origination fee.

When to Pay a Mortgage Broker's Fee   Once again, the key to realize is that if you don't see a mortgage broker's fee listed, you are still paying it some way, somehow. The pros and cons of paying a mortgage broker's fee are the same as for an origination fee.

Pay It

- If you plan to stay in the house a long time.
- If you have a choice between this and some other fee that is not tax deductible.

Avoid It

- If you don't plan to live there long.
- If you don't have enough cash for closing.

Yield Spread Premiums

If you are working with a mortgage broker, something called the yield spread premium (YSP) may be listed on line 1303 of your

Good Faith Estimate. You will also see fine print there, in parentheses, which says "Not paid out of loan proceeds." You might think, "Phew, one fee that I don't have to worry about because *I'm* not paying it," but you would be wrong. You *are* paying it—many times over.

Here's how it works. If a broker can get you to agree to an interest rate that is higher than the going rate on the open market—called the par rate—the broker earns a bonus called a yield spread premium. In other words, the wholesale lender is rewarding the broker for the difference—the spread—between the par rate and the rate they sold you.

This yield spread premium bonus is calculated as a percentage of the loan amount, usually 1 percent—often more. You don't pay the actual YSP fee, but you pay a higher interest rate each and every time you make a mortgage payment over the life of your loan, which could cost you tens of thousands of dollars. Think this won't happen to you? Think again. Yield spread premiums are regular, routine. For example, according to the Center for Responsible Lending, 85 to 90 percent of subprime mortgages are yield spread premium deals.

If you are working directly with a bank, they do not have to list their yield spread premium. In fact, often bankers deny that they have yield spread premiums, but many do. If you are not paying an origination fee to the bank, then you are probably paying a yield spread premium. It's one or the other, unless the bank makes its up-front profit in some other way, like large application and closing fees.

So what's a savvy borrower to do? In her book *Mortgage Rip-offs and Money Savers*, Carolyn Warren suggests asking three simple questions:

1. *What is the par rate on this loan?* If the lender tells you the par rate on the loan is 6 percent, when you were offered 7 percent, then you'll know you are paying a full percentage point more than the rock-bottom rate of the day.
2. *What is the yield spread premium on this loan?* If the yield spread premium is $5,000 on a $250,000 loan, you know the broker is making a 2 percent yield spread premium bonus on your loan.
3. *If rates go down, will you lock the loan in at a lower rate or pocket the YSP?* If *they* know that *you* know that many mortgage brokers

fail to lock in lower interest rates for their customers just so they can make a bigger yield spread premium for themselves, chances are they won't do that to you.

Just by asking these questions, you will be putting the lender on notice that you know what you're doing—and, more importantly, that you know what *they're* doing. I wouldn't be surprised if you shame them into making you a better offer. Getting those three Good Faith Estimates also helps protect you from paying an exorbitant interest rate with a yield spread premium. After all, the lenders are competing with each other. But if you learn all the offers you've received are higher than par rate with juicy yield spread premiums for the broker, either negotiate them down or get additional offers.

When to Pay a Yield Spread Premium I've probably made yield spread premiums sound so evil that you're wondering why there is a section about when to pay them. Well, there are certain narrow circumstances when YSPs are actually helpful. Even though you don't pay the yield spread premium bonus directly, I'm deliberately using that wording, because you *do* pay it in the form of an inflated interest rate.

Pay It

- If you need to keep your closing costs down because you are short of cash, you can compensate the broker or loan officer by paying a yield spread premium instead of a loan origination fee. You pay less up front, more later.
- If you have no money at all for closing costs, you could pay an even bigger yield spread premium in exchange for the broker crediting you enough money to cover all your closing costs. The credit is given at closing.

Avoid It

- If you are already paying an origination fee or broker's fee on the front end, there are very few circumstances in which you should also pay a YSP on the back end. That's double dipping—unless the YSP is helping you with closing costs. Add up the total commission the broker is making and decide whether it's fair.

- If you plan to live in the home for a long time, a YSP is bad for you because it means you will be paying an inflated interest rate for a long time. You want the rock-bottom rate, because you will be paying that mortgage for years to come. You'd be better off paying a one-time loan origination fee than a YSP.

How to Compare Good Faith Estimates

Now that you have three Good Faith Estimates from three different types of sources in your hands—and you know how those sources get paid—you need to figure out how to compare the GFEs effectively. The Good Faith Estimate is a standard government form (don't accept GFEs that come in some other format), but lenders still manage to vary the wording and numbering enough so that you're stuck comparing apples to oranges.

Never fear! I buckled down and did the hard work for you so you can compare one lender to another. I divided the Good Faith Estimate into the three key categories that you should compare and contrast:

1. Loan terms.
2. Lender profit.
3. Miscellaneous lender fees.

I have grouped items together that you should consider together, but they are not always in the same order on the GFE itself. What can I say? It's an illogical government form. To overcome this, I've noted the section or line item where each charge is usually found. Use my list to deconstruct your three Good Faith Estimates so you can compare apples to apples—or maybe a better metaphor is compare watermelons to watermelons, since some of these fees are huge!

Loan Terms

Make sure the following loan terms are the same from lender to lender so you are making an accurate comparison.

- **Loan Amount**—top of form. Make sure your loan amount is accurate and that all three lenders have used the same amount.

- **Interest Rate**—top of form. Duh. Of course, you want to know what interest rate each lender is offering.
- **Loan Discount,** also called "Discount Points" or "Discount Fee"—top of form or usually item #802. Make sure all three lenders are basing their interest rates on paying zero discount points, for easy comparison. You can add points later if you wish.

Lender Profit

Add up the total amount of profit each lender is making, by gleaning the numbers from these line items:

- **Loan Origination Fee**—usually item 801. This is one place where the lender's profit will be listed. Compare and contrast.
- **Mortgage Broker's Fee**—usually item 808. This line item is for third-party brokers, not bankers. It is part of the broker's profit.
- **Yield Spread Premium**—usually item 1303. This is the YSP, that back-end broker's fee I told you about. As I explained, the wholesale lender pays the broker this fee, but you are really the one covering it by paying a higher interest rate.

Miscellaneous Lender Fees

Add up all of these smaller charges—miscellaneous lender fees—without worrying about the specific wording from lender to lender.

- **Items Payable in Connection with Loan**—section 800. This line shows the lender's miscellaneous charges. If, by chance, the loan origination fee, mortgage broker's fee, or discount points are listed here, count them separately, because we have dealt with those previously. You're left with a series of smaller charges like application fee, processing fee, appraisal, credit report, and tax service fee. Total them up.
- **Additional Settlement Charges**—section 1300. If there is a yield spread premium, it will be listed in this section, but separate it out and compare it when you are comparing lender profit, as shown earlier. Lenders often list some of their other miscellaneous fees down in this section, perhaps to break them

up a bit so they look less imposing. Common charges in this section are survey fee and pest inspection. Add all fees listed in this section to the "Items Payable in Connection with Loan" and then compare the miscellaneous lender fees from one GFE to the next.

Charges You Don't Need to Worry About—Yet You will see other charges on your Good Faith Estimate, like hazard insurance (section 900), property taxes (section 1000), title charges (section 1100), and government transfer charges (section 1200). You can ignore these for purposes of comparing loans because these prices are set by other entities.

BIG TIPS

- Get three full-fledged Good Faith Estimates.
- Don't tell a mortgage professional that you were referred to him—at first.
- Consider the interest rate *and* the closing fees before choosing a lender.
- Pay either a loan origination fee/broker's fee or a yield spread premium, depending which is more advantageous to you.
- Compare and contrast the lenders' Good Faith Estimates, using the breakdown I provided.

CHAPTER

Cut Your Closing Costs

I wore a power suit to my first closing—and I needed it. The closing costs on my HUD-1 settlement sheet were $2,000 more than had been listed on my Good Faith Estimate. Good faith, huh? They pulled that bait and switch even though they *knew* I was a television reporter specializing in consumer investigations! Imagine what they do to people without a job like mine. I marched into the mortgage manager's office and demanded that he waive these ambush fees. I had my paperwork and I had my power suit and I won.

Ever since then I have been passionate about teaching people to cut their closing costs, which are the endless charges you have to pay in order to finalize your mortgage and your property purchase. Here I will expose the two problems of closing costs: real fees that are inflated and junk fees that are just plain made up. I'll break down lender fees, title company fees, and government fees and show you how you can SAVE BIG—thousands of dollars—by fighting them.

In this chapter, learn to SAVE BIG by:

- Knowing which settlement fees are junk and which are justified.
- Asking for a written guarantee that your closing costs will not rise more than 10 percent.
- Shopping around for title services, something nobody does.
- Making sure you're not up-charged on government real estate fees.
- Bringing key documentation to your closing to fight up-charges.

Lender Charges

As we discussed in Chapter 5, lenders are required by law to give you a Good Faith Estimate of your closing costs. But it's *not* required to be accurate! How's that for an example of tortured government logic? For years, the federal government has been trying to come up with a way to make sure lenders don't lowball their closing charges on their estimates and then jack them up at settlement time. There is still no law that truly protects consumers from this bait and switch. A 2006 *Money* magazine investigation suggests these days Americans pay eight times the closing costs they paid 40 years ago.

Beth and Robert G. love their house outside Minneapolis, but they hate that the lender jacked up their closing costs sometime between when they got their estimate and when they went to the settlement table. Beth and Robert ended up paying $500 for a mysterious "processing" fee and $575 for an official-sounding "administration" fee. They didn't notice these junk fees at the settlement table, but they now calculate they paid a total of $1,265 in bogus add-on charges.

Lenders are now required to inform you if they're going to raise their fees before you close, but they can still raise them. The feebs—I mean feds—did have one promising idea. There was talk of a law that would require lenders to guarantee that the prices quoted in their Good Faith Estimates would not rise more than 10 percent. That's so simple, so logical. No wonder they couldn't pass it.

It's time to take the law into your own hands. When you choose a lender, ask them to drop all the junk fees in their Good Faith Estimate, using the guidance I give you in this chapter.

Junk Fees

If you scrutinize your three Good Faith Estimates, you will see all sorts of official-sounding fees that have no purpose except to pad the lender's profit. They are junk fees. What lenders and brokers do is charge for things that ought to be included in their service. It would be like an accountant charging extra for doing math to prepare your tax return, or a mechanic charging extra to put your car up on the lift. They do those things in the course of performing their jobs and they shouldn't charge extra. Lenders shouldn't either, and if you stop them you will SAVE BIG. Here is a list of the most common junk fees and what action you should take to combat them:

Application fee. Where would lenders be without applications? Come on, their entire mission in life is to get prospects to apply. You shouldn't have to pay as much as $550 for the privilege. Here's what more insidious: The reason some lenders charge several hundred dollars for their application fee is so you will feel obligated to stick with them rather than switching to another lender. As of 2009, lenders cannot charge you an application fee until after they have disclosed all the details of their loan to you, but I worry there will still be abusive application fees, just later in the process. Watch out.
    Action: Fight this fee.

Document preparation fee. Lenders have to prepare several documents in the process of granting you a loan. Some charge as much as $200 for it. That's ridiculous. We're talking about filling in forms and printing them out. Give me a break.
    Action: Fight this fee.

Appraisal review fee. Appraisals are an important service performed by an outside expert, but if you see "appraisal review" as a separate line item, you can fight it. Some lenders hire a second appraiser to read over the appraisal and make sure the first one did a good job. They're trying to protect themselves from risk. That's fine, but let them pay for it—not you. This fee can be as much as $400. You shouldn't have to pay it.
    Action: Fight this fee.

Administrative fee. This is a catch-all fee that could cover anything from evaluating you as a potential customer to preparing your loan documents. Don't pay it, especially if it's at the high end, such as $500.
    Action: Fight this fee.

Processing fee. This is another word for an administrative fee.
    Action: Ditto.

Courier fee. Um, in the age of e-mail, does anybody actually *use* couriers anymore? From the looks of people's settlement sheets, you'd think the streets would be teeming with them.

If your antiquated lender actually hires a courier to schlep your loan documents somewhere, it's part of their cost of doing business. They should pay for it themselves. Besides, many lenders pad this fee, charging about $50 when an overnight FedEx only costs $15.

Action: At least ask for receipts that prove they really did hire a courier.

Funding fee. This fee, also called a wiring fee, is supposed to cover the cost of wiring your loan money to whoever is conducting your closing. Lenders never used to charge this fee. Getting the money to you is the lender's main job. It should not cost $30.

Action: Fight this fee unless you are fighting so many others that you want to ignore this one as a negotiating tool.

Lender closing fee. Your closing is conducted by a title company, an escrow company, a settlement attorney, or some combination of these. I don't see the word *lender* anywhere on that list. Banks don't need to charge a lender closing fee, which is also sometimes called a lender settlement fee, and yet some do—as much as $800! The high price makes it seem important, but keep in mind, the bankers desperately want to close your loan. They don't get paid until they do.

Action: Fight this fee.

Now that you have fought your battles, ask your broker to sign a letter stating that the remaining fees will not rise more than 10 percent above what's listed in their Good Faith Estimate. That's your new Leamy law!

How Junk Fees Add Up   The following list shows typical charges for the most common junk fees, though they vary by region. As you can see, junk fees really add up, so you can SAVE BIG by demanding the lender drop them. I suggest you attack the biggest ones and let the little ones slide.

On this list, I would probably ignore the courier and funding fees and maybe the doc prep fee. That's a good negotiating tactic because it allows the lender to save face and make a little bit of profit. But let's say you're merciless and you demand that the company drop every single bogus charge. Here's how your efforts would add up:

Junk Fees

Application fee	$ 550
Document preparation fee	200
Appraisal review fee	400
Administrative/processing fee	500
Courier fee	50
Funding/wiring fee	30
Lender closing fee	800
BIG SAVINGS =	**$2,530**

There you have it: $2,530 saved by junking the junk fees you were charged.

Justified Fees

Okay, enough bank bashing. There are also plenty of justified fees you will encounter in the course of closing on your new home. After all, the bank is basically buying you a house! The bankers certainly deserve to check you out and check the property out. But even the legitimate fees are often padded or misused, so here's a list of the most common charges, what they are for, and when to take action.

Credit report fee. Of course, the lender will want to pull your credit report before "buying" you a house. Perfectly understandable. Just know that this fee is often padded. Bulk credit reports probably cost lenders a couple of bucks, but they may charge you more like $50.

Action: If your lender has not charged you a bunch of other junk fees, leave it alone. If it has, then request a lower fee. Really mad? Request a receipt that shows the true amount the lender paid an outside vendor for your report.

Loan origination fee. As we discussed in Chapter 5, a loan origination fee is a way for the lender to make a portion of their profit up front. By far the most common origination fee is 1 percent of the purchase price. I think that's fair. But sometimes brokers and bankers charge much more.

Action: Add up the loan origination fee, loan discount points, yield spread premium bonus, and all the other fees that go directly to the lender as profit. If you have excellent credit, you should expect to pay the lender 1 percent of the loan amount for the total of these fees. You may pay a bit more, like 1.25 percent, if the loan is less than $100,000. If you have subprime credit, your loan takes more work and you can expect to pay the lender 3 percent of the loan amount—up to 5 percent if it's a small loan. If the percentages are much higher than what I've described here, demand answers.

Mortgage broker fee. Some mortgage brokers openly call their commission a mortgage broker fee instead of the more mysterious loan origination fee. Others charge you some of each. Expect to pay 1 to 1.25 percent for the total of these fees if you have excellent credit, 3 to 5 percent if you have subprime credit.

Action: If the percentage is any higher, ask hard questions and shop around to see if you can get a better deal.

Loan discount points. These are the true points, the type that buy you a lower interest rate. As I mentioned previously, a point is 1 percent of the loan amount and usually gets you a quarter-point discount on your rate.

Action: Make sure that if discount points are listed, they are real—not fake. You can go back to Chapter 4 for a detailed explanation of how to tell the difference. Also scan to make sure that you are not paying both discount points and a yield spread premium. If there's a YSP, that means you are paying an above-market rate for your loan, which is a direct contradiction of paying a discount point, which is supposed to get you a *below*-market rate. It should be one or the other.

Underwriting fee. Some lenders charge a fee to weigh the risk of doing business with you. Critics say this fee shouldn't exist, because underwriting is an integral part of what lenders do and they do it to protect themselves—not you. But I have left this fee in the "justified" column. Here's why. The majority of mortgages are obtained through independent brokers these days. The actual loan comes from a wholesale lender and that lender undergoes an underwriting process to check the broker's work and make sure you are a good risk.

Action: You may be able to negotiate a lower underwriting fee.

Appraisal fee. Lenders require a professional appraisal so they will know if the home you are buying is worth the amount of money they are lending you. If you are refinancing, the lender may be satisfied with a drive-by appraisal, which is much less expensive.

Action: Either way, you can ask your broker or lender for a receipt showing which appraiser did the work and how much it actually cost. You shouldn't have to pay an inflated fee.

Survey fee. A survey is performed to make sure the boundaries of your property are clean and clear. Surveyors look for things like misplaced fences and shared driveways that may cloud property lines and cause a dispute. Lenders ask you to pay for a survey if you are buying a new home. If you are refinancing, they are usually willing to recertify the existing survey. Surveys do not apply to condominiums, but watch out, because some lenders tack them on anyway.

Action: If the seller hasn't owned the home long, you may be able to get their survey recertified for free. Even without recertification, many home buyers have had success getting this fee waived. At least try to get it reduced. Surveys can cost a few hundred dollars, so it's worth it.

Flood certification fee. If you are buying a single-family home, the lender will want to have a flood survey done to see if the house is in a flood zone. It's required, even if the house sits on a hill. An outside company will review government charts to find out the home's flood status.

Action: Let it be. It costs less than $30. Exception: If you are buying a condo on an upper floor, you should not have to pay for a flood certification, but some lenders charge for it out of habit. Look for this line item.

Tax service fee. This is also called an escrow fee. Lenders want to make sure you are paying your property taxes, because if you're not, the county can seize your home and the lender won't get paid. If you put down less than 20 percent, your lender will make you send extra money each month and will use it to pay your property taxes for you. If you make a big down payment, you're allowed to pay your property taxes yourself, but the lender still hires an outside company to monitor whether you're paying your taxes. This fee covers that service.

Action: Let it be.

Less Homeowner's Insurance

You probably don't have to pay for a full year's homeowner's insurance at closing. Lenders require you to purchase homeowner's insurance to protect your new property since it's the collateral for their loan, and some automatically put you down for a full year's coverage. But if you ask, they will probably be satisfied if you take out a policy that is paid quarterly. That way you won't have to pay as much at closing when you have so many other overwhelming expenses.

Title Charges

Most people don't quite know what title insurance is, let alone that they can shop around and SAVE BIG on it and other title charges. Here's the deal. Title insurance protects you if somebody comes along and claims they have a legal right to your property. Maybe a divorcing wife sold you the house and now the ex-husband shows up and says she shouldn't have. Title insurance will pay your legal fees in a case like this and even pay for your loss if you end up having to give up the property.

Most people just go with the title company (also called an escrow company) that their real estate agent or lender recommends. At this point in the home buying process, you're exhausted from looking at 200 houses and vetting three lenders, so it's understandable. But it's a big mistake that will cost you.

I saved $1,200 by shopping around for title services when I bought my house. I made up a big checklist of every possible title charge and called around to title companies asking how much they charged for each. Once you find the lowest price, just as you did with the lender, ask the title people to send you a letter guaranteeing their fees will not rise more than 10 percent.

Justified Fees

Here's a pretty exhaustive list of title-related fees. I've listed the justified ones first this time, because that makes the junk fees easier to explain. I tell you what each fee is for and whether there's any action you can take to get the cost down.

Title insurance. Your chosen title company will perform a title search to try to make sure the seller has the right to sell the home to you. But if they miss something, that's when title insurance kicks in. Lenders require you to buy a lender's policy to protect their interests in the property, and most people purchase a homeowner's policy to protect themselves as well.

In some states title insurance pricing is unregulated, which means there's competition and you can play title companies off of each other to get a better rate. Just ask. In other states, title insurance premiums are set by the state government and title companies must obey.

Even in regulated states, you can still SAVE BIG by asking for what's called the reissue rate on your title insurance. If you are refinancing—or buying a house that the seller purchased less than 10 years ago—the reissue rate is available to you. The idea is that a shorter time period means a shorter title search so a smaller fee is in order. The discount ranges from 25 to 60 percent off, with 40 percent being the most common.

Homeowner's Insurance for Less

While we're talking about insurance, choose a $2,500 homeowner's insurance deductible and save 40 percent. Yes, $2,500 is high, but you should avoid making claims where you would have to pay that deductible anyway. Why? Just one or two petty claims and your insurance company will cancel you these days. You should be prepared to pay for small incidents yourself. How? With the gobs of money you will save on your annual premium by having a higher deductible. If you can't stomach $2,500, then go with a $1,000 deductible, which will save you about 25 percent.

Many title companies won't offer the reissue rate unless you ask, and believe it or not, the government doesn't require them to. So ask. Inquire. Demand! In order to qualify for the reissue rate, you may have to provide proof that there is a valid title insurance policy in place. If you are refinancing, that's easy. Just dig up your old policy. If you are buying, ask the seller if they can provide a copy of their title policy. Most sellers will happily do this because they love sticking it to the man and helping you save money.

Let's use an expensive place as an example, for a change. My New York friends need some love. How much could Debbie S. save by getting the reissue rate on title insurance for a $450,000 New York City condo? (I wonder if you can even get a Manhattan apartment for that?) Here's how the savings would look if we assume the most common 40 percent discount:

 Benefit of Asking for the Reissue Rate

Full title insurance rate	$2,594
Reissue rate	1,556
BIG SAVINGS =	**$1,038**

A savings of more than $1,000 is worth striving for.

Action: Ask title companies point-blank, "Are you quoting me the lowest-cost policy I am eligible for? Is it the reissue rate?" They won't want to lie to you because then you could sue them for fraud.

Title search. You may also see this called an abstract fee. This charge covers the cost of sending somebody down to the courthouse to research the history of the property you want to buy. They're checking to make sure the seller really owns the property free and clear and has a right to sell it to you. Some title agents have somebody in-house who does this work. Others hire an outside company.

Action: This fee is usually in the range of $150 to $250, but it can vary regionally. If your title company hires an outside company for this, you can ask for a receipt to verify there is no up-charge.

Closing fee. Your closing is the meeting where you sign all the paperwork to finalize your loan and purchase the home. This meeting is also sometimes called a *settlement.* Closings can be conducted by escrow agents, title agents, or real estate attorneys. Their fees are not regulated by the government. That's good! It means everything is negotiable. A typical closing ceremony costs $150 to $350, again with geographical differences in price. The fee is split between the buyer and seller.

Action: Beware of shady operators who charge you for a closing *and* a settlement even though they're the same thing. If the title company can't or won't reduce your title insurance premium, because it involves an outside company or is regulated by the state, see if it will reduce this fee instead.

Attorney's fee. If your escrow or title company employs an attorney who works on your home purchase, you may be charged an attorney's fee. It could be in place of the closing fee or it could be additional.

Action: Ask what services the attorney will be performing for you and how long they will take. Then assess whether the fee makes sense on an hourly basis.

Notary fee. Some of your loan documents must be notarized. Every title company has somebody in-house who does this, but some pass along the cost to you.

Action: It should be less than $20. If so, let it be.

Release of lien fee. This is the fee for getting the county to change the records so the old homeowner and old lender are no longer listed as owners. Some title agents include this service under another heading. Others list it separately so you know exactly what you're getting. Good title agents often complain that the bad apples in their industry charge for this service but don't actually do it. That leaves multiple ownership records in place for the same property.

Action: It's important and pretty cheap. Pay it, then check your property records online or in person to make sure it's been done.

Junk Fees

Okay, now that you understand what title services are and the important ones that are justified, you'll have a better grasp—and more rage—when I reveal the junk fees some title companies charge. Once again, I also suggest the action you should take.

Title administrative fee. Just like with lenders, this is another one of those ridiculous catch-all fees that are meant to boost profits.

Action: Fight this fee.

Title document preparation fee. This is similar to the lender's doc prep fee: a crock. Most people pay it anyway, to the tune of as much as $200.

Action: Hopefully if you shop around aggressively you will find a title company that does not charge this fee. If they all do, ask them to waive it.

Title examination. This is the fee some title agents charge to analyze the results of the title search done at the courthouse. Many title professionals consider this just an extension of the title search and charge nothing. Others consider it a separate function and charge as much as $400.

Action: Tell your top choice that the other companies you're interviewing don't charge this fee and see if the company will drop it. If not, consider going elsewhere.

Title insurance binder. This may sound like a three-ring binder that your title policy comes in, but it's actually a commitment by the insurance company to cover you. Title insurance is provided by big national insurance companies, but brokered by small local companies, so this document bridges the gap.

Action: This is usually about $50 and some title agents include it in the cost of the title search or title exam, so try to get it waived. It's the cost of doing business.

Courier fee. Sound familiar? Ditto what I said about lender's courier fees.

Action: Ask for receipts. I bet they'll be so embarrassed that they can't produce any that they'll offer to waive this fee.

Government Charges

Years ago I did a story on Cleo S. of Maryland, a dignified, older woman who was desperate to refinance her longtime family home to save it from foreclosure. It was the kind of home where four generations of family members had carved their names in the oak tree in the front yard, so it had deep sentimental value.

The lender charged Cleo a bunch of junk fees. And then, to add insult to injury, somebody inflated the *government* fees she owed, the one type of charge she should have been able to count on. Cleo's county only charges $25 to record a deed, but the title company charged $125. The new loan was so bloated with fees that she couldn't afford it and lost the home after all.

Every time a property changes hands, there are government fees and taxes for recording the new deed and so on. Here I list the most common ones, so you'll have an idea what they are for. Keep in mind that unscrupulous operators could try to inflate these set government fees to pad their own profits.

> **Recording fee.** This is simply the amount the county clerk charges to make a record of the fact that you are purchasing the property. If you're refinancing, typically you still have to pay this fee because the county has to record the new lender's name.
>
> > *Action:* Check the true cost with your county recorder of deed's office.
>
> **Tax stamp.** This is a tax charged when a property changes hands. It's also sometimes called the recordation tax or transfer tax. The amount is based on the purchase price. It's sort of like a sales tax. It's just a chance for the county or state to collect a little revenue—or a lot. If you're a first-time home buyer, the amount may be less. Some jurisdictions do not charge tax stamps when you refinance. Others base the charge on the difference between the amount of your old loan and your new one.
>
> > *Action:* Call your county office of taxation and revenue to learn the formula and whether it's different for first-time home buyers or refinances.

Going to Closing

Despite all your prudent preparations, you could find that the broker, lender, or title company will try to stick it to you at closing. Remember, it happened to me, the (supposedly) intimidating investigative reporter. Unfortunately, it's common—even mundane—for these professionals to slip in extra fees at the settlement table. So here's what you do.

Ask your title company to provide you with a copy of your HUD-1 Settlement Statement at least a day in advance, so you can study it without time pressure. Any title company that cannot do this for you is not worth hiring. Pore over the HUD-1, which is a government form very similar to your Good Faith Estimate. The line item numbers should correspond.

If you detect differences, demand an explanation before your closing. For this reason, don't close on a Monday. I did that the first time and learned the hard way that there's nobody to argue with over the weekend!

Next, bring all your key documents with you to the closing so you have ammunition if there are mysterious changes you need to shoot down. This includes:

- Your rate lock guarantee.
- Your Good Faith Estimate.
- Your Truth in Lending form.
- The lender's 10 percent fee guarantee that you obtained.
- The title company's 10 percent fee guarantee that you obtained.

Oh, and don't forget to wear your power suit!

BIG TIPS

- Scan your GFEs for junk fees and ask the lender to drop them before signing.
- Ask your lender to sign a letter guaranteeing its remaining closing fees will not go up more than 10 percent.
- Shop around for title insurance and services.
- Make sure standard government charges are not padded.
- Bring all your key documents with you to closing.

CHAPTER 7

Appeal Your Property Taxes

So you're in. Great! But just because the purchase is complete doesn't mean you are done saving money on your house. One of the first targets to SAVE BIG is your property taxes. Let me throw out a couple of statistics from the National Taxpayers Union that, taken together, spell opportunity:

1. Sixty percent of homes are overvalued for property tax purposes.
2. Only 2 percent of homeowners appeal their property taxes.

The beauty of these two figures is that since so *many* properties are overassessed, but so *few* property owners file appeals, the chances are very good that *your* appeal will work!

In this chapter, learn to SAVE BIG by:

- Being one of the few homeowners who appeal their property taxes.
- Pulling comparable home sales data that proves yours is worth less.
- Escalating your appeal from letter to meeting to hearing.
- Hiring help—for free—if you don't have time to appeal on your own.

Look for the Opportunity to SAVE BIG

In hot real estate climates, property taxes can double or triple in just a few years as home values rise. That's pretty overwhelming, but consider this: Since so few people appeal, it's cheaper for the city or county to give the few squeaky wheels what they want than to maintain a massive bureaucracy to tell them no. In fact, the National Taxpayers Union says the majority of homeowners win at least a partial victory. Be one of the 2 percent and you can SAVE BIG.

For that reason, think of property taxes as an opportunity to save rather than an obligation to pay. You need to look for that opportunity in the mail. Some cities and counties issue new property tax assessments every year. Others change their assessment only once every few years. Find out when you can expect it and be ready to appeal. Some people brazenly appeal their tax assessment every single year!

Once you receive your property tax assessment and realize it's too high, you need to move quickly because the window to appeal is usually very short. Depending on the rules where you live, you will only have 30 to 120 days to let the local government know you intend to appeal. Send your appeal application by certified mail or hand-deliver it and get it stamped, so you will have proof that it arrived by the deadline.

Follow the tax office's appeal instructions to a T, so your case won't be thrown out on a technicality. And don't neglect to pay your taxes! You still owe while you are appealing. If you win, the difference is refunded or comes off your next tax bill.

Understanding Property Taxes

It would be easy to glance at your property tax assessment when it comes in the mail and see that the assessed value of your home is lower than what you paid, and think you have no grounds for appeal. But wait! Most jurisdictions base their assessed value on a *percentage* of the property value, so it's *supposed* to be way lower than what you paid. You have to work backward from the assessed value to figure out if the government has overassessed your home.

Here's how it works. Some jurisdictions base your tax on 100 percent of the property's value, but most assign a lower assessment ratio. According to the National Taxpayers Union, 60 percent is the average assessment rate. Here's an example: If your house is worth $100,000 on the open market and your town's assessment ratio is 60 percent, that means the assessed value of your home is $60,000.

If you got a tax assessment notice stating your assessed value was $80,000 you might think you don't have a case because you know your home is really worth $100,000. But you've neglected to factor in the assessment ratio! In this case, by giving an assessed value of $80,000, the assessor is really saying your home's *market* value is $133,000. That's 33 percent too high!

Once the assessed value is set using the assessment ratio, then most jurisdictions tax you a certain amount per $100 of assessed value. Back to the house with an assessed value of $60,000. If the town charges $1 for every $100 of assessed value, the property tax bill on that home would be $600.

While We're Talking Taxes, Let's Talk Federal Income Tax Deductions

Years ago a wise accountant gave me a way of thinking about tax deductions that turned me into an itemizer-bunny. Say you're in the 25 percent tax bracket. For every $100 worth of deductions you can claim, you will save $25 on your taxes! It's such a concrete way of looking at it! I love it.

Appealing Your Tax Assessment

Once you've determined that your property has been assessed too high, the next decision is whether to handle the appeal yourself or hire help. Even pros who do this for a living admit that homeowners can easily appeal their property taxes on their own. They say the level of effort is similar to appealing a traffic ticket or going to small claims court, but with a much higher payout. You can expect to spend somewhere in the neighborhood of 5 to 20 hours working on your appeal.

If you absolutely cannot spend the time it takes to appeal your tax assessment yourself, I have good news! Many property tax consultants and tax attorneys will take these cases on a contingency basis. If you lose your case, it costs you nothing. That should tell you how good your odds of winning are—since lawyers don't generally like to work for free!

A typical contingency fee is a third to a half of the amount you save in taxes the first year. Contact your local bar association for a referral or just search for attorneys on the Internet using the name of your city or county and the words "property tax" and "appeal."

The Government Will Reduce Your Income Taxes If You Save Money and Save the Environment

Yes, you heard that right! There are programs in place that give you a tax deduction for installing energy-efficient furnaces, air conditioners, insulation, windows, and appliances. The government offers separate bonuses for going solar. So the home improvement *saves* you money and the government *gives* you money. Sweet! Here are some websites that show you what programs are available: www.dsireusa.org and www.energystar.gov/taxcredits.

How to Appeal on Your Own

If you decide to appeal your taxes by yourself, the first step is to ask your city or county tax assessor's office for the materials it used to evaluate your property. As an example, in Washington, D.C., where I live, the Office of Tax and Revenue will send you the property worksheet, which consists of its notes on your property; and also a sales list, which is the list of recent home sales that it used to set the value of your property. Once you get these internal government documents, you should scrutinize them, looking for errors that give you a great argument for your appeal.

There are really only three basic arguments you can make to appeal your tax assessment. That keeps it nice and simple. See if one applies:

1. **The assessor made a mistake in describing your house.** This argument covers situations where the assessor made simple math mistakes. Maybe he got the square footage wrong (only heated, livable areas should be counted), or stated that you have five bedrooms when you have three. If you uncover

these errors, lucky you—you will win. All you have to do is describe the errors in writing or in person.

2. **You just bought the house for less.** If you recently purchased your home for less than the assessed value would indicate, lucky you. If the assessment is wrong, and grossly inflated, you will win your appeal. (If the assessment is right, you will lose, but it means you got a tremendous bargain when you bought the place!) This is pretty cut-and-dried, and can probably be taken care of with a simple letter or phone call.

3. **The assessor made poor comparisons in valuing your house.** In this third situation, the assessor put a value on your house by using comparables that aren't, well, comparable. If this is the case, you will argue that the houses the city or county used as comparisons are far better and nicer than your house. It's the one time you want your home to be as crummy as possible! According to attorneys who handle these cases, the difference between your house and the comparables needs to be at least 10 percent for you to have a good case. Some jurisdictions will actually tell you what percentage difference they consider actionable.

Attacking the Assessor's Comparables

Not to get all sci-fi on you, but if you are using argument number three—that the comparables are wrong—you have to establish an alternative reality. Insert twangy alien music here. First you must show why the comps the assessor used are all wrong. Are you living in the modest original farmhouse surrounded by McMansions? That's not a fair comparison. Does the house across the street have a new state-of-the-art kitchen, while you are content with pink Formica? Then the two shouldn't be valued at the same price.

After you knock down the assessor's comps, you need to build up others that are more favorable to you. You need three to six comps that bolster your case. They must be of about the same size and age as your house for your argument to persuade.

Here are some sources of comparable information:

1. **www.Zillow.com.** This fun, fabulous real estate website shows how much your neighbors are paying for their property taxes. In the "Charts and Data" section, Zillow lists property tax bills for most homes.

2. **Real estate agent.** Another option is to ask a real estate agent. Many will pull a few comps as a courtesy since they are in a service business.

3. **Appraiser.** If you are fighting a hyperinflated tax assessment, then spring for a professional appraiser to evaluate your property and provide comps. This will cost a few hundred dollars, but will help you SAVE BIG in the years to come.

Once you find your alternative comparables, you need to evaluate them. It's the opposite of putting your house up for sale. You want to look for anything and everything that makes other homes seem better and yours worse.

Beware of Fake Property Tax Assessment Services

I first heard about this when I was a reporter in Florida, where con artists love to live. Every few years crooks somewhere in the country pose as the local tax office and do mass mailings either promising to help people reduce their property taxes or threatening to raise them. Of course, they charge a fee for their nonexistent services, then disappear. If you get such a notice, look up the number for your local tax assessment office and call to see if it's for real.

Escalating Your Appeal

Now that you've got your ammunition, it's time to shoot down your property tax assessment. You can start with a little warning shot, then ramp up as you see fit. There are five typical levels in the process, but the vast majority of people manage to get some satisfaction just by taking the first or second step.

1. **Put it in writing.** There's a really strong chance you will be able to lower your property tax rate just by sending a well-written, well-documented letter. Many jurisdictions accept appeals by mail (or even e-mail). This will probably work best if your appeal is based on errors the assessor's office made or on the fact that you purchased the home for less than the

assessed price. These are straightforward arguments, which are easy to make in writing.

2. **Request a meeting.** Another option is to arrange an informal meeting with the tax assessor's office. Not all localities allow this, but if yours does, the National Taxpayers Union says it works 95 percent of the time! Often the assessment staff would rather work quietly with you than see their work criticized in a public hearing.

    Yes, you are coming face to face with the dreaded tax man, but don't be too angry and aggressive. Instead, adopt the tone that you are "asking for their assistance" and you're "grateful for their attention." You know the drill. This is not a binding hearing, but you should still be prepared to present your argument in an organized manner. Wouldn't it be nice to just end the process right here? Most people do and I hope you do, too.

3. **Hold a hearing.** If letters and meetings don't work, you may have to make your case before a panel at a formal hearing. Sounds scary, but it's no big deal. Just be sure to get a copy of the panel's procedures so you are prepared to follow them.

    Go to this hearing armed with a spreadsheet showing why the government's comparables are inappropriate and another showing why yours are more accurate. Hand out packets to each panel member, complete with photos you have taken of the properties in question. Lead the panel through a 5- to 10-minute presentation, no more—you don't want to be a bore.

    Conclude with the taxable value you believe is fair. Rather than telling the tax board, "My tax assessment is unfair, please lower it," it's more effective to say, "My tax assessment is unfair, please lower it *to X.*" You may not get your precise wish, but naming a number helps frame the debate.

Sit In on a Hearing

BIG SECRET

A hot tip: Attend somebody else's hearing a few days before your own to get a feel for the process and the questions you are likely to be asked. Listen carefully, because some panel members repeat the same questions and objections in every single case. Be prepared to answer!

4. **Appeal to the state.** If you lose at the local level, you can usually take your case to a state appeals board. Whether you do this will probably depend on just how egregious your tax bill is. The nice thing is that these boards typically try to dispense with most cases without holding an in-person hearing. To accomplish that, they often offer some sort of tax reduction, even if it's not all that you had hoped for.

5. **Last stop: court.** I doubt you're going to go all the way to court. I think the government will knuckle under well before that, but remember those tax attorneys who frequently take property tax cases on contingency? If you have a strong claim for a lot of money, why not hire an attorney who agrees to be paid only after winning your case? That's a great vote of confidence that you will win big and SAVE BIG.

Results That Last Years

If appealing your property taxes seems labor intensive, remember that a successful appeal resets your rate for years to come. My neighbors Kris and Roxanne H. appealed their property taxes and won. All they did was write a letter and fill out some forms. Their case was pretty straightforward because they had just refinanced and had a current appraisal which showed their home was worth less than the city thought.

Voila! Kris and Roxanne persuaded the city to lower their home's assessed value from about $600,000 to $550,000. The value began to creep up again after that, about 4.5 percent a year, but because it was creeping from a lower starting point, they were able to SAVE BIG. Here's an approximation of their five-year savings:

Kris and Roxanne's Property Taxes over Five Years

Assessed Value	Tax Bill
$600,000	$ 31,511
$550,000	28,885
BIG SAVINGS =	**$ 2,626**

Wow! Just by spending a little bit of time one year, Kris and Roxanne were able to save themselves $2,626 over five years. They figure they spent about two hours appealing their property taxes, so their hourly wage for the work was $1,313! A BIG SAVINGS like that is definitely worth your time and effort.

BIG TIPS

- Find out when to expect your tax assessment, then work fast so you don't miss the deadline.
- Work backwards from the assessment ratio to figure out if the tax assessor has overvalued your home.
- Get the property worksheet and sales list that the government used to assess your home.
- Gather your own comparables that prove your house is worth less or others are worth more.
- Work your way through the system from a written appeal to a hearing and beyond.

CHAPTER

When to Refinance

Another way to SAVE BIG while you own your home is to refinance into a new mortgage with a lower interest rate. You should always be on the lookout to refinance because it is one of the truly unique chances to save. Oh goodie, you get to reuse all that new-found knowledge about loans, lenders, and closing costs that you learned in the previous chapters!

I'm glad I brushed up on all these details myself in order to explain them to you, because I am in the process of refinancing into a new mortgage right now. As I write this, my closing is a week away and the new loan will cut our payments by about $7,000 a year. Now *that* is SAVING BIG!

In this chapter, learn to SAVE BIG by:

- Always being on the lookout to refinance.
- Going for it if the circumstances meet the Refinancing Rule of 5s.
- Refinancing into a shorter-term loan.
- Recognizing that so-called no-cost refis are a bunch of baloney.

Should You Refinance?

I want you to be ever vigilant about the possibility of refinancing, but don't worry, tracking mortgage rates is not much effort, because some-body else is going to do it for you. Remember how hard you worked to find your lender? All you have to do is ask that person to watch rates for you and let you know if there's a good opportunity to refinance.

Trust me, they will follow through because they want to make some more commissions off of you. When your broker or banker alerts you that rates are down significantly, you will say, "Thank you very much" and ask for a Good Faith Estimate, plus get two from other sources, just like before. Loyalty has its limits when big bucks are involved!

Then look at your three GFEs and ask yourself, is it time to refinance? To help you answer this question, I came up with the Refinancing Rule of 5s. Here it is:

Refinancing Rule of 5s

- Your new interest rate should be at least **0.5 percent** lower than your current rate.
- You should add **5 years** or less to the length of your loan. Reducing the years would be even better.
- You should be able to recover your closing costs in **5 years** or less—preferably much less.

If you plan to sell the house before you have recovered the closing costs you must pay to refinance, that is the number one deal breaker. To figure this out, all you do is divide the cost of closing by your monthly savings to see how long it's going to take for the new loan to pay for itself. To really understand this, let's delve into an example. Meet Kristin and Emmet H. of Indiana. Here's their refinancing dilemma:

- Kristin and Emmet owe $200,000 more on their mortgage.
- There are 28 years left of their current mortgage term.
- They are considering refinancing into a 30-year fixed-rate loan.
- They can reduce their rate from 7 percent to 6 percent.
- Their closing costs are $1,300.
- Kristin and Emmet plan to move in five years because they have two toddlers and want to relocate to a better school district.

Let's see how the 1 percent reduction in interest rate plays out for this couple:

 How Much Will Kristin and Emmet Save?

Monthly payment at 7 percent	$1,331
Monthly payment at 6 percent	1,199
Monthly Savings =	**$ 132**

Now we need to apply the Refinancing Rule of 5s to see if refinancing is a good financial decision for them.

✔ The interest rate is going down by more than 0.5 percent.
✔ Kristin and Emmet can recoup their closing costs in less than 5 years—10 months, in fact—well before they plan to move.
✔ Kristin and Emmet are adding less than 5 years to their loan term—two years, in this scenario.

Kristin and Emmet should go for it! At first glance, their $132 monthly savings may not seem like much, but let's see how it plays out over time:

 Kristin and Emmet's Savings

Monthly	$	132
Yearly	$	1,584
Five years	$	7,920
Thirty years	$	47,520

Since Kristin and Emmet want to move in five years, is it still worth it? Yes! They will easily earn back their closing costs in just 10 months, so they're fine in that regard. And even in five years, a one percentage point rate reduction will save them $7,920 worth of interest! If they change their minds, stay in the house, and send their kids to private school, they could save $47,520 over the life of the 30-year mortgage.

Reduce More Than Just the Rate

Often when people refinance, they focus solely on getting a great new rate and leave everything else the same. If they originally went with a 30-year fixed-rate mortgage, they do so again out of habit. Depending on how many years there are left on your loan, that can defeat the entire purpose of the refinance. Why? Because even if you get a lower interest rate, stretching out those interest payments over additional years will eventually cost more.

That's why the last point in the Refinance Rule of 5s is that your loan term should not increase by more than five years. In Kristin and Emmet's case, a 30-year mortgage is okay because they're only two years into their existing 30-year mortgage. But what if you were 10 years in? Refinancing into another 30-year mortgage would be like having a *40-year* mortgage and, as you may remember, I told you never to get one of those. That's just too long to pay for this product we call credit. It's even worse for people who are near retirement. If that's you, you should be looking to finish off your mortgage ASAP, not extend it.

Again, when you refinance, don't increase your loan term by more than five years and, if at all possible, *reduce* it instead. Here's the strategy: Use the savings you get from the lower rate to pay for a shorter, more aggressive loan term.

Let me show you what would happen if Kristin and Emmet refinanced into a 20-year mortgage instead of a 30-year. Their monthly payment would go up by $102—which isn't much, so if they can swing it, here's what will happen:

Kristin and Emmet's 20-Year Savings

Interest at 7 percent (28 years)	$247,216
Interest at 6 percent (20 years)	143,680
BIG SAVINGS =	**$103,536**

So you see, if you can stretch your budget and switch into a shorter mortgage, you SAVE BIG. By cutting eight years out of their time as mortgagees, Kristin and Emmet save $103,536! That might be enough money for them to stay put and pay for private school!

Beware the Contractor Con

BIG SECRET

If you're refinancing so you can remodel, be aware of how contractors can con you. First of all, never hire an unlicensed contractor. Ask to see his license and then verify its validity with your state. Never pull permits for the job yourself. If you do, you are assuming liability for the job. Don't let your payments get ahead of the contractor's progress. Some just disappear! Get lien releases, which are letters stating the contractor has paid the subcontractors so they can't come after you. If all this fails, find out if your state has a contractor guarantee fund. If so, the state will reimburse you for shoddy work!

Refinancing Fees

Since closing costs—and whether you can earn them back in a timely fashion—are the big sticking point of refinancing, a no-cost refi might sound tempting. Red alert! This is one of those too-good-to-be-true situations. If you go this route, it's true that you don't have to come up with any *cash* for the closing costs on your refinance loan, but you *do* pay for them. Trust me, they always make you pay.

One way lenders get their money is by tacking the closing costs onto the end of your loan. That increases the principal owed and can actually defeat the purpose of the refinance by raising your monthly payment and lowering your savings.

The other way they charge you for so-called no-cost refinancing is with a higher interest rate. The lender charges you an interest rate high enough to more than make up for the closing costs you are not paying. Once again, that defeats the purpose. The whole point is to refinance into as low an interest rate as possible.

Bottom line: Come up with the money to pay your own closing costs when you refinance. Under the Refinance Rule of 5s, you are going to make up those costs in a short time, anyway.

BIG TIPS

- Apply the Refinancing Rule of 5s to decide whether to refinance.
- Reduce your loan term when you refinance, if possible.
- Divide your closing costs by your monthly savings to see how long it will take to recover your costs.
- Don't fall for a "no-cost" refinancing. It will cost you. A lot.

CHAPTER

Pay Off Your Mortgage Early

Throughout Part I, I've alluded to the exponential savings that come from paying your mortgage off early. Remember all the hints I dropped? In Chapter 2 we talked about my Fourth Wall of Home Ownership, which is using your mortgage interest tax deduction to prepay your mortgage. In Chapter 4, I warned you never to sign up for a mortgage with a prepayment penalty because prepaying your mortgage is exactly what you want to do and a penalty will cut into your profits. Okay, enough foreshadowing. It's finally time to focus on how paying your mortgage off early guarantees you will SAVE BIG.

In this chapter, learn to SAVE BIG by:

- Paying your mortgage off early, the one guaranteed return on investment you can make.
- Using your mortgage interest tax deduction to pay extra toward your mortgage.
- Skipping services that promise to help you prepay your mortgage.
- Making sure your mortgage company credits your extra payments accurately.

A Guaranteed Gain

If your stockbroker told you he had an investment that was *guaranteed* to get you a 5 to 10 percent return, you would call him a crook. After all, we've been taught that no investment is a sure thing. But that's exactly what prepaying your mortgage is: an investment that's *guaranteed* to get you a return equal to the amount of your interest rate.

There are lots of books about how to make money, but if you think about it, *not losing* money is just as good. That's where that expression "a penny saved is a penny earned" comes from. Make $100,000. Save $100,000. It's the same amount of money in your bank account that you wouldn't otherwise have. Plus, you have to pay income taxes on *earned* interest but not on *saved* interest.

Don't believe me? Let me show you an example. Deb F. of California has a $200,000 mortgage. It's a 30-year fixed at 7 percent. Her monthly payment is $1,331. Here's how much money she can save by sending in just $50 extra each month.

Deb's 30-Year Mortgage Prepayment Plan

Total interest paying minimum	$279,013
Total interest paying extra $50/month	242,586
BIG SAVINGS =	$ 36,427

Presto! Deb is able to save $36,427 over the 30-year life of the loan just by sending in 50 bucks extra per month. Surely, you can find an extra $50 lying around somewhere. How does so little achieve so much?

Here's how it works. When you pay your monthly mortgage, you send in extra money and specify that it is to go toward reducing your loan amount—the principal. The bank bases its interest charges on that principal, so by reducing the amount of principal, there is less for it to charge you interest on. Another way of putting it: The extra $50 you sent in is $50 the bank will never get to charge you interest on. Not now. Not over the 30 years of your loan. Never.

BIG SECRET Make Sure You Get Credit for Your Mortgage Payment

Some banks intentionally overlook on-time mortgage payments so they can charge you late fees. I once did a television investigation about this. A major national bank was routinely failing to record people's payments, so some consumers started sending them certified mail out of desperation. This is where it might be worth having an automated payment set up through online banking. That way you know you've paid on time each month and there's a written record.

When you send in extra money to pay down your principal, it doesn't change your monthly payment (except with special mortgages). Rather, it comes off the back end of your loan. The bank doesn't get to charge you interest for *as long*, because once the principal is paid off, there's nothing *left* to charge interest on. So that extra $50 a month will save Deb *time* in addition to money. In fact, she will be finished paying her mortgage more than three years early!

But you don't have to wait 27 years to see the benefit of mortgage prepayment. Every time you send in extra money for your mortgage, you will save, even if you don't keep the loan for long, because each extra payment causes less money to go toward interest and more to go toward principal.

Let's say Deb sells after 10 years. Here's how prepayment would still benefit her:

 Deb's 10-Year Mortgage Prepayment Plan

Loan balance left after paying the minimum	$171,624
Loan balance left after paying an extra $50/month	162,970
BIG SAVINGS =	**$ 8,654**

In just 10 years, Deb will have saved $8,654 by paying just $50 extra per month. That's all additional equity she can put toward her next home. It's kind of fun to plug in different prepayment numbers and time frames and see how much you can save by prepaying your mortgage. I've posted an excellent prepayment calculator at my website, www.ElisabethLeamy.com.

Silencing the Naysayers

I know I've made mortgage prepayment sound like a no-brainer, but there are plenty of eminent experts who raise doubts. Here are their agitated arguments and my reasoned comebacks.

> **Their argument:** "You can make more by investing the money."
> *My response:* Yup, you can. But you can also lose more money. When you invest in the market, your investment has the *potential* to go up, but it can also go down. There's risk there. Mortgage prepayment has a guaranteed return. No other

investment does. And the higher your mortgage rate, the more competitive an investment prepayment is.

I'm not sure why, but whenever financial whizzes debate this topic, they always frame it as an absolute, like you either have to put *all* your money in the market *or* all of it into prepaying your mortgage. Why can't you do a bit of both? Prepaying your mortgage could be one of many investments you make, a way of diversifying your portfolio. Or you could switch back and forth over time, putting your money in the market when it's hot and in your mortgage when it's not.

There's also the discipline factor. Yes, if you have extra money, you can make a greater return by investing it, but many of us will just spend the money instead. Investing takes willpower and effort. You have to hire a financial adviser, find a stock to invest in, and hope it's a good choice. Any idiot can prepay their mortgage—and I mean that as a *good* thing!

Their argument: "You should save for retirement and college first."

My response: Okay, go for it. But, being the savvy consumer that you are, you can probably pay down your mortgage *while* saving for retirement and college. Yes, max out your retirement plans before prepaying your mortgage. You should at least make sure you are contributing enough to get your company's 401(k) match, if it offers one, because that is a 100 percent return. There are great college savings plans with lucrative tax benefits as well. But remember, any amount—$100, $50, or even $25—you send in to pay your mortgage off early makes an impact. Besides, you have to pay your mortgage off eventually. It's a debt you took on. You can either pay it early—and SAVE BIG—or pay it later and save nothing.

Their argument: "You lose part of the mortgage interest tax break."

My response: Yes, you do. When you spend less on interest, you have less to write off. But please, people, by prepaying your mortgage, you are slashing tens of thousands off of your interest payments. By contrast, the mortgage interest tax deduction only saves you a *fraction* of those thousands. It's always better to save the whole thing than part of the thing.

Their argument: "You should save up six months' worth of living expenses first."

   My response: Good idea. Do that . . . and also prepay your mortgage. After all, if you lose your job but you have paid your mortgage off early, those living expenses will be next to nothing because you won't have a mortgage payment to make. This is exactly what happened to the "Most Frugal Mom in America" whom I mentioned in the Introduction to this book. She lost her job, but managed to putter along for two years without one because she had no mortgage payment.

Their argument: "Money prepaid into a mortgage is not liquid."

   My response: This is the most compelling argument against mortgage prepayment. I suppose it is the one risk of prepayment as an investment. A couple of thoughts: I always believe in taking the *sure* savings over the *possible* problem. You may never have an emergency that forces you to tap the cash that is stashed in your house. If you suddenly do, you will have to refinance or take out a home equity loan and your chances of approval are much greater if you have substantial equity in the home—which you can get by, you guessed it, prepaying your mortgage.

Home Equity Loans Are the Best of the Worst

I am anti debt, because credit costs money, but if you need to take on debt, a home equity loan is the best kind because the interest on it is tax deductible. For example, if you are in the 28 percent tax bracket and you take out a home equity loan at 10 percent interest, your after-tax cost is only about 7 percent.

Their argument: "What if the homeowner doesn't plan to keep this house anyway?"

   My response: That's fine. There is no rule that says you can't sell a home that is already paid off. It gives you more equity to put toward the next one. And remember, I already proved to you that prepayment creates substantial savings even if you sell early.

Their argument: "Real estate prices are falling."

> *My response:* That's irrelevant. The amount of money you invested in real estate was determined back when you made an offer on the home. If values have fallen, you still owe the same amount, whether you pay it now or pay it later when you sell. By prepaying your mortgage, you can save thousands in interest payments and at least cut your losses.

Their argument: "You could lose your equity through foreclosure."

> *My response:* If you get behind on your house payments and you have no equity, *that's* when you are forced into foreclosure. If you get behind on your payments and you *have* equity—especially the extra equity you gain by prepaying—you can sell the house before the bank forecloses.

Where's the Money Going to Come From?

If I've convinced you that prepaying your mortgage is a savvy move, then let me help you find the money to do it. The nice thing is, as I've shown, even a tiny amount of money makes a significant difference through the power of time and reverse compounding.

Using Free Money to Save Money

Remember the Four Walls of Home Ownership that I shared with you in Chapter 2? The fourth point was this:

> **Wall 4: Tax deduction = Mortgage prepayment fund**. The final wall of your sound financial structure is using the "free money" you get from your mortgage interest tax deduction to prepay your mortgage, saving thousands and paying the loan off years early.

Yes! I've been planning this for several chapters now. Many people use the mortgage interest tax deduction to stretch and strain for a fancier house. But in my four-part plan, you make your mortgage equal your rent, which means this tax deduction is *found money*—money you didn't have when you were a renter—that you can use to SAVE BIG.

Back to Deb in California. Remember, she has a $200,000 mortgage at 7 percent. Her mortgage interest tax deduction is roughly $3,000 a year for the first decade of her loan; $2,000 a year for the second decade; and $1,000 a year for the third decade. Again, I've rounded for easy math. I've posted an easy-to-use calculator to help you determine the amount of your mortgage interest tax deduction at my website, www.ElisabethLeamy.com.

Let's see how much Deb could save if she put her annual mortgage interest tax deduction toward prepayment. This is going to be mind blowing!

Using Deb's Tax Deduction to Prepay Her Mortgage

Interest owed making minimum payment	$ 279,013
Interest owed adding tax deduction funds	164,435
BIG SAVINGS =	**$114,578**

Woo-hoo! $114,578 is *serious* money that Deb saved by using *free* money—the mortgage interest tax deduction the government gives us just for buying a house—to prepay her mortgage. Not only that, she will get her mortgage paid off 10 years early! Imagine the financial freedom of not having a house payment, your single biggest expense.

Only Make Renovations That *Make* You Money Until Your House Is Paid Off

If you are ultradisciplined about paying your mortgage off early, one tactic is not to spend any money decorating or remodeling your home until it is paid off. The only exception: upgrades like new energy-saving windows or a fuel efficient furnace that *make* you money. Honestly, I'm a home improvement nut, so I wouldn't be able to pull this off! But that's how the most frugal mom in America did it. You met her at the beginning of the book. Her name is Kathy S. She lives in Illinois. And she paid off her mortgage in just five years!

Paying Your Mortgage Biweekly

The most popular mortgage prepayment system is to pay biweekly. It's simple: You make half a mortgage payment every two weeks instead of the full payment once a month. You end up making 13 mortgage payments a year this way, rather than 12, because there are more than four weeks in some months. This appeals to folks because so many of us are *paid* biweekly, so you can plan your mortgage payments around your paychecks. Biweekly payments are especially easy to arrange in the era of online banking because you can set it up with a few clicks. Here's the math if Deb were to pay her mortgage biweekly:

 **If Deb Pays Biweekly Instead of Monthly**

Interest owed paying monthly (12 payments)	$279,013
Interest owed paying biweekly (13 payments)	208,115
BIG SAVINGS =	**$ 70,898**

Another round of impressive savings, just by tweaking your habits so you can afford to pay a little bit of extra money toward your mortgage. You can pay off your loan about six and a half years early by doing it this way.

Cancel PMI and Pay It toward Your Mortgage

As you know, I recommend making a 20 percent down payment on your home, but if you just couldn't do it then you are paying private mortgage insurance. You're entitled to drop PMI when you have 22 percent equity in the home. That means you own 22 percent of its value and the bank owns the rest. You get to the 22 percent point either by diligently making payments (and prepayments!) or because home values have risen in your area, giving you more equity.

When your bank drops the PMI premium, you should keep paying that amount, but not toward PMI—toward paying your mortgage off early. You are used to paying this amount anyway, so it's one of those great painless strategies.

Petition Your Bank to Drop PMI

Lenders are required by law to stop charging you for private mortgage insurance when you have 22 percent equity in your home, but some have been known to conveniently forget. What's more, if you reach the 22 percent threshold because real estate prices have gone up, you're going to have to prove your case. Ask your bank what proof it requires. You may have to gather comparable sales figures or hire an appraiser to determine the new value of your home. Do it! Dropping PMI is worth it.

Let's see how this repurposed payment helps you SAVE BIG. The PMI premium on a $225,000 loan is about $100 a month. Let's say you get to drop PMI after year 5. What would that extra $100 a month do for you if you used it to prepay your mortgage? Take a look:

Putting PMI Premium toward Prepayment

Total interest making minimum payment	$252,072
Total interest adding PMI funds	228,029
BIG SAVINGS =	**$ 24,042**

Not too shabby. By applying your previously used PMI premium to your mortgage, you save $24,042. That is pretty darn good, considering that in this example you didn't get started making extra payments until year 6 of your mortgage.

The Logistics of Prepaying Your Mortgage

There's no right or wrong answer if you're choosing when to prepay your mortgage or how to come up with the extra money. Starting at any time in any amount will help you. However, there *is* a right and wrong way of sending in the actual payment.

Don't Pay Somebody Else to Be Your Conscience

Your lender or an outside company may offer to help you prepay your mortgage by enrolling you in a biweekly payment program. Yes, paying biweekly is a great system, but you don't need anybody's help to do it. Don't fall for this rip-off! Here's the catch: The company charges you $400 to $600 to enroll in the program, plus as much as $40 for each payment!

Worse yet, these corporate con artists don't send in the extra payments as you make them. They hold them either until the end of the month, or until the end of the year, all the while earning interest on *your* money. Plus, do you really want to send your mortgage payment—the biggest chunk of your income—to some outside company? What if the company is tardy in making your payment, wrecking your credit? What if the company doesn't forward your payment at all? What if the company folds?

Online banking makes it so easy to create your own prepayment program. If you still use paper checks, that's doable, too. Just add extra to your payment each month. Bottom line: Never pay somebody else for what you can do for free.

Protecting Your Extra Payments

Banks are notorious for crediting people's prepayments wrong. What a nightmare. You make this huge push to send in extra money and then they screw it up? They are losing tens of thousands of dollars when you prepay, so don't expect bankers to be the best stewards of your extra payments. Here's what you can do to protect yourself.

- Contact your bank to see how it prefers that you make your prepayments. You may be required to make a special notation on your check or online payment noting that the extra is for principal.
- It's safer to send an identical extra payment every month. That makes it easier for the bank to understand what you're doing and easier for you to track.
- You may want to consider making your extra payment via a separate check or separate online transaction, so that it is not lumped in with your base mortgage payment.
- You should print out an amortization table from the Internet that shows how each extra payment affects your principal and interest, then check it whenever you get a new statement to make sure the bank's calculations are in line with yours.

There is an excellent amortization calculator at www
.DecisionAide.com.

- Keep your online banking summaries (or canceled checks)
as proof of your extra payments.
- If you do have a dispute, don't send it where you send your
payments. That's just an automated processing center. Call
the bank and get a proper address where real human beings
read mail.

BIG TIPS

- Use your mortgage interest tax deduction to prepay your
mortgage.
- If you are paying PMI, cancel it as soon as possible and
use that amount to prepay your mortgage.
- Don't pay some service to prepay your mortgage for you.
- Check with your mortgage company to see if it has any
rules about how your prepayment must be made in order
to be credited accurately.

CHAPTER

Sell Your House Yourself

We've come full circle in the journey of home ownership—from buying to owning and maintaining—and now it's time to sell. Heads up, because this is one more opportunity to save tens of thousands of dollars. How? By doing a For Sale by Owner or *FSBO* (pronounced "fizz-bo") deal. Selling your house yourself is not easy, but it's not that hard. I helped my husband sell his house without an agent, and I bought and sold my condo without one.

If you can do this just once, you will get ahead financially. According to the National Association of Realtors, most people own six homes in their lifetime, so you have half a dozen chances to SAVE BIG. FSBOs work best if you have a cool head and a hot housing market. Look for the opportunity.

In this chapter, learn to SAVE BIG by:

- Pricing your house right for sale. If you get this wrong, nothing else matters.
- Welcoming buyers' agents to your home, but offering them less than full commission.
- Negotiating strategically to make the most money on your home.
- Asking a seller's agent to accept a lower commission if all else fails.

It's the Price, Stupid

Just as candidate Bill Clinton once figured out how to get himself *into* the White House, by reciting "It's the economy, stupid," you can get yourself *out* of your house by reciting, "It's the price, stupid." Nothing else really matters. You must set the right price for your home to succeed in selling it yourself and making a profit. But hey, no pressure! Below are several ideas for how to zero in on the perfect price point for your home.

Check Comparables

The most important factor in deciding the selling price of your home is how much similar homes have sold for in the past six months. Fortunately, in the age of the internet, this is easy to find out. Just go to a website like www.Zillow.com or www.Domania.com, enter your address and then follow the links to homes sold recently nearby. Concentrate on those homes that are closest to yours in terms of geography, size, and amenities.

When using these sites, you need to make sure you are looking at actual sales figures rather than the sites' own estimates. For example, Zillow's "Zestimates" are great fun, but the site itself acknowledges it has a margin of error of about 7 percent. That is too big a margin for purposes of pricing your home.

Moving Estimates Given by Phone or Online Are Useless Scams

If you go with a phone or Internet moving estimate, you're just setting yourself up to be lowballed. Many companies lurking online are not even movers. They're moving *brokers* infamous for cheating people. You must invite three or four reputable movers to come to your home, view your belongings and give you *written* estimates. Insist on *binding* estimates. The best kind of binding estimate is one that is "guaranteed not to exceed." In other words, the mover promises to move your household for a set rate. If your move involves *more* weight or takes *more* time than the mover thought, you *still* pay the estimated amount. If your move involves *less* weight or *less* time than the mover originally estimated, you pay *less!* Never hire a moving company without first checking it out at www.bbb.org and www.movingscam.com.

In addition to studying sales over the past six months, you should also be aware of how houses on the market are priced right now. In order to get a sense, scan your local paper's website and classified ads and spend a couple of Sundays visiting open houses. This will enable you to see what the houses have to offer compared to yours. Compare based on square footage, number of bedrooms and bathrooms, architectural style, features, and finishes.

Call In the Experts

Okay, that all sounded very nice, but now it's time to call in the experts. The reason I suggested that you do some research of your own is so you will be prepared to *listen* to what the experts have to say! In the end, pricing the house is your own decision, and you will be better able to appreciate expert advice if you have a first-hand feel for the market.

Ask an Agent   One strategy is to ask real estate agents how you should price your home. I know, I know, this is a chapter about selling your house yourself, but if you can get some advice from a pro (gracefully and gratefully), you should. When I was selling my condo, I ran into my neighbor Barbara B. while out walking my dog. Barbara happens to be *the* expert agent who sells most of the condos in my old community. I explained that we needed to squeeze every bit of profit out of our condo in order to afford our next home, so we were going to try to sell it ourselves. I went on to say that if we failed, we planned to give her the listing. Then I asked what price she would recommend.

She cheerfully suggested a price and I went with it. I am grateful to Barbara to this day because I would have priced the condo about $5,000 higher. With the price she suggested, it sold in four weeks. So if you have a friend who is a real estate agent, find a way to approach her politely and ask for advice.

If you can't fall back on a friend, interview three agents who are experts about your neighborhood and ask them to do a pricing analysis for you. I know this doesn't sound like the world's classiest move, but I can rationalize it. When you try a FSBO, I believe you should set a deadline for yourself. For instance, if the house hasn't sold in, say, three months (or whatever time frame works for you), you will hire an agent. When you interview these agents for their pricing suggestions, you will also be choosing who to give the listing to should you fail to make the sale on your own.

Don't Hire an Agent, But If You Do, Sign Up for a Three-Month Contract

Most real estate agent contracts are for six months, but three months is preferable. You want to give this agent a sense of urgency about selling your house. If they are doing a great job, but it just hasn't clicked, you can extend for another three months. But if you are disappointed in the agent, you will be able to bail out sooner and hire somebody else

Pay for an Appraisal   If you can't stomach this minor deception, fair enough, I have another idea for you. Hire a professional appraiser to put a price on your house. The appraiser will perform a comparable analysis of recent home sales, and—better yet—will tackle the tricky task of evaluating how those homes are different from yours and what dollar value to put on those differences. Try to find an appraiser who has worked in FSBO situations before. You can find an appraiser at www.appraisalinstitute.org.

Be Aware of Benchmarks

Another important factor to consider when setting your price is benchmarks, pricing cutoffs that buyers are likely to pay attention to. Here's what I mean: It has always seemed dumb to me when a candy bar is priced at $.99. I mean, everybody knows that's the same thing as a dollar! But with real estate, there is a sound rationale for goofy prices like $499,000. Many sellers will instruct their agent that they want to buy a house "under $500,000." Or they may search online and choose the search category that says "$475,000–$499,000." You don't want your home to be excluded from their search because you priced it at a round number of $500,000.

Know Your Minimum

As you price your home, you need to establish the rock-bottom minimum price that you are willing to accept. It's best to start thinking about this now rather than when you are under pressure because you have just received an offer and you have 24 hours to respond to it. In addition to considering comparable sales, think about the amount of money you need to get out of the house in order to recover your own purchase price. And don't forget about the closing costs you paid when you bought the home and any major money you have spent on upgrades. You want to try to recover those costs, too. Memorize this bottom price and keep it in mind as you receive offers.

Underpricing Your FSBO

Once you know your home's value, the great thing about selling it yourself is that you can afford to underprice it and still make money. Having a house languish on the market because it is overpriced is considered the worst danger in real estate. In a FSBO situation you have a built-in mechanism for avoiding that blunder. Deliberately underpricing your house is your number one strategy for a painless FSBO process. The discounted price makes your home appealing, making up for any disadvantage you may face because you are selling without the help of an agent.

Don't worry, you can still make money if you underprice your home. Since you are selling the house yourself, you can price it *under* what you would with an agent, but make *over* what you would with an agent. You can afford to do this because real estate agents traditionally make a 6 percent commission. Since you don't have to pay an agent, you can play around with the price within that 6 percent that agents usually make.

For instance, Cindy G. of California was moving because she wanted to send her son to the wonderful private school she herself had attended as a child. She needed to squeeze as much money out of her house as possible to pay for that private school so she decided to try to sell it herself. Cindy knew she could afford to underprice her home a little bit to make it attractive and still make more money than if she paid an agent.

After doing her homework, Cindy learned that an agent would have priced her house at about $250,000 (actually the agent suggested $249,999!) and charged a 6 percent commission. So Cindy priced her home at $247,500, a 1 percent discount. This pricing strategy worked! In fact, she got multiple offers and received her asking price for the home because it seemed so reasonable to buyers. Here's how much money Cindy saved by selling her house herself, even though she discounted it a bit:

The Power of Underpricing Cindy's FSBO Home

Proceeds after discounting house 1% and selling it herself	$247,500
Proceeds at higher agent's price with 6% commission	235,000
BIG SAVINGS =	**$ 12,500**

To buyers, Cindy's house looked alluring—downright sexy— because it was priced $2,500 below others around it. But despite that discount, she actually made $12,500 *more* than she would have with an agent because she didn't have to pay a commission.

Remember, "It's the price, stupid." For those who live in more expensive real estate markets, you can save even more. What if you were selling a pricier house that an agent would list for $500,000? Here's how you would SAVE BIG if you discount the price 1 percent and sell it yourself.

The Power of Underpricing a More Expensive FSBO Home

Proceeds after discounting house 1% and selling it yourself	$495,000
Proceeds at higher agent's price with 6% commission	470,000
BIG SAVINGS =	**$ 25,000**

That's $25,000 saved! As you can see, in this example I assumed you get your asking price, just to make the math easy. There's no guarantee that will happen. It depends on the real estate climate. But if you sell a house yourself, even if it sells for less than you had hoped, you are saving the 6 percent commission. Depending on the market, you can play around within that 6 percent range that is the agent's typical commission—lowering your discount when it's a seller's market and increasing it when it's a buyer's market.

Hire a Lawyer Instead of an Agent

If you are selling your house without an agent, you will do the work of advertising and showing your home yourself, but you will still want help with the unfamiliar details of the offer. Long before you get an offer, you should hire a good real estate attorney. Your attorney will be able to advise you on the proper protocol, review offers, and be present at your closing. Whether you pay a lump sum or an hourly fee, it will still be much less than what you'd pay a real estate agent.

Agents Welcome

At this point you've set your price and you're waiting for buyers to come tour your home. True, you chose not to hire an agent to help you *sell* the house. But if there is an agent who can help somebody else *buy* your house, you should consider it. According to the National Association of Realtors, 86 percent of home buyers find their property with the help of a real estate agent, so you don't want to exclude this constituency.

Welcoming agents simply means that instead of saving 6 percent in commissions, you may save 3 to 5 percent. Traditionally, real estate agents split commissions in half—3 percent to the seller's agent and 3 percent to the buyer's agent. So the low-friction option is to agree to pay the buyer's agent that 3 percent bounty for bringing you a buyer.

Just when Kendell A. of Illinois finally bit the bullet and bought her own condo, she met her soulmate and they decided to move in together and get married. Ah, life. Suddenly Kendell needed to sell her condo. She wanted to try to do it herself so she could make enough money on the place to recoup her closing costs. Kendell considered paying a buyer's agent 3 percent, because she knew she would still make a tidy profit on her $495,000 home if she did that.

Here's how paying a 3 percent commission compares to paying the traditional 6 percent commission:

 If Kendell Pays a Buyer's Agent 3 Percent on Her $495,000 Condo

Proceeds after 3 percent commission	$480,150
Proceeds after 6 percent commission	465,300
BIG SAVINGS =	**$ 14,850**

As you can see, if Kendell paid the full 3 percent to a buyer's agent, she would still save $14,850 compared to the cost of paying both a seller's agent *and* a buyer's agent.

Offer a Lower Percentage

Kendell might have been willing to sacrifice the 3 percent in a lopsided buyer's market, but her home was in a hot Chicago neighborhood, so she figured she could save even more.

She also knew that many real estate agents will accept a commission of 2 percent. It's pretty routine. So Kendell decided to offer buyer's agents 2 percent instead of 3 percent. Kendell's plan paid off! She still compensated a buyer's agent for bringing her a sale, but she preserved more profit for herself.

 If Kendell Pays a Buyer's Agent 2 Percent on Her $495,000 Condo

Proceeds after 2 percent commission	$485,100
Proceeds after 6 percent commission	465,300
BIG SAVINGS =	**$ 19,800**

There, that's better. A $19,800 savings for all your hard work seems more like it. Call me greedy. The smart thing to do is raise or lower the percentage you are willing to pay a buyer's agent, depending on the real estate climate. It's a nice safety valve that you can adjust to the times.

Flat-Fee Commissions

Hang on. There's one more option! In a hot real estate market, where sellers have the upper hand, you may be able to offer a flat fee to buyer's agents instead of a percentage of the sales price. Choose a flat fee that is still attractive to agents but far less than a percentage commission would be.

This is what my husband and I did when we sold our condo. We advertised that we were offering a flat fee of $5,000 to buyer's agents. The strangest thing happened. The agent representing the couple who bought our place tried to get us to pay 3 percent instead. He made it sound like his clients wanted it that way and the deal was in jeopardy if we didn't pay.

I called up the couple, because we had established a rapport, and they were horrified at their agent's deception. My husband and I stood our ground and the sale went through with just a $5,000 flat commission. I felt no guilt, because this couple found our home through an open house. The only service this agent performed was filling out the offer form for his clients. That's not worth 3 percent!

BIG
SECRET

Have Your Lender Help You

Remember the lender you carefully chose in Chapter 5? That pro can help you sell a house as well as buy one. Normally your real estate agent would qualify potential buyers to make sure they have the financial means to buy your home. Instead, send prospective buyers to your lender for vetting. This mortgage broker or banker will be happy to have the referral and will pull a credit report, and so on. If the buyers are mortgage-worthy, this pro will let you know and also offer them a loan, a free service to both sides.

Negotiating the Deal

When you're selling without an agent, it's easy to feel so relieved and grateful to receive an offer that you don't want to jinx it. But as long as the buyer is financially fit, you should always make a counteroffer. Don't be insulted if what you've received is a lowball offer. Unfortunately, you don't have an agent to shield you from this sort of thing, so you'll have to shrug it off on your own. It's worth making a counteroffer because this is somebody who has shown a strong interest in your home.

Fortunately, counteroffers are simple to prepare. You simply state the price that you would accept and list the other items in the offer that are *not* okay with you. Then you list what you would accept instead. You may be able to use a standard regional form designed for counteroffers to make it even simpler. Your lawyer will know. Be sure to give a deadline by which the buyer must respond.

As you go back and forth, here are a few strategies to consider:

- If you have the upper hand because it's a seller's market, make your price reductions smaller than the buyer's price increases. But if it's a buyer's market or a balanced market, consider splitting the difference. There's something about meeting in the middle that seems profoundly fair to people.
- Consider tabling smaller matters, like who's going to fix the leaky faucet, until you have settled on the big stuff like price and closing date. (*Note:* Tighter closing schedules are better because less can go wrong.)
- If you and the buyer are close but can't quite meet on price, find out how much your higher price will cost the buyer per month (ask your lender). When they hear that a $10,000 difference only amounts to about $60 more per month, they may concede.

If none of these strategies works, you may want to consider paying for some of the buyer's closing costs. Offering to pay some closing costs can save a sale—and it doesn't have to cost you anything. Some buyers have diligently amassed a down payment, but just can't quite scrape together the closing costs. So here's what you do: Offer to pay some or all of their closing costs, but raise your price by an equal amount. This may seem like just a psychological ploy, but it's not. You net the same amount, but the buyers get the all-important cash they need to close their loan.

This transfer of funds is done painlessly at the closing. You never have to front any money. Just be sure to set a dollar limit on your closing cost contribution, in case the buyers haven't read this book and don't know how to cut their closing costs!

Pretend to Be a Curmudgeon

When negotiating the sale of your house, pretend to have certain ironclad sticking points that are not open to compromise. Then, when you concede those items later, the buyers will think they have really scored!

If All Else Fails

If you manage to sell your house yourself, you're a genius—a richer genius! If you don't, you're right back where you started. So what? *Now* you will hire an agent. You gave yourself a workable deadline at the beginning, so you still have time to sell before you need to move.

Since you have done so much work already polishing your house for sale, there's one last-ditch chance to save: See if your new agent will agree to take your listing at a discount. According to Real Trends, a real estate consulting firm, a commission of 5.2 percent is now the national average, and for that to be the case, plenty of agents must be agreeing to take *less* than 5 percent.

If your agent accepts a 5 percent commission instead of 6, even though your FSBO didn't work out, you still SAVE BIG! Don't believe me—check out the numbers for a $250,000 house:

Paying a Lower Commission on a $250,000 House

Proceeds after 5% commission	$237,500
Proceeds after 6% commission	235,000
BIG SAVINGS =	**$ 2,500**

There you have it, a final last-ditch savings of $2,500 in the life cycle of getting a mortgage, buying a home, paying taxes on the place, and finally selling it again. You were able to SAVE BIG at every step along the way. Now, you can start the entire process all over again and save even more!

BIG TIPS

- Look up comparable homes and see what they sold for.
- Attend open houses to scope out your competition.
- Interview real estate agents or hire an appraiser to help price your house.
- Discount your house slightly to make it alluring to potential buyers.
- Welcome buyer's agents but try to pay them less than 3 percent.
- Hire a real estate attorney and ask your lender to help.

CARS

The Cheaper Road

A car is the second biggest thing we buy. Auto website Edmunds.com says Americans spend an average of $5,637 on car payments each year. Then we add on another $8,095 for license, registration, taxes, insurance, interest, and depreciation, according to AAA.

Here's the conventional wisdom for saving money on your car: Inflate your tires adequately. It's a great step to take for safety. But for savings? Come on. Inflating your tires to the optimum level will save you an average of $9 a month, according to Edmunds.com. Yup, that's it. Small Stuff Savings again. And yet plenty of people preach proper tire inflation as a key cost-saver.

Instead, follow my advice and you will SAVE BIG. Not small. Shall we put this in perspective? Don't mind if I do. There are $152,417 in car savings in the next seven chapters. You would have to properly inflate the tires of five cars for 282 years to match that!

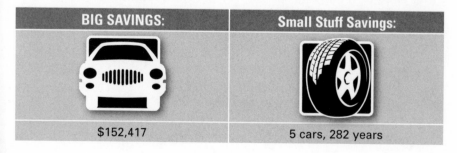

BIG SAVINGS:	Small Stuff Savings:
$152,417	5 cars, 282 years

> That's the key to the car: Don't buy new. Get a snazzy car if you want, but get a used one. Then keep it as long as you can stand it.

If you can SAVE BIG like this on your car, it's a triumph because cars are terrible investments! In fact, they're *not* investments. Cars depreciate an average of 45 percent in the first three years, according to *Consumer Reports*. They're supposed to get you from point A to point B safely and efficiently. Period.

Think of your car as just a giant appliance. Don't think of it as a status symbol. Blenders aren't status symbols. Cordless drills aren't status symbols. It's funny, people put bumper stickers on their cars to express their most fervent political and religious beliefs. Nobody puts bumper stickers on their washing machine. You would never trade in your lawn mower every three years to get the newest model, and you shouldn't get a brand-new car, either.

That's the key to the car: Don't buy new. Get a snazzy car if you want, but get a used one. Then keep it as long as you can stand it. In this section, we're going to travel down the cheaper road in the logical order you'll encounter with your car, from buying it to making it last and insuring it.

- **Chapter 11:** First we'll talk about the type of car you should buy. I'll make my argument that buying used is the way to go. If you follow my advice, you can SAVE BIG—45 percent—and have so many more car choices.
- **Chapter 12:** You're also going to need to know what type of car you can afford. I'll prove you can save thousands of dollars by paying cash for your car or limiting the loan to two years. I'll also teach you where to get the best car loan, another major money-saver.
- **Chapter 13:** Did you know you could save nearly $4,000 by buying your car from the right source? In this chapter, we'll discuss the pros and cons of superstores, new and used car dealers, individuals, and auctions.
- **Chapter 14:** When you buy a used car, it's already relatively affordable, so reliability is more important than the precise

price. I'll take you through the steps to make sure your used car is not a rebuilt wreck.

- **Chapter 15:** In this chapter, we discuss bargaining for the best purchase price. Savvy negotiators pay 10 to 15 percent less for their vehicles, so you'll want to become one. I tell you, step-by-step, how to haggle.

- **Chapter 16:** Since the second part of SAVING BIG on cars is to keep them as long as possible, you're going to need a great mechanic. I'll give you proven tips for finding Mr. Right. I'll also share three techniques for getting your car repaired for free. Yup, I said *free!*

- **Chapter 17:** The final piece of the puzzle is car insurance. I will show you how shopping around for this boring but essential product could save you as much as $1,500. We'll also talk about insurance coverage you can afford to cancel and how to squeeze the most money out of your insurance company.

Let's step on it and start talking about how to SAVE BIG on that big appliance you call your car. Hang on—$152,417 here we come!

What to Buy

I've owned two brand-new cars in my life. The first one I had for five months and then somebody crashed into it. The second lasted for five years, and then I crashed it myself. That latter story is a long, embarrassing one, so I'll skip to the point: What a waste of money! If those had been used cars, the amount of money lost when they were totaled would have been far less. But even if you have better luck (or better driving skills!) than me, a brand-new vehicle loses so much value the moment it's no longer new that it's just a terrible deal. I now happily drive a nice used car that I bought after some sucker bought it new, drove it for three years, and then turned it in.

I'm in good company. In the groundbreaking book, *The Millionaire Next Door*, Thomas Stanley and William Danko point out that people who truly understand how to save money don't believe in displaying their wealth. Their interviews with self-made millionaires revealed that only 23.5 percent of them own new cars. That's right: The millionaire next door drives a used car. As Danko and Stanley put it, "You aren't what you drive."

In this chapter, learn to SAVE BIG by:

- Buying used instead of new.
- Purchasing a less expensive dark horse vehicle.
- Being smarter than the suckers who get a new car every three years.

Never Buy a New Car

You know that cars go down in value, but did you know that a car's steepest depreciation occurs between ages zero and three—an average of 45 percent? The depreciation from year three to year six is much more modest, more like 25 percent, according to *Consumer Reports*. If you were psychic and knew a stock was going to go way down in value for three years and then level off, wouldn't you wait until year four to buy it? And yet, for some reason, people persist in sinking money into brand-new vehicles.

Dave Ramsey puts it more pithily in his book *The Total Money Makeover*. "You can't afford a new car unless you are a millionaire," he says. To drive the point home, Ramsey then tells people who want to buy a new car that you might as well "open your window on your way to work once a week and throw out a $100 bill."

Thanks, Dave. Now I'll pile on. Despite the overwhelming stats on depreciation, millions of people still buy brand-new cars every year. Here are the most frequent new-car rationalizations I hear and my snappy comebacks:

> **Your argument:** You take comfort in knowing that your brand-new car has never been in a wreck.
>
> > *My comeback:* Actually, sometimes new cars *are* wrecked coming off the delivery truck or during test drives. What's more, dealers are not required to disclose the damage unless it's more than a certain percentage of the vehicle's value. So brand-new cars *can* be damaged.
>
> **Your argument:** Used cars don't have the latest safety features.
>
> > *My comeback:* I'm not suggesting that you buy a used car from the 1980s! I'm talking about buying nearly new vehicles here, which have the latest safety features. For instance, LATCH child car seat connectors have been mandatory since 2001. Electronic stability control is now common and will be in all vehicles by 2012.
>
> **Your argument:** You crave that fragrant-new car smell.
>
> > *My comeback:* It's the scent of offgassing plastics. Seriously. I once did a story for *Good Morning America* on the possible toxicity. If you love new-car smell so much, you can buy it in a bottle.
>
> **Your argument:** You are grossed out by what my girlfriend Alicia calls "other people dirt."

My comeback: My two-year-old daughter will grind Cheerios into the seats so fast it will make any new car instantly look used. I used to freak out about "other people dirt" too, but I've now been forced to conclude my own dirt is just as bad as—and maybe worse than—other people's!

Your argument: You want the long new-car warranty.

My comeback: If you buy a certified preowned vehicle you *can* get a long manufacturer warranty on a used car. And if you do your research right, you'll choose a car so reliable that you won't need warranty protection. More in Chapters 13 and 14.

Don't Lease, But If You Do, Haggle

Leasing is a terrible move. But if you are going to go behind my back and lease a car despite my advice, know this: You should negotiate the price of the car just as if you were buying and *then* reveal that you want to lease. The lease payment is based on the total price of the car, so the lower that price, the lower your payment.

Always Buy a Used Car

Diane B. of Georgia came to me with a dilemma. Her car had conked out. It was dead, done. The timing was terrible because Diane had just quit her traditional job to start her own business. In the past, Diane had always bought brand-new vehicles *and* she had always driven a convertible. It was part of her persona, her lifestyle. But now she couldn't afford a brand-new convertible. What should she do?

I recommended that Diane buy a *used* convertible. "No way," she countered, "I don't want to buy somebody else's problem." I told her to think about it because if she were to buy used, she would be able to afford most any convertible on the road. We never discussed it again. But a couple of weeks later, Diane pulled into my driveway in a sleek, silver convertible. Was it used? Shhh! Yes it was. I'm proud to say Diane's business is now flourishing and she can probably buy any car she chooses, but she's still driving that beautiful used convertible.

Check the Insurance Rate and Save

It may sound strange to bring up insurance, when you haven't even purchased your car yet, but checking the insurance rate early is a way to SAVE BIG. Joe M. of Arizona bought a muscle car back in his younger days without checking. The insurance ended up costing him $14,000 a year! To prevent this from happening to you, call your insurance agent with your short list and ask how much it would cost to insure the various vehicles on it. Insurance premiums can vary dramatically based on a car's safety rating and whether that vehicle seems to attract risky drivers.

The point is, buying used is not a bummer. It's a benefit. It opens up a whole new range of vehicles to you. For instance, which would you rather drive, a Lexus or a Taurus? Gosh, I'm going to go out on a limb and guess that the vast majority of you said a Lexus. Well, guess what? You *can* drive a Lexus for the *same* price as a Taurus. (It's just that it will be slightly used.)

I am going to take a quick break from writing and tool around on a car-buying website. Aha! Look at the price comparison I found between a Taurus and a Lexus:

 Which Would You Rather Have?

2009 Ford Taurus Ltd. sedan, brand-new	$24,999
2006 Lexus GS300 sedan with 38,046 miles	$24,999

Amazing. You can get a three-year-old Lexus with low mileage for the same price as a brand-new Taurus. That's the story of vehicle depreciation. Dramatic, isn't it? Of course, if you *really* want to SAVE BIG, it's the *Taurus* that you will buy used. Watch this:

 New versus Used Taurus

2009 Ford Taurus Ltd. sedan, brand-new	$24,999
2008 Ford Taurus Ltd. sedan with 40,085 miles	14,990
BIG SAVINGS =	**$10,009**

$10,000 is a huge savings and this used Taurus is only one year old. Buy a *three*-year-old Taurus and you would see the price drop even more. Buying a nice used car is a perfectly painless way to SAVE BIG and it can be done at any price point.

Let's go back to that Lexus we had our eye on. Maybe it's a little over-the-top to use a Lexus as our comparison car, but remember, I'm the savings author who lets you have fun! Why not drive a more prestigious car, if you can get it for the same price? We're pinching dollars here, not pennies.

Even if you spring for the used Lexus, you will SAVE BIG compared to buying new. Watch this:

New versus Used Lexus

2009 Lexus GS350 (replaced GS300), brand-new	$56,278
2006 Lexus GS300 with 38,046 miles	24,999
BIG SAVINGS =	**$31,279**

A $31,279 savings is spectacular. Just remember, the math works with all sorts of vehicles if you compare used to new. Used trucks are cheaper than new trucks. Used American cars cost less than new American cars. And so on. The moral of the story is simple: Let somebody *else* be the chump, buy the brand-new car, and lose thousands on it.

Shhh, Nobody Has to Know

BIG SECRET

If you are still clinging to cars as status symbols, then do this: Buy the first model year of a redesigned body style. That way, nobody will even know your vehicle isn't new! On average, car manufacturers build the same body style for four to five years before changing it.

Save Even More: Dark Horse Vehicles

I think I've proved my point that buying used is a great way to SAVE BIG. Now, you can save even *more* by picking and choosing wisely among used cars. You should try not to buy the most popular makes and models, because they are in demand so they can command a higher price.

Auto website Edmunds.com suggests shopping for what it calls dark horse cars. These are vehicles that are similar to the most popular models but are less well known. For example, Edmunds says the Nissan Altima is similar in features and quality to the Toyota Camry, but less expensive because it doesn't have the famous name. Edmunds says dark horses can be as much as 20 percent cheaper.

Let's test that premise. Back I go to a car-buying website for today's prices. Okay, I found two used vehicles—one famous, one dark horse—with nearly identical mileage. Let's compare the prices:

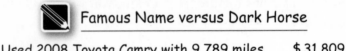 **Famous Name versus Dark Horse**

Used 2008 Toyota Camry with 9,789 miles	$ 31,809
Used 2008 Nissan Altima with 9,851 miles	24,995
BIG SAVINGS =	**$ 6,814**

As promised, you are able to save 21 percent if you buy the dark horse Nissan instead of the famous Toyota.

To help cement your understanding of dark horse vehicles, here are a few other dark horse pairings, courtesy of Edmunds.com:

Famous Name Vehicle	Dark Horse Alternate
BMW 5 Series	Cadillac CTS
Chevrolet Silverado	Dodge Ram
Chevrolet Tahoe	Buick Enclave
Dodge Caravan	Kia Sedona
Honda Civic	Mazda 3
Honda Fit	Suzuki SX4
Honda Odyssey	Ford Flex
Lexus GS	Hyundai Genesis
Toyota Camry	Chevy Malibu
Toyota Prius	Honda Insight

 ## BIG TIPS

- Never buy a new car.
- Always buy a used car.
- Consider purchasing a dark horse make and model to save even more.

CHAPTER

What Can You Afford?

The number one way to SAVE BIG on cars is to buy them used. The number two way is to pay cash for them. It may sound ambitious to pay cash for a car, and I realize not everybody can—yet. If that's your situation, don't worry, there are two painless plans for paying cash for your *next* car. Cash is king because financing a vehicle is such a terrible deal. When you take out a car loan, you are paying an *increased* price for the vehicle in the form of interest and you are getting a *decreased* value in the form of depreciation. Nevertheless, if you have to finance for now, you can still SAVE BIG by limiting the length of your loan. And whether you're paying cash or taking out a loan, there are concrete steps you can take to figure out what you can afford.

In this chapter, learn to SAVE BIG by:

- Paying cash instead of using credit to buy a used car.
- Limiting your loan term to two years if you must finance.
- Figuring out—really figuring out—what you can afford.
- Shopping for a loan before you shop for a car.

Cash Is King

I want you to pay cash for your car. The best kind of car loan you can get is no car loan. Paying interest on something that is definitely going down in value is a horrendous waste of money. Worse yet, your car could depreciate faster than you pay it off, putting you underwater in your car loan. That means you owe more on the car than it is worth. Pay cash instead and you will never have that sinking feeling. In fact, you will SAVE BIG.

Let's get right to an example. Say you decide to buy that one-year-old Ford Taurus we talked about earlier for $14,990. Let's compare the cost of paying cash for it with the cost of financing it. According to Edmunds.com, the most popular auto loan term in America is five years. Horrifying but true. I just found a five-year car loan online with a 6.5 percent interest rate. That's a pretty good rate, but even at that rate, financing the Taurus is way more expensive than paying cash for it. Here's the comparison:

Used Car Loan versus Cash

Cost over life of loan	$17,598
Cost if you pay cash	14,990
BIG SAVINGS =	$ 2,608

What a rotten deal! It costs $2,608 extra to finance the vehicle. And we know the Taurus will have lost as much as 65 percent of its value by the time this five-year loan is paid off because of depreciation. So by financing, we will have paid more than $17,500 for a vehicle that is now worth only about $5,000. Not good. And yet most people finance their cars. In fact, most people finish paying off one car loan and immediately trade that vehicle in for another one with *another* loan. A car payment is a permanent part of their lives. Bad move! Cash is king. *Pay* cash now and you can *live* like a king later.

What Can You Afford If You Pay Cash?

If you heed my call to arms and pay cash for a car, then figuring out what you can afford is a really, really simple formula. Here's how it goes:

How much cash do you *have?*
That's what you can afford to pay.

If you're lucky enough to have piles and piles of cash, go read some *other* book. Kidding! If that is your situation, you'll want to spend less than you have available on your car. I repeat: Cars are terrible investments. Correction: They're *not* investments.

Make Loans Short and Sweet

Okay, I realize not everybody will be able to pay cash for a car—at first. Fortunately, if you must take out a car loan, there is still a way for you to SAVE BIG. Here are the two parts of the plan:

1. **Big down payment.** Make as big a down payment as you can. The national average is less than 20 percent. You can do better —40 to 50 percent is more what I have in mind. The more you put down, the less you will be paying interest on. If you already own a car, a big down payment may not be as hard as it sounds because you might be able to combine your trade-in value and some savings to come up with the money.
2. **Two-year loan term.** Limit your loan term to two years. A two-year loan should assure that you are paying the car off faster than it depreciates. And it will limit the amount of interest you shell out. Let me make this point with some more math. Once again, we will use our used Ford Taurus for $14,990 and our low interest rate of 6.5 percent for this example. Here's how much you can save by choosing a two-year loan instead of a five-year one.

Comparing Loan Lengths

Term	Cost
Five years	$17,580
Two years	16,032
BIG SAVINGS =	**$ 1,548**

Yes, $1,548 saved! Even though the interest rate is the same, by shortening the number of years you pay that interest, you SAVE BIG.

Watch the Clock at the Parking Garage

Once you get your new used vehicle, you've got to park it somewhere. Many garages set their "in" clock slow and their "out" clock fast so it seems like you've been there longer than you really have. They are trying to bump you up into the next price level. Keep an eye on the time elapsed. It's fun to bust scams like this!

What Can You Afford If You Finance?

I showed you the two steps that will help you SAVE BIG if you must finance your vehicle. Now we need to drill down and figure out what you can actually *afford* within those guidelines. Let's follow Carolyn D. of Florida as she cruises through this process.

Carolyn comes from a big, boisterous family where people hand their cars down to each other. But her latest freebie just broke down on the freeway, and nobody else in the clan is quite ready to give up their old vehicle yet, so for the first time in her life Carolyn is going to take out a car loan.

Carolyn has $4,000 in cash and her old car is worth $3,000. She can combine the two and make a big down payment, as I've suggested. She likes the idea of limiting her loan to two years given that she's never even had a car loan to worry about before.

That leaves just one other moving part: her monthly payment. I don't believe in starting with abstract formulas to figure out the monthly car payment you can afford. Instead, what Carolyn—and you—should do is create a detailed budget that includes every single essential (from mortgage payments down to birthday presents) and see how much is left over for a car payment. After doing this, Carolyn thinks she can swing $375 a month. Once you've determined your monthly payment, if you want to cross-check it to make sure it's not too high, then it's fine to use a formula. Your monthly car payment should be no more than 20 percent of your monthly after-tax income. The less the better.

When you have these numbers in hand—down payment, loan term, and monthly payment—then you can go to an auto loan calculator and plug them in to see what price range you can afford. Be sure to use a calculator that does *not* list the price of the car as one of the factors. Most of the calculators I have seen online start with the vehicle price. That is just wrong! Totally backwards! *First* you should figure out what you can afford, *then* which car you're going to buy, not the other away around. ConsumerReports.org and Edmunds.com both have calculators that do it right. I will link you to them from my site, www.ElisabethLeamy.com.

I plugged in Carolyn's numbers and this is what we learned:

What Can Carolyn Afford?

Down payment	$ 4,000
Trade-in	$ 3,000
Monthly payment	$ 375
Loan term	2 years
Interest rate	6.5%
Loan she can afford	**$ 8,418**
Car she can afford	**$15,418**

By these calculations, Carolyn can afford a vehicle that costs $15,418. She shouldn't buy anything that costs more than that, but that gives her lots of choices, including the 2008 Ford Taurus we've been using as an example.

Of the four factors involved—down payment, monthly payment, loan term, and vehicle cost—only one should be adjustable: the vehicle cost. Many people change the wrong variables. They go for a higher-cost vehicle because they fall in love with it. Then they make the loan term longer so that they can afford the monthly payment. Whoops! Wrong. And wrong again. If you do this exercise and find you cannot afford the car you've had your eye on, guess what? You should downgrade what you're considering. Seriously. Sorry!

BIG SECRET

Two Easy Plans to Pay Cash for Your Next Car

1. **Plan one:** After you've figured out a monthly car payment your family can afford, subtract $50 from it. In other words, if you can afford $400 a month, resolve to spend only $350. Then use that $50 a month to immediately start a fund for your next car.

2. **Plan two:** Save nothing now, but *after* you've finished paying off your car loan, continue putting a payment of that same size into a savings account each month. You're used to it, so it's easy. Since you're going to keep your car long past when it's paid off, you should have enough money saved to pay cash for the next one.

Shop for Outside Financing First

If you must finance your vehicle, there's another crucial rule you should know to SAVE BIG: Never shop for a used car at a dealership without first getting outside financing quotes. It's one more factor the dealership can play around with in the messy math equation of buying a car. The process is torturous enough. Don't add to the angst.

Here are some outside sources that you should consider:

- **Credit Unions.** If you belong to a credit union, that is a terrific source for auto loans. Not a credit union member? Never fear, they are accessible to far more people than they used to be. Find one at www.FindACreditUnion.com.
- **Banks.** Check local banks in your area. The bank where you have your checking account may even offer you a special deal for opening a second account there.
- **Websites.** For good measure, try out a website that gives instant quotes like www.Bankrate.com.

I just checked today's available rates at all of these outside sources and here's what I found:

 Car Loan Interest Rates from Different Sources

My credit union	4.25%
A small bank in my area	7%
Online quote	9.14%
Bank where I have my checking account	11.22%

As you can see, by shopping around for an auto loan, I found a low interest rate of 4.25 percent, almost a third the size of the highest quote of 11.22 percent. The best deal was at a credit union, which is often the case. Now let's see how that helps us SAVE BIG on a $25,000 car loan, the national average.

Shopping Around for an Auto Loan

Rate	Amount Owed
11.22%	$28,032
4.25%	26,112
BIG SAVINGS =	$ 1,920

There you have it. Close to $2,000 in savings achieved through half an hour's worth of work comparing interest rates. I love it when I make a small effort but achieve a BIG SAVINGS!

Dealer Financing Deals

With outside financing information in hand, now you can walk into the dealership with some knowledge that gives you power. Don't ignore what the dealer has to offer; just don't consider it on its own. Now you have a point of comparison. If you have excellent credit and the dealer is offering a special to get people in the door, you may get a great loan at the dealership. If you are interested in the dealer's financing, be sure to negotiate the price of the car first and then terms of the loan. Keep the two transactions separate.

Know the Score

Used car salespeople have been known to tell customers their credit scores don't measure up even though they do. It's their excuse for charging you a higher interest rate or claiming you don't qualify for the hot financing deal being advertised. So you should pay to find out your own credit score at www.MyFico .com before going car shopping (more on getting your credit score in Chapter 19). That way you cannot be bamboozled into believing your score is lower than it is.

Always remember that car dealers can often make more money on the vehicle financing than they do on the vehicle itself! People seem to know that they need to hustle and haggle for the best deal on a car, but they forget to hustle and haggle for the best price on the car *loan*. As you saw, doing so will help you SAVE BIG.

BIG TIPS

- Pay cash for a car if you can.
- If you can't, make at least a 20 percent down payment.
- Limit your loan term to two years.
- Use the right kind of calculator to find out what you can afford.
- Shop for financing at banks, credit unions, and websites before heading to the dealership.

CHAPTER

Where to Buy a Car

Just as there are lots of places to shop for car loans, there are lots of places to shop for cars. And where you buy can help you SAVE BIG. I'm sensitive to the fact that most of us also want to save *time*. So first I'll lay out the pros and cons of the places where you can get a car *fast*—used car superstores, new car dealers, and used car dealers. Then I'll tell you where to get your used car for *even less*—namely from an individual or an auction.

In this chapter, learn to SAVE BIG by:

- Shopping at a used car superstore first.
- Getting a certified used vehicle at a new car dealer.
- Avoiding bogus used car warranties.
- Skipping small used car lots.
- Taking the extra savings you get by buying from an individual owner.
- Attending a wholesale auto auction.

Getting a Used Car Fast

Congratulations. Just by choosing to buy a used car you are going to SAVE BIG. Now you need to decide if you want to whittle that price down even further. It could be that at this point speed is more important to you—the speed of the search, silly, not the speed of the car! If that's the case, superstores and dealerships are your best bet.

Superstores

One place to shop for cars is at a used car superstore. I like to begin at a superstore like Carmax because you can test drive lots of different makes and models all in one spot. It's fast and efficient when you're still at the stage where you're honing in on exactly which type of vehicle you want. I'm not saying you will necessarily buy at Carmax, but it's a handy place to start.

Carmax prices probably are not the very best you can get. The superstore has a fixed-rate, no haggle policy. The price you see on the window sticker is the real deal. You can most likely snag a lower price *if* you bargain expertly at a regular dealership. However, many people hate to haggle and appreciate the low-key atmosphere. Remember, you're already saving thousands by buying used, so if you fail to save a couple hundred more by bargaining, that's your choice.

Just don't forget that even though they call it a "store" and the salespeople wear polo shirts instead of shiny suits, Carmax still sells *used* cars. You must make sure the one you choose is in good shape. More on that in Chapter 14.

New Car Dealers

The other easy option for buying a used car is a new car dealership, especially since they have their own in-house shops and can service the vehicle before they sell it. A quick tip: Deals are better at the end of the month, when they are trying to make quotas. So you may want to wait until then to walk into a new car dealership.

There are some great benefits to buying your used car at a new car dealership. For starters, new car dealers typically have first dibs on good used vehicles, as their (foolish!) customers trade them in for new ones every three years. Another bonus: The used car you're looking at may have been serviced at the dealership. If it was, then you may be able to get copies of the service records, which can be a gold mine of insight into the car's performance and any problems.

There are probably multiple dealers in your area that sell the same kind of car. One way to choose one is to check their reputations through the Better Business Bureau, at www.BBB.org.

Don't Be Put on the Spot by *Spot Delivery*

Many car deals are done on weekends when the finance company isn't open. So the salesman may send you home in a car even though he's not really sure your loan has been approved. Days or weeks later you get a call demanding that you return the car. If you finance through the dealership, ask if it's a done deal or a spot delivery. Just knowing the lingo will put them on notice!

Another benefit of buying at a new car dealership is that you might be able to get a certified preowned vehicle (don't you just love that ridiculous euphemism?). This can be a particularly great deal for consumers who want the comfort of a written guarantee. Certification means the people at the dealership have checked the car out, made the necessary repairs to bring it up to standards, and will now stand behind it by extending the factory warranty.

The best certified vehicle programs give you at least 24 months and 24,000 miles worth of coverage. Don't accept less. Yes, certified cars cost a bit more than other used cars, but again, you have already achieved your big savings by buying used. The website www.Intellichoice.com rates car certification programs. Check it out.

Request Certification

If you are interested in a used car at a dealership and that car is not certified, you may be able to negotiate for the dealer to certify it in exchange for a slightly higher price.

One red alert: Never fall for a phony certification program offered by some outside company instead of by the dealership and vehicle manufacturer. It's confusing because many dealers do sell these third-party certification programs to trusting consumers. To be sure that you aren't getting a bogus certification, ask if the guarantee you are being offered is backed by the dealership itself or an outside company.

Used Car Dealers

Paradoxically, used car dealers are not a great place to buy used cars. I do not mean to malign an entire industry. It's just a structural situation: Used car dealers typically get the less desirable used vehicles that new car dealers dump at auctions. Even if they are reputable, they can't help it. They mostly sell the leftovers. Used car superstores like Carmax are the exception because they are so big that they are able to buy clean used cars in bulk. "Buy here, pay here" lots are in another category altogether. They're in the business of selling predatory financing, not cars.

Getting a Used Car for Less

We all need to balance saving time with saving money. You're already going to SAVE BIG by buying used. But you can SAVE BIGGER by buying from an individual owner or finding a way to attend a wholesale auction. You'll need a combination of time and ingenuity to make this happen.

Buying from Private Owners

You can get a better price on a used car—some say 10 to 15 percent less—by buying from an individual vehicle owner. If you don't have time to slog around the metropolis looking at individual cars, I understand. But this is one of the rare opportunities in life to save thousands all at once. Remember the used Lexus that we talked about in Chapter 11? Well, it was being sold by a dealer. What if we could find the same car in somebody's driveway? We can. I just checked the classified ads, and look what I found:

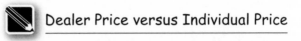 Dealer Price versus Individual Price

2006 Lexus GS300 from a dealership	$24,999
2006 Lexus GS300 from an individual	21,249
BIG SAVINGS =	**$ 3,750**

You can achieve a $3,750 savings by buying from an individual instead of a dealership. But there are some precautions that I urge you to take when you buy from a private owner. After all, the sellers don't have a reputation to uphold like a business does.

Ask the owner if you can look at the record of the original purchase and all the service records. My husband and I once test-drove a used car that an individual was selling, and while he was driving, I pored over the service tickets. At the bottom of the stack were a bunch of records that showed the owner had had to take the car back to the dealer for the same serious repair again and again. That's the definition of a lemon!

You must also take a look at the title before committing to the deal. You're trying to avoid buying a car the seller doesn't really have the right to sell you! Compare the name on the title to the name on the seller's driver's license to make sure they match. Also match up the VIN number from the dashboard with what is written on the title. If you see a bank listed on the title as the lien holder, you and the seller should call the bank together and verify how the loan is to be paid off.

Finally, write up a formal bill of sale and keep a copy for as long as you own the car. Pay for the vehicle with a cashier's check instead of cash. That way there is a traceable record of your purchase if you run into trouble down the road.

Beware of Curbstoners

Curbstoners are illegal, unlicensed used car sellers who sell cars from the curb—or the strip mall parking lot. Curbstoners typically pose as individual owners and try to unload rebuilt wrecks. Investigators estimate as many as 80 percent of the cars for sale in the classifieds are sold by curbstoners. If you see the same phone number listed for several cars or the seller refuses to show you the title before making the sale, steer clear.

Auto Auctions

Probably the cheapest way of all to buy a car is to get a friend in the auto business to take you to one of the wholesale auctions. You'll need this connection because only licensed dealers can buy at these auctions. They are not open to the general public. You can find out about them through the National Auto Auction Association, www.naaa.com.

My husband is fortunate to have a friend who is a former car dealer and maintains his license. He once purchased a vehicle for us at one of the wholesale auctions. It was three years old and just coming off of a lease. I kicked and screamed because we were taking a risk since there was no way to have a mechanic check the vehicle out, but our friend is an old pro and he eyeballed the vehicle carefully before bidding on it. It's been a great vehicle for us, which goes to show you how consistent today's cars really are. Here's how much money we saved:

Buying at a Wholesale Auction

Retail price	$23,300
Auction price	18,300
BIG SAVINGS =	**$ 5,000**

One caution: Don't confuse the big wholesale auctions with fake auctions. Some clever used car lots now call themselves "auctions" to generate excitement. They're not. They're just used car lots that sell people cars without letting them test-drive or inspect them first. Holley C. of Washington, D.C., has the worst car luck of anybody I have ever met. Her dad bought her a car at a fake used car auction and later learned it wouldn't drive in reverse! The auctioneer had driven the car forward when it came up for a bid, and Holley's dad had driven it forward right off the lot. Oops.

BIG TIPS

- Shop a superstore first so you can test-drive multiple vehicles.
- Buy a used car from a new car dealer if you are in a hurry and want certified preowned protection.
- Find out who is behind the extended warranty before paying for one.
- Buy from an individual and save another 10 to 15 percent.
- Try to find somebody knowledgeable who can get you into a wholesale auto auction.

CHAPTER **14**

Choosing a Reliable Car

When you buy a new car (which I hope you will never do again!), your focus is on negotiating for the best possible price. By contrast, with used cars, the price is already low, so the real key is to buy a reliable one. Getting a really solid used car is even *more* important when you consider that another way to SAVE BIG is to keep that car as long as possible. You need a car that will last. The first step is to make sure the model you choose was well engineered. After that, you must scrutinize the individual cars you are considering to make sure they have never been in a crash and have always been well maintained.

In this chapter, learn to SAVE BIG by:

- Using just two resources to research used cars.
- Knowing that you do not have three days to return a used car.
- Getting a vehicle history report but knowing its limitations.
- Having a mechanic scrutinize the car before you buy it.

Narrowing It Down

You can start your used car search in your slippers, by consulting the car resources available right on the Internet. If anything, there are too many choices—umpteen gazillion sources of information about used cars. Since I'm into saving *time* as well as money, I will tell you that you can learn all you need to know by cross-referencing just two resources:

1. *The Consumer Reports Used Car Buying Guide.* This is the most trusted source of information about which vehicles are the most reliable.
2. **Edmunds.com.** On this auto website you will find nitty-gritty information about vehicle pricing and more.

Consumer Reports

The *Consumer Reports Used Car Buying Guide* has been an essential resource for decades. You can get it instantly online at www.ConsumerReports.org or buy a hard copy in a bookstore.

Advice from *Consumer Reports* stands out because the publication doesn't accept any advertising dollars from car companies or anybody else. You also get the benefit of *Consumer Reports'* own anonymous testing of vehicles. I've been to their state-of-the-art facility in Connecticut and man, is it impressive!

The *Used Car Buying Guide* also polls millions of readers about their vehicles and how they have held up over time. This will give you a sense of which cars require the fewest and cheapest repairs.

If you want a shortcut, *Consumer Reports* puts out a list of Used Car *Best* Bets and a list of Used Car *Bad* Bets. Steer clear of the bad, go for the best. It's that simple.

Edmunds.com

Auto website Edmunds.com also puts out an annual Best Bets list. It weighs reliability and safety, but also availability. That can be key, because if a vehicle is more widely available, by the law of supply and demand it will be cheaper.

Edmunds.com is best known for its vehicle pricing tools. The website offers what it calls the True Market Value (TMV) price. Edmunds gathers sales data from dealerships around the country to see what cars are selling for in the real world.

When you've narrowed your choices down to a handful of cars, then it's time to utilize another neat Edmunds feature: the True Cost to Own calculator. It shows what you will pay to own the car for five years, including taxes, gas, maintenance, repairs, and financing. You may find that a car with a lower purchase price is not worth it because it is expensive to own. Or you may find that a more expensive vehicle is so reliable and repair-free that it's actually a better buy.

I tried it out, comparing two SUVs, a 2006 Buick Rainier and a 2006 Honda Pilot. The purchase price of the Buick is about $1,000 less than that of the Honda. But the Edmunds' True Cost to Own calculator reveals a hidden price tag. The Buick Rainier costs much more to maintain over a five-year period. Take a look:

True Cost to Own over Five Years

Buick Rainier	$42,262
Honda Pilot	39,087
BIG SAVINGS =	**$ 3,175**

Pick a Research Threshold for Your Purchases

BIG SECRET

Make up your mind that you will research the heck out of anything over X dollars—like a car—to make sure it's good quality. Anything below your threshold? Risk it. The research isn't worth your time. My threshold used to be $100. When I got older, busier, and a bit more prosperous, I raised it to $200. I no longer research purchases under $200.

The Number One Consumer Myth of All Time

Cover your ears because I'm about to shout at you: *YOU CANNOT RETURN A CAR!*

The number one consumer myth of all time is that you have three days to return a car—new or used. I'm always amazed how many of my suave, intelligent, well-educated friends still believe this lie. So let me say it again: Once you sign the sales contract, that car is yours. You cannot return it. That's why the next section on how to check out a used car is so crucial.

There are a few minor exceptions. Carmax stores give you five days to return a car. A few private dealers have internal policies—which they can revoke at any time—allowing returns. And the state of California enacted a law that allows you to pay $500 extra for the right to return a used car within two days of purchase.

But it's better if you just operate on the assumption that YOU CANNOT RETURN A USED CAR, because people who buy a vehicle knowing they can return it often fail to get it checked out during the short window of time they are allowed.

You Can't Give a Car Back, But You Can Give One Away

D onating a vehicle is now a mainstream way of disposing of one because you don't have to go through the hassle of selling it and you can get a tax deduction. Just be cautious. It's the biggest charitable donation many of us will ever make. Many car donation programs are run by for-profit brokers who give only a tiny fraction of the proceeds to charity, if they give any at all. Make sure the program you donate to is legitimate or your tax deduction might not be legitimate.

Checking It Out

As a consumer reporter, I can't tell you how many people have called me over the years complaining that they bought bad used cars. My first question is always, "Did you check it out before you bought it?" The answer is almost always a sheepish "No."

Since you have already researched the best makes and models of used cars, now it's time to check out the *actual* used cars you are test-driving. Here's how to do it:

Step 1: Order a vehicle history report. That's an easy one.

Step 2: Get a physical inspection. This one may take a little more effort, but is utterly crucial.

Step 1: Vehicle History Reports

Years ago, when I was doing a television story about how to buy a used car, I heard about this obscure start-up company that would *fax* you a vehicle history report. Doesn't that sound quaint? Although times have changed, Carfax reports remain a godsend to used car buyers. Don't buy a car without one.

There are other vehicle history websites out there now, including some affiliated with the government, but Carfax is still way ahead of the pack. Carfax charges $30 for a single report and up to $50 for unlimited reports. You can get a Carfax vehicle history report at www.Carfax.com.

Here's the drill: You enter the vehicle identification number of the car you're considering, and the company will spit out a report in seconds. It will tell you if the car has ever been in a flood, whether it has a salvage title, whether the odometer's been rolled back—and so much more. Carfax even promises to buy the vehicle back from you if it misses something major.

If only Henry M. of Maryland had had that Carfax guarantee. He bought a used Acura luxury sedan for $12,000. The car looked good on the surface, but when he received the title in the mail, Henry was shocked to see an ugly red brand stamped across the title that said "Rebuilt Salvage." This is the sort of thing that a vehicle history report will catch.

What vehicle history reports do not always catch are traffic accidents. If the car you're considering was in an accident that was not large enough to generate a police report, it may not show up on the vehicle history report. Carfax now has agreements with some collision repair facilities and insurance companies to try to fill this information gap. And the U.S. Department of Justice (DOJ) recently got involved and is trying to compel insurance companies and salvage shops to report accident data to a central authority.

That's good news and means we may soon have a more complete picture of whether the used cars we are looking at have been in wrecks. Regardless, it's crucial that you have the car checked by a mechanic who can spot evidence of a crash.

Step 2: Make the Mechanic Mandatory

This is the other crucial step that you *must* take: Get the vehicle inspected by a qualified mechanic. Please, people. I hate to sound preachy, but over the years I have gotten hundreds of calls and e-mails from consumers who were stuck with cars too dangerous to drive because they failed to take this basic precaution.

Take Reese F., who bought two trucks for the price of one, but quickly learned that it was no bargain. The Ford truck he bought for $15,000 was actually two totaled trucks welded together. The frame was hopelessly twisted and, by law, he had to disclose the problems if he sold the vehicle. He lost thousands of dollars on the deal. If only he had had the vehicle checked out before he bought it, a mechanic would have spotted the glaring evidence.

So please, take the used car to a mechanic before you buy it. It may sound like a pain, but it's really not. Ideally, you have a trusted mechanic who can inspect the vehicle for you, and if you don't, I tell you how to find one in Chapter 16. There are also mobile mechanics who can bring their diagnostic tools right to the car.

AAA-approved repair shops offer AAA members a free 24-point inspection of their vehicle. You can get this same inspection for a vehicle you are considering buying. If the dealer or owner won't allow you to get the vehicle inspected by a mechanic, I think you know what to do. Run—don't walk—away from the deal.

Besides, you can use this diagnosis as a bargaining chip. Ask the mechanic to write up an estimate showing what is wrong with the car and how much it will cost to fix it. Take this back to the seller and use it to talk the price down. More on how to do that in the next chapter.

BIG TIPS

- Cross-reference ConsumerReports.org and Edmunds.com.
- Order a vehicle history report *before* you buy the car.
- Have a mechanic check out the vehicle *before* you buy it.
- Remember that you do *not* have three days to return a car.

CHAPTER 15

Bargaining for the Best Price

You will SAVE BIG by buying used. You may even SAVE BIGGER by buying a dark horse car from an individual owner. But if you want to SAVE BIGGEST, know this: Skillful negotiators pay 10 to 15 percent less, on average, than those who just accept the seller's price, according to Edmunds.com. The key is to research pricing carefully, down to the nickel for every option on the vehicle you want. Then it's time to haggle.

In this chapter, I'm going to tell you, step-by-step, how to bargain for the best price. We'll make it a game—a game where you save more than just Monopoly money! You SAVE BIG!

In this chapter, learn to SAVE BIG by:

- Researching pricing down to the last detail.
- Keeping your trade-in vehicle a secret.
- Setting the opening offer just right.
- Haggling with daring and drama to win!
- Saying no to pricey add-ons you don't need.

Research Pricing

Here's how to proceed if you want to get an A for effort and SAVE BIG. When you researched the best and worst used vehicles through *Consumer Reports* and Edmunds.com, you also learned a lot about vehicle pricing. I like Edmunds' True Market Value price quotes because they attempt to factor in what vehicles are actually selling for in the marketplace. I also like them because they're usually lower!

It's not enough to look up the base price. These websites will tell you how much to add for every last option—like the sunroof, the souped-up stereo, the fancy wheels, and so on. You will also see how much to add or subtract based on the vehicle's mileage and condition.

I recommend that you research the pricing of more than one car. It's a good idea to identify multiple cars at different locations that you're interested in. That way, when it's time to haggle, you won't be in love with just one vehicle. You'll be able to walk away if you don't get the price you want.

That reminds me of what my friend Terri T. says about dating. Her philosophy is "Date a pair and keep a spare." In other words, have *three* options! For Terri, it works with men and she drives a hard bargain on vehicles, too!

Keep Your Trade-in a Secret

Do not tell dealers you have a vehicle to trade in until after you have negotiated a price for the car you're buying. (Of course, you'll want to consult some of the same car websites to determine the value of your old vehicle.) When the trade-in is part of the deal, the salesperson can use that as one more number to play around with. It's a sliding scale. They give you an enticing low price on the vehicle you're buying, but a corresponding low offer on your trade. Or they may offer big bucks for your trade, then charge you more for the car you're buying. You want to conduct two separate transactions to avoid all this rhetoric.

How to Haggle

Once you've researched pricing, it's time to talk price with the seller. Try to relax and enjoy haggling. It's a game. After all, as I've said a zillion times, you are already SAVING BIG by buying used. That takes the pressure off. Remember, the person selling the vehicle needs you more than you need them. There are more cars than there are customers. This should give you confidence. Dealerships may be expert negotiators, but they are desperate to make their

minimum sales quotas. And if you're negotiating with private owners, they are probably desperate to get their weekends back.

The Opening Price

Your goal is to pay a price somewhere between the low trade-in
(wholesale) value and the high retail value listed in the pricing
information you have gathered. Set a firm number that you will not
exceed. Obviously, the closer you get to the trade-in value, the more
of a rock star you are and the more you SAVE BIG.

Some experts recommend making your first offer 15 percent
less than what you are really willing to pay. Another technique is
to take the seller's price and knock it down based on all the repairs
your mechanic has told you the vehicle needs. Whatever you do,
keep in mind, the first number you throw out defines the negotiation. You can't go any lower after that.

After you make your initial offer, bite your lip, dig your nails
into your hands, or do whatever it takes to make yourself shut up
while the seller ponders your offer. You *want* that pregnant pause,
that uncomfortable quiet. *Do not* fill it. Your goal is for the seller
to be the one to squirm and shatter the silence by accepting your
offer.

Uncle Sam Will Pay Part of Your Parking

If the vehicle you're bargaining so hard for is a commuter car,
did you know that the federal government lets you use pretax
dollars to pay for parking? It's true. You'd think the feds would
only subsidize commuters who use green options like mass transit. But no. The
money is automatically deducted from your paycheck. Ask your employer and
parking vendor to participate if they don't already. One company that processes
the paperwork required is Wage Works, www.WageWorks.com.

The Next Move

After you have stated your offer, the seller will either accept your
offer, make a counteroffer, or reject your offer. If you get a flat-
out rejection, then simply ask "Okay, so what's your best price?"

If the seller counters, make a show of flinching, of wincing, like the counteroffer is painfully unreasonable. (That's right, folks, this is your big chance to make money as an actor!) Never accept the first counteroffer. Instead, name your next price, which you should raise by a smaller increment than they just lowered theirs. For example, if the seller just dropped his price by $500, you would raise yours by $400.

Feeling uncomfortable? Blame your hard-nosed negotiating on somebody else. As in, "I'm sorry, but my spouse will kill me if I pay more than X dollars." This is the same good cop/bad cop technique many car salespeople will try to use on you, only they'll say "My manager said no." Sound familiar? Why not turn the tables? It works on private owners too.

If your negotiations stall, one fabulous theatrical tactic is to leave. You don't have to turn on your heel and walk out in a huff. Simply tell the seller you were prepared to buy a car today but you just don't feel the price is appropriate. Some experts recommend leaving three times during the process. That's a lot of drama, but it's quite possible, especially in the post-2008 economy, that you will receive a callback soon with an offer to drop the price some more.

Closing the Deal

If you are *just over* the maximum price you want to pay, but can't quite get there, there's one last option before you bail out. Instead of trying to get the car for less money, try to get the money to buy more car. In other words, ask for extras like new tires, a great stereo, replacement floor mats, or anything else you genuinely want.

If you're buying at a dealership, be sure you and the dealer are clear on whether tax, title, and fees are included in the figures you are slinging back and forth. Years ago, when I was more tender and naive, I thought I had negotiated a great deal on a car, but I hadn't specified that mine was an out-the-door offer, meaning I wanted it to include taxes and fees. The dealer added those in at the end and I was so exhausted from the whole skeevy process that I agreed. That cost me more than $1,000.

Once you make a deal, don't sign anything until you've read it carefully. Ideally, take the paperwork out to your old car, to a coffee shop or some place where you have privacy and no pressure. Look for pricey add-ons like "paint protection," "undercoating," and credit life insurance. You don't need or want these. Cross them off. If you want other things added to the deal, insist that they be put in the contract, in writing. Verbal guarantees are worthless.

Once everything is in order, take a deep breath and sign on the dotted line. And remember, YOU CANNOT RETURN A CAR!

Real Results

Since effective negotiators knock an average of 10 to 15 percent off the price of a used vehicle, let's do some math to get an appreciation of how much some good haggling helps your bottom line. I'll pick a percentage in the middle—12 percent. Let's see the savings:

 Benefits of Bargaining Hard

Original asking price	$15,000
Price after haggling	13,200
BIG SAVINGS =	**$ 1,800**

I'd say all the drama is worth it! A couple of hours outside your comfort zone can save you nearly two grand or 12 percent off the purchase price.

BIG TIPS

- Pursue more than one vehicle, so you have options.
- Negotiate the price of the vehicle you are purchasing before revealing you have a vehicle to trade in.
- Bite your tongue, shut up, and even walk out when you are negotiating.
- Study the contract for pricey extras before signing on the dotted line.

CHAPTER

Make Your Car Last

Most Americans replace their car every five years. That's right, they ditch a remarkably sturdy vehicle capable of cruising along past 200,000 miles. They treat it like a starter wife and trade it in for a newer, younger model. To me, that is just silly. After all, you will have just spent all this time and effort finding the perfect car at the perfect price and now you are going to get rid of it and start the process all over again? What a waste of time! If you want to SAVE BIG you need to make your car last.

In this chapter, learn to SAVE BIG by:

- Keeping your current car as long as you can stand it.
- Finding a good mechanic and being faithful to him (or her!)
- Keeping the shop from jacking up the initial price you are quoted.
- Not paying the bill—legally—if you have been wronged.
- Searching for secret warranties that get your car repaired for free.

Repair or Replace

There comes a time when your older car needs more maintenance. Belts start to go. Fluids are leaking. Brakes are squealing. Suddenly, you panic and think, "This car is costing me a fortune! Maybe I should replace it!" Wrong!

Here's what costs a fortune: replacing your car.

Let's say your old car needs a whopping $3,500 worth of repairs. A rebuilt engine! Transmission overhaul! Sounds awful! But compare that to the cost of getting a new vehicle, even a used one. Here's an example, using the purchase price of our old standby, the used Ford Taurus:

Replace versus Repair

New-to-you used car	$ 15,000
Repair	3,500
BIG SAVINGS =	**$11,500**

I spared you by not even including the additional cost if you were financing the vehicle, but I'm sure you remember that discouraging waste of money from Chapter 12. Now, before I start to sound like a huge bore, let me say that I realize you're going to replace your scruffy old car with something new-to-you at some point. That's fine. The idea is that the longer you stretch out the current car's life, the more money you'll save.

In her book *Spend Well, Live Rich*, Michelle Singletary, the savvy, sassy personal finance columnist for the *Washington Post*, writes about a woman at a seminar who asked her whether she should replace her car. The woman's car needed a $1,500 repair, and she had been looking at a $25,000 replacement. What should she do? Michelle wrote the two numbers down on the blackboard as if she was making some kind of careful calculation. Then she asked the lady, "Which number is smaller?" And that was her answer!

Beware of Tow Truck Bounties

If your car breaks down and needs a tow, don't let the tow truck driver choose the shop. I once did an investigation and proved that some shops pay tow truck drivers a bounty to bring them business. We went undercover and tow trucks took our car past a dozen decent shops to get to the one where they could make a personal payday. We had to pay more to be towed farther and the shop in question had a terrible reputation.

Bottom line: Keep your car as long as possible. Most people turn their cars over every five years, according to Edmunds.com. Let's say you get your first car when you're 18 and stop driving at age 78. That means you would own about 12 vehicles during your lifetime. If you keep each vehicle just one year more, you'll only need 10 vehicles. Keep it 10 years—twice as long as the national average—and you'll only need 6 vehicles, which will cut your car-buying costs in half.

So exactly how much can you save by keeping your car longer? Let's pick a number in the middle for the sake of fairness. If you keep you car seven and a half years, that's 50 percent longer than most people do and means you will need eight cars in your lifetime. Let's say each car you buy costs $15,000, the price of the Ford Taurus we've been using throughout our discussion. Here's the math:

 **Making It Last**

12 cars at $15,000 each	$180,000
8 cars at $15,000 each	120,000
BIG SAVINGS =	**$ 60,000**

Another bonus of keeping your car as long as you can stand it: You won't have to reread and follow my advice as often on how to find and purchase a good one!

Finding a Great Mechanic

If you're going to keep your car around longer, you must make it your mission to find an honest and skillful mechanic. Car repairs are one of the most expensive services that we spend money on, so working with an honest mechanic will help you SAVE BIG. Good mechanics are like good husbands. It's hard to find one, and once you do, you shouldn't cheat on them. The bit of hassle I am going to suggest is well worth it compared to the angst of wondering if you've been ripped off by the mechanic of the moment.

Every consumer book tells you to ask friends and family for referrals to find a good mechanic. I've given that advice myself in the past, but it's not very satisfying. What if *you're* the organized one in the bunch? They're probably asking you! So here is a list of possible sources of shops.

You Don't Have to Use Premium Gas

If your owner's manual recommends regular unleaded, premium doesn't do a darn thing to help your car. Even if your owner's manual *does* list premium, is it "recommended" or "required"? That wording is key. Ask your mechanic if you can just use regular.

Ways to Find Mr. Right

- **Ask a mechanic.** One creative alternative is to ask a mechanic about mechanics. Huh? Find a reputable shop that doesn't work on your kind of car, and ask them who they would recommend.
- **Check *Consumer's Checkbook* magazine.** If you are fortunate to live in one of the large metropolitan areas served by *Consumer's Checkbook* magazine—Boston, Philadelphia/Wilmington, Seattle, San Francisco, Minneapolis/St. Paul, or Washington, D.C.— you are in luck. *Checkbook* surveys hundreds of consumers in the area and uses their responses to rate shops for quality and price. Learn more at www.Checkbook.org.
- **AAA-certified auto repair facilities.** AAA shops are another possibility. They're required to offer members a 12-month, 12,000-mile warranty on their work. Their estimates are guaranteed. And if you still have a problem, AAA will investigate your claim and resolve it. Visit www.AAA.com to find a member mechanic in your area.
- **Automotive Service Association.** Another source of shops that have pledged to uphold high standards is the Automotive Service Association (ASA—not to be confused with ASE, Automotive Service Excellence, a series of exams mechanics take to prove their competence). I have often turned to ASA mechanics to be the good-guy experts when I am doing an undercover investigation of crooked mechanics. Check them out at www.ASAShop.org.

- **Better Business Bureau.** Continuing through the alphabet, you can test out mechanics who are members of the Better Business Bureau (BBB). There are certainly some bad businesses that join the BBB to camouflage themselves, but most are good companies that have pledged to uphold a code of ethics. If you have a problem, the BBB will help mediate it for you. Go to www.BBB.org to search for members. Check the shop's reputation while you're there.
- *Car Talk.* Do you ever listen to Click and Clack and their hilarious talk show *Car Talk* on NPR? *Car Talk* listeners swap referrals with each other at www.Cars.com in the *Car Talk* section. Just search by zip code and then read with a critical eye.

Google 'em

In addition to checking the reputation of a shop—or any kind of company—with the Better Business Bureau at BBB.org, I always suggest that people Google 'em. This is a technique I use for any new company I'm about to do business with. Google the name and city of the business with words like "scam," "rip-off," or "complaint" and see if anything comes up. It's a quick, easy cross-check and could help you SAVE BIG.

The Estimate

Once you've chosen a reliable mechanic, its time to talk to him about the anticipated cost of your repair, the estimate. When you tell your mechanic what sort of problem you're having with your car, be sure to describe symptoms, not diseases. For instance, say, "It's stalling at stoplights," not, "I think there's a problem with the alternator." Remember, *you're* not the mechanic! You don't want to end up paying for some goofy repair that you dreamed up yourself.

Your mechanic should be the one diagnosing the problem and that diagnosis should be in writing. Most states require mechanics to give you a written estimate. That estimate should state the problem to be repaired plus the parts and labor needed for the job. You don't want an estimate that just lists the work the mechanic is going to do. The reason? What if it's the wrong work? You want the mechanic to be obligated to fix the root problem rather than performing some specific procedure that may be off-base. For the same reason, avoid estimates that are just a long laundry list of parts, because who's to say those parts will fix the problem?

Red alert! The number one problem people have with car repair is that they are expecting to pay the price the mechanic estimated and then that price goes up—way up. In many states it's actually against the law for the mechanic to perform the extra work without your approval, but it happens all the time. You can avoid this by knowing the law. In most states, once the shop gives you a written estimate, it's required to contact you if that estimate is going to rise more than 10 percent.

Put a Stop to Upcharging

If your state doesn't require shops to ask your permission before doing additional work, take the law into your own hands—with a pen! Write on the service ticket either "Not to exceed X dollars" or "Mechanic must contact customer if price is going to rise more than 10 percent."

Get a Second Opinion

Remember how I said not to cheat on your good mechanic? The idea is to build mutual trust, but sometimes I can be a fickle woman. If your mechanic says your car needs major work, it might be time for a quick affair. I'm not saying your mechanic is lying to you. It's just that mechanics, like doctors, can diagnose more than one problem from the same set of symptoms. So pick a price that's comfortable for you and resolve that you will get a second opinion for any repair over X dollars.

When Mark L. of Florida noticed his car was pulling to the left, he went to a shop that recommend complicated, expensive repairs to the tune of $1,400. Since Mark was skeptical, he decided to get a second opinion. So he took his vehicle to another mechanic who simply recommended new tires. That bit of extra legwork helped him SAVE BIG. Here's the math:

Getting a Second Opinion

Complicated repairs	$ 1,400
New tires	400
BIG SAVINGS =	**$1,000**

Deduct the Deductible

Ask if you can skip the deductible when you need body work. If you get in an accident, you have the right to choose which collision repair facility you use, so negotiate. Some body shops will do the work for just the amount of your insurance company's payment, without charging you the deductible.

Two Ways Not to Pay

If you take the wise and wonderful steps I've described and still have a dispute with the shop over your repairs, pay with a credit card. Then drive your expensively repaired car straight home and dispute the charges. Often you don't have to pay the bill while the card company is going to bat for you.

There's also another way not to pay that is truly novel and creative. In some jurisdictions, you can go down to the local courthouse and post a bond for the price of the repairs. The law varies from place to place, but either you or the mechanic must then file a small claims suit over the money. In some states, if the mechanic doesn't bother to file, you automatically get your money back. Talk about a way to SAVE BIG!

I know some of these steps sound over-the-top, so just remember, the more time you spend *finding* a shop, the less time you'll have to spend *fighting* one.

Secret Warranties

There's another way to SAVE BIG on your car repairs and that is getting them gratis. There are about 500 secret warranties available at any given time, according to the Center for Auto Safety. Secret warranties are agreements by automakers to fix a particular problem in a particular car because that particular problem is happening in a lot of those particular cars. It's a chance for you to SAVE BIG—but they don't tell unless you ask.

Automakers sometimes offer secret warranties in order to avoid issuing a full-fledged recall. The manufacturer alerts its dealers that if customers complain about the problem, the manufacturer will pay for the repair. A few states require automakers to alert consumers to these opportunities, but if you obeyed me and bought the car used, the company won't have a record of your ownership, so you'll need to ask.

As you can imagine, the people in the auto industry don't call them secret warranties. They use euphemisms like goodwill adjustment, warranty adjustment, and after-warranty assistance. They also refer to them as extended warranties, because your car does not have to be in its initial factory warranty period to be covered.

Getting In on the Secret

How do you find out about a secret warranty? One way is to bluff. My buddy, Michael Finney, the brash and brilliant consumer reporter at KGO TV in San Francisco, says in his book *Consumer Confidential* that he just *assumes* there's a secret warranty. Michael suavely drawls to the service manager, "I think there is a warranty adjustment on this repair." And often there is! He gets the work done for free.

Here's an example of a recent secret warranty. A certain European luxury carmaker now equips its vehicles with run-flat tires. These are tires that can limp along for several miles, allowing you to get to a service station instead of changing your tire by the side of the road, but they're a newer technology that hasn't been perfected yet. The luxury car company's customers started complaining that the run-flat tires on their swanky cars were failing after just a couple thousand miles, giving the vehicles a rough ride like a diesel dump truck. The manufacturer instructed dealers to replace the tires for free *if* customers asked and, voila, a secret warranty was born. For the savvy customers who inquired, look at the savings:

 It Pays to Ask

Cost of new tires	$1,200
Cost with secret warranty	0
BIG SAVINGS =	**$1,200**

The more mundane way to sleuth out secret warranties is to look up *technical service bulletins* on cars. These are notices that automakers send to dealers alerting them about emerging problems and giving guidance on how to handle them. You can find technical service bulletins on Edmunds.com.

BIG TIPS

- Squeeze as many years out of your car as you can.
- Do the work to find a good mechanic.
- Cheat on your mechanic and get a second opinion for pricey repairs.
- Write "Not to exceed X dollars" on your service ticket.
- Inquire about secret warranties.

17

Car Insurance for Less

After buying used, paying cash and haggling hard, car insurance is the next best opportunity to SAVE BIG in the car category. According to Ratewatch Auto Insurance, the average annual auto insurance premium is $1,872. When you consider that most Americans live in two-car families, you're talking nearly four grand a year for something you hope you never have to use. What a dull thing to spend money on. Ugh! I'd rather buy shoes! Fortunately, I've got lots of ideas for how you can cut the cost of your car insurance.

In this chapter, learn to SAVE BIG by:

- Shopping around to see if there are big price differences between companies.
- Buying insurance through a warehouse club.
- Raising your deductible as high as you can afford to.
- Lowering or dropping insurance coverage that you don't need.
- Getting compensated for the diminished value of your vehicle if you're in an accident.

You'd Better Shop Around

You can save thousands of dollars by shopping around for car insurance. It's one of the few areas of your financial life that can make a quadruple-digit difference. Oh, I admit, it is a *boring* project, but saving thousands is exciting, right? We tend to just go with the same company that insured our parents' vehicles. That can be a big mistake.

So you must shop around. One caution: You don't want to switch to a company so cheap and cheesy that you have trouble getting your claim paid after an accident. If you do that, then you have saved money but stripped away the whole purpose of the insurance. *Consumer Reports* rates auto insurance companies for quality. Go to www.ConsumerReports.org and check reputations before committing. Once you know the companies you're considering are all top-notch, then you can SAVE BIG by comparing and contrasting rates.

Compare Prices Online

Martin G. of Washington State is really Web savvy, so when he got his first car, he shopped around for insurance on the Internet. If more people would do that they would SAVE BIG. Martin is 18 years old, drives an SUV, and, like many young guys, he's had one minor fender bender that resulted in about $500 worth of damage. His grades are solid, but not enough to qualify him for a good student discount. Martin got two quotes and made sure both were for the exact same coverage. So did this sweet, but flawed, young driver save some money? You bet! Take a look:

Benefit of Shopping Around for Car Insurance

Insurance company 1	$ 7,308/year
Insurance company 2	5,830/year
BIG SAVINGS =	$1,478/year

Isn't it amazing that there could be a $1,478 difference in the rates charged by two different insurance companies for the same coverage? You may be wondering if insurance company number 2 is "Bob's Taxidermy and Car Insurance," an unknown company in a trailer somewhere that's unlikely to pay if Martin makes a claim. Not so. Both quotes came from big, national insurance companies that advertise like crazy. If you want to shop online for car insurance, here are some helpful websites: www.Geico.com, www.Esurance.com, www.NetQuote.com, and www.Progressive.com.

Hire an Independent Agent

If you don't trust the quotes you're seeing online, another good way to shop around is to check with an independent insurance agent who

More Ways to Save

There are lots of other ways to save on car insurance, according to the Insurance Information Institute. Get your car and homeowner's insurance through the same company and save 10 percent. Buy car insurance through a group plan, perhaps offered by your employer, and save 5 percent. Tell your insurance company some other company has offered you a better deal and save 15 percent.

---

sells policies for several different companies. With one phone call or e-mail, an independent agent can give you quotes from a bunch of different carriers. To find an independent insurance agent, go to www.TrustedChoice.com, the website of the Independent Insurance Agents and Brokers of America. Just keep in mind that these agents don't represent companies like Allstate and State Farm that have their own, in-house agents. If you want quotes from those companies, you will have to approach each one directly. There's no harm in getting multiple quotes, because they are free of charge.

Join the Club

Here's a more creative source when you're shopping around for car insurance. If you belong to a wholesale warehouse like Costco, BJ's, or Sam's Club, you may be able to get auto insurance there. They partner with some major insurers to offer group discounts to their members. Sounds weird to pick up bulk toilet paper, cheap electronics, and auto insurance in one place, but it's true. Some warehouse club members have cut their car insurance costs in *half* by signing up.

Gregory P. of North Carolina is one of them. He says the warehouse club car insurance policy was actually more generous than his old policy yet cost half as much. Gregory switched both his family's cars to the new policy and bragged about his savings online. Here's how he did:

Warehouse Club Car Policies

Individual car insurance policy	$2,832
Warehouse club car policy	1,392
BIG SAVINGS =	**$1,440**

Change Your Coverage

Changing companies is one way to slash your car insurance premiums; changing your coverage is another. You can raise certain parts of the policy, lower others, and even cancel some to SAVE BIG.

Raise Your Deductible

It was my dad who taught me that insurance is supposed to be just that: insurance—not a maintenance plan. In other words, you buy insurance to protect yourself in extreme situations. You pay for the little scratches and dings yourself. With this in mind, I've always been a big believer in high deductibles. The deductible is the amount you must pay yourself before insurance kicks in. When you raise your deductible, the insurance company faces less risk that it will have to pay for petty claims, so it gives you a generous discount.

Many people sign up for deductibles of just $100 or $250. I suggest you set your deductible way higher than that. Just don't sign up for a deductible so high that it will ruin you financially if you have to pay it.

You will SAVE BIG if you raise your deductible. For instance, you can save up to 30 percent by signing up for a $500 deductible instead of a $200 one, according to the Insurance Information Institute. Hike the deductible up to $1,000—which I think is more like it—and watch the premium drop by 40 percent or more.

Here's an example, using the average annual premium that I mentioned earlier—$3,744 for a two-car family. Since the typical savings when you switch from a $200 deductible to a $1,000 deductible is 40 percent, here's how you SAVE BIG:

 Raise the Deductible, Lower the Premium

Average annual premium for a two-car family	$ 3,744
Premium after raising deductible to $1,000	2,246
BIG SAVINGS =	**$1,498**

Yes, it's true that if you get in a wreck, you will have to shell out $1,000 of your own money, possibly at a painful time. But the discount is so substantial that you can save up the $1,000 needed for the deductible in less than a year.

Here's another way of looking at it: Take the sure savings and risk the possible costs. After all, there is a good chance you will never be in a car accident. And if you *are* in one, it may be the other driver's fault, in which case that person will be the one worrying about their deductible—and the repairs won't cost you a cent.

Not only will raising your deductible save you money, it could save you from having your insurance policy canceled. These days insurance companies are tight with their funds. Have you ever heard of nonrenewal? That's their silly euphemism for canceling you as a customer, but the result is no joke. Insurance companies have a central database where they share information with each other. If you make a bunch of frivolous claims and your company cancels you, other insurance companies may well review your record and choose not to insure you, either. High deductibles discourage frivolous claims and keep your coverage safe.

Involuntary Car Insurance

If you don't buy car insurance, your finance company may buy it for you. That's right. Some lenders check to see if you have proper insurance, and if you don't, they will buy an overpriced policy for you—or really for *them*—to protect their investment. When you think you're finished making your car payments, surprise! You get socked with an insurance bill for thousands.

Cancel Your Collision and Comprehensive Coverage

Since I'm advising you to keep your car as long as you can stand it, there's one more way to save on car insurance. At some stage your car will depreciate to the point that it is not worth repairing. That's when it may be worth your while to drop the collision and comprehensive coverage on your old car. Collision is the insurance that pays to repair the vehicle after a wreck. Comprehensive car insurance covers repairs if your car is damaged in something other than a car accident—like if a tree falls on it.

Experts suggest that you should consider nixing that coverage when your annual collision and comprehensive premium equals more than 10 percent of your car's value. If you cancel these options, instead of fixing your vehicle after it's mangled, you will just kiss it off and get a new (used) one. Canceling collision and comprehensive can reduce your premium by 30 to 40 percent, according to www.Autoguide.com. Don't worry—you will still have the truly important mandatory car coverage like liability insurance, the kind that covers you if you hurt somebody else.

Jacqueline M. of Hawaii drives a fast, loud, older car that she loves. Her boyfriend has a somewhat aged vehicle, too. Jacqueline has moved around a lot for her career, so the belongings she brings with her are what make each city feel like home. It was hard for Jacqueline to admit that it wouldn't be worth repairing her old rocket. But when she finally got around to canceling the collision and comprehensive coverage on her vehicle and her beau's, she quickly changed her mind. Let's see how much she saved per year by dropping her collision and comprehensive coverage:

 Cancelling Collision and Comprehensive

Average annual premium for two-car family	$3,744
Policy without collision and comprehensive	2,434
BIG SAVINGS =	**$1,310**

Wow! With savings like that, she can start putting money toward buying a new (used) car.

Diminished Value

Here's something I wish I had known about when another driver plowed into my five-month-old car: diminished value. The other driver's insurance company paid to fix my vehicle, but just the fact that it had been in an accident diminished its value. Rightly so. It was no longer as sound. One former general manager says his dealership used to automatically offer 30 percent less for a trade-in if it had frame damage.

Sure enough, when I went to sell the car, the pros could easily tell that it had been wrecked and rebuilt. That other driver—or her insurance company—should have paid me for that. I couldn't get as much for the car, so I didn't have as much to put toward my next car.

Many people don't think about the new, lower value of their vehicle in the aftermath of an accident. Instead, we just worry about how long it's going to take for the body shop to fix the darn car so we can get back to our lives. If you have a newer vehicle or an expensive one, you must ask to be compensated for diminished value. The insurance company won't offer to do this. Insurance companies try to avoid paying for diminished value. It's important to pursue a diminished value claim right away, because most states have a statute of limitations on property damage claims, often three years.

Most insurance contracts prevent you from making a diminished value claim against your own insurance company. Where you may succeed is by going after the other driver's insurance company, because you don't have a contract with them. Plus, the whole point is that the accident wasn't your fault, right?

Towing Troubles—and Tricks

If you are towed from an unmarked parking lot, it's probably illegal. Specific signage is required. If you return to your car right before it's hooked up, most jurisdictions allow you to drive away for free. If you return and your car is *already* hooked up, it depends. Some jurisdictions make the driver cut you loose for free, others allow him to charge you. Learn the law where you live.

If the other driver's company resists, consider small claims court to collect diminished value. It should be a fairly easy case to prove: What was your car worth before the crash? How much less is it worth now because it was in an accident? You can also find a bunch of law firms online that specialize in getting people paid for diminished value.

Some of those firms estimate that the average value lost when a vehicle is in an accident is 33 percent. So we return to our old friend, the 2008 Ford Taurus, to see how that 33 percent difference looks in real dollars. If you succeed with your diminished value claim, that 33 percent difference becomes your savings. Take a look:

 **Why Diminished Value Matters**

Ford Taurus value before accident	$14,990
Ford Taurus value after accident	9,893
BIG SAVINGS =	**$ 5,097**

$5,097 is a meaningful amount of money that you deserve to put toward your next car. Pursue diminished value and you can SAVE BIG.

BIG TIPS

- Shop around for insurance every few years. It really does work.
- Raise your deductible to get the sure savings.
- Cancel collision and comprehensive if your car is not worth much.
- Fight for your right to be compensated for diminished value.

PART

CREDIT

Loans for Less

Credit is one of the top five things we spend money on. It's really very logical. We already know that houses and cars are our top two expenses, and how do most of us pay for them? With credit. Big expenses bring big credit. For example, the interest owed on a $200,000 mortgage at 7 percent is $279,160 over the life of the 30-year loan. The *credit* costs even *more* than the house! In other words, it costs money to get money.

The classic tip for saving money on getting money is to go to your own bank's ATM to avoid fees. I don't like the idea of having to pay a fee to access my own money either, but we're talking Small Stuff Savings with that: an average of $3 per transaction, according to www.Bankrate.com. Utterly underwhelming.

There's a better way to save money on getting money and that is to zealously protect and promote your credit rating so you can get credit for less. In the coming pages, I will unveil $177,340 worth of credit savings. You would have to avoid some other bank's cash machine 59,113 times to achieve that kind of savings!

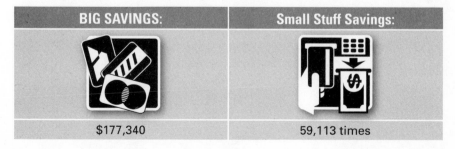

BIG SAVINGS:	Small Stuff Savings:
$177,340	59,113 times

Why am I making a big deal about how much credit costs? Because you can SAVE BIG on credit by using less of it or getting it for less.

Remember, my premise is that if we can identify the areas where we spend the most money, that's where we can save the most money. I encourage you to start thinking of credit as a product with a price. We purchase it just like we purchase houses and cars. The price of credit is the interest. Why am I making a big deal about how much credit costs? Because you can SAVE BIG on credit by using less of it or getting it for less.

In Parts I and II we talked about how to use less credit by making a 20 percent down payment on a home and paying cash for a car. In the following chapters, I am going to show you how to get credit for less.

- **Chapter 18:** First we'll cover credit reports. I'll explain what they really are and why they can be riddled with errors. Then I'll detail how to fight ferociously to correct your credit reports and provide the single best method for protecting them in the future. Inaccurate credit reports cost you money.
- **Chapter 19:** Next, we'll talk about credit scores and how they're derived from credit reports. This is where good credit helps you SAVE BIG. I show how a solid credit score can save you more than $90,000 on a mortgage and car loan combined.
- **Chapter 20:** If your credit score needs work, we'll tackle that, too. First I give you the fundamentals for raising your score, but then I share some flashy moves to speed up the process. I'll show you how raising your score 100 points could save you about $100,000.
- **Chapter 21:** The logical topic after that is credit cards. Where there are credit cards, there is often credit card debt. But I've

got slick strategies that will get you out of debt faster while saving thousands along the way. Then you can get your credit cards working for you instead of working for them.

Want to learn how to SAVE BIG on the cost of credit? We're going to cash in over the next four chapters as I reveal $177,340 worth of savings!

CHAPTER 18

Protecting Your Credit Reports

To SAVE BIG on credit, the first thing you need to do is order your credit reports regularly. Here's why: The information in your credit report makes or breaks whether you can get loans and how much you will pay for them. Unflattering errors in your reports cost you money. Shoot down those errors and you will SAVE BIG.

I am always shocked at how many savvy, sophisticated people have never laid eyes on their own credit report. An acquaintance in her 40s, name withheld to protect the ignorant—I mean innocent—just asked me how to order a credit report the other day. Hey, it's a start. According to the National Foundation for Credit Counseling, only 34 percent of the population orders their credit reports each year. Amazing, given that it's free. Normally we *love* free stuff.

In this chapter, learn to SAVE BIG by:

- Ordering your credit reports strategically so your identity is protected year-round.
- Scanning for the most critical errors on your credit report and going to war over them.
- Understanding how the credit report dispute process is supposed to work—and how it *really* works.
- Taking a little-known step that prevents crooks from opening accounts in your name.

What Is a Credit Report, Really?

Have you ever Googled yourself to see if there's anything floating around about you on the Web? It's fun, in a queasy-curious kind of way, right? Ordering your credit report is the same—except that it *matters.* "Sticks and stones may break my bones, but words will never hurt me"—unless they're in my credit report.

Your credit report is like a record of all the gossip about you, but in this case it's what people are saying about your finances. (And, like gossip, it is often inaccurate and unflattering.) In the case of credit gossip, the town tattlers are the big three credit bureaus:

1. **Experian:** www.Experian.com
2. **Equifax:** www.Equifax.com
3. **TransUnion:** www.TransUnion.com

They talk about where you live, where you work, and, most of all, how you manage your money. They know about every bank account, credit card, mortgage, and car loan you have. And they tell people whether you pay those bills on time. Bankrupt? They'll gossip about that for 10 years.

Yet the credit bureaus themselves don't make decisions about whether to loan you money or how much interest to charge you. They are simply conduits who receive information from companies you do business with, organize that information, and make it available to others.

These days, in addition to banks and credit card companies, you can expect landlords, employers, cell phone companies, department stores, car dealerships, insurance underwriters, student loan programs, and the government all to look at your credit reports to get a sense of your reliability. So don't *you* want to know what's in that report?

Getting Your Credit Report

The big three credit bureaus are all now required by law to provide you a free copy yearly of the report they have compiled on you. The government set up a website with the not-so-intuitive Internet address of www.AnnualCreditReport.com, where you can access your report.

Beware of Fake Credit Report Sites

Beware of copycat websites run by private companies that claim to be free but aren't. They have more obvious names than the government credit report site and they snare people, then market expensive, unneeded financial products to them. The poor Feds tried to counteract this by creating clever musical TV commercials about the real site, www.AnnualCreditReport.com. So what did the copycats do? They spoofed those, too.

A good technique is to order one of your free reports every four months, so that you are monitoring your credit year-round to guard against identity theft. For example, you could stagger your requests, ordering from Equifax in January, Experian in May, and TransUnion in September. In addition, it's especially important to review your credit reports before a big purchase to make sure there are no inaccurate entries that will hurt your chances of being approved.

If you *are* turned down for a loan, you're entitled to a free credit report at that time. The institution that told you no is required to list the reason for your rejection plus the name of the credit bureau it used. You then have 60 days to request your free report.

You can also qualify for a free report if you believe your file is inaccurate due to fraud. If you want to pay for reports in between freebies, it will only cost you about $10 for each one. Just be sure to order only the report unless you want to pay the credit bureaus more for other bells and whistles.

Soft Inquiries Don't Hurt You

Many people worry that when banks check their credit reports to consider offering them a credit card, those inquiries hurt their credit rating. It's a myth! Those are called *soft inquiries* because you have no control over them, and they are harmless. Only hard inquiries, where you actively apply for credit, have an impact on your credit rating. So don't apply for several credit card accounts in a short time.

Lies, Damn Lies

As many as 79 percent of credit reports contain erroneous information, according to a study conducted by the U.S. Public Interest Research Group. Nasty, negative, harmful information. That is a sobering statistic, since your credit report is the foundation of every move you make financially. As a journalist, if I say something derogatory—and inaccurate—about somebody, I can be sued for slander. But decades ago, Congress granted the credit bureaus immunity from such claims. I can see why, because a free flow of credit histories is essential to our economy, but it certainly doesn't give the bureaus the maximum motivation to ensure accuracy.

The first time I ordered my credit reports years ago, they were thick with errors. For example, the same credit card was listed three different times—so it looked like I had triple the debt that I really did. I filled out dispute forms and got the credit bureaus to correct my record. Then, when I ordered my reports again a year later, some of the same errors had resurfaced. Argh! I filed disputes again and it worked the second time.

How Does It Happen?

It's easy to see how mistakes happen. After all, the credit bureaus take in more than two billion new pieces of information every month. That's why I think it's helpful to know the most common credit report mistakes. Following are the top three errors that may occur, according to a study by the National Consumer Law Center:

1. **Mixed or merged files.** Your report may be combined with somebody else's, often because of similar names or birth dates. And, sorry to say, I've never heard of somebody lucking out and seeing their credit rating soar after learning their report was mixed up with Warren Buffett's.
2. **Identity theft.** This is the second largest source of mistakes, since crooks create accounts in your name and don't pay those bills. Because they are pretending to be you, their debt becomes your debt.
3. **Furnisher errors.** Furnisher errors are number three on the list: mistakes inserted into your record by the banks and businesses that report information about you.

Which Entries Should You Dispute?

The following are the most damaging types of entries that are worth going to war over because they can lower your credit score, which is based on your credit report.

- **Old bankruptcies.** Bankruptcies remain on your report for 10 tough years. If a bankruptcy entry is still there after that, complain.
- **Debts disposed of in bankruptcy.** If you declared bankruptcy in the past, debts covered by that bankruptcy settlement should not appear on your report as past due or still payable because bankruptcy wipes the slate clean.
- **Outdated lawsuits and judgments.** If you paid a legal judgment, it should not be in your records anymore. If you didn't pay, it's still supposed to disappear after seven years.
- **Inaccurate tax liens.** Tax liens you have paid remain on your report for seven years. Unpaid ones last 15 years, longer than anything else. (Guess who makes the laws!) If there's a lien on there for longer than those two parameters, dispute it.
- **Outdated demerits.** Late payments and charge-offs, where a creditor writes your bill off because they have given up on you, are not allowed to remain on your report after seven years.
- **Duplicate debts.** The same debt should not be listed more than once, particularly by more than one debt collector.
- **Your spouse's bad debts.** If your spouse failed to pay bills before your marriage or after your official divorce, as long as your divorce filing was handled properly, these should not be on your credit report.
- **Other people's accounts.** Other people's account information—good or bad—should never appear on your credit statement. A cynic might say to keep the stranger's entries if they are positive, but who's to know when that person will face a financial crisis that will ruin their credit—and yours.
- **Old credit applications.** Hard inquiries, where you apply for credit, count against you. They shouldn't remain on your report for more than two years.
- **Credit you didn't apply for.** If you spot hard inquiries that you didn't authorize, dispute them. Soft inquiries, where banks check your credit report in order to offer you a preapproved card, are harmless. Checking your own report is also harmless.

Disputing Errors

If you find mistakes on your credit reports, fight to the finish or you could be finished financially. It's time to go into pit bull mode, lock your jaws on the problem, and don't let go until you have won. Sound intense? I mean it. I'm not asking you to pack your lunch every day, or turn the lights off when you leave the room, but you must fight for your good credit. Unlike those Small Stuff Savings measures, good credit saves you tens of thousands of dollars.

Basic Method

When you find an error on your credit report, the big three bureaus ask that you fill out a dispute form on their websites. Hopefully that alone will take care of the problem, but if you're trying to prove a *crucial* point—like that you never made a late payment—you should take the additional step of providing documentation that proves your case. Do whatever it takes to get your hands on that documentation.

Under the Fair Credit Reporting Act, the credit bureau has 30 days to research your claim and get back to you. If the original bank or business that reported the false item can't prove it is true, the bureau is supposed to correct it.

If a creditor wants to reinsert negative information into your file later, the bureau is supposed to require that creditor to certify that the negative entry is accurate. The bureau is also supposed to give you a toll-free number where you can call to dispute the reinsertion. This is where the process starts to sound ridiculous. I mean, where does it end? Will they re-reinsert the item you have recorrected?

If the credit bureau decides that you didn't make your case—initially or after the reinsertion—the next step isn't very satisfying. You're allowed to write a 100-word statement, which will be attached to your credit file, explaining the inaccuracy. To give you a feel, this paragraph you're reading contains about a hundred words. It's not much. The bigger problem is that many businesses considering you for a loan never actually read your credit report anyway. They just look at the three-digit credit score that is derived from it. So they'll never see your carefully crafted statement.

I have personally seen the basic credit report dispute method work beautifully. But it can get ugly. You can't sue a credit bureau for libel, but you can sue for negligence. That's what Judy T. of

Beware of So-Called Credit Repair

If there are unflattering entries in your credit report and they are *true*, there is no legitimate way to remove them. Late payments, lawsuits, and judgments stay on your report for seven years. Bankruptcies are reported for 10 tough years. So-called credit repair businesses that claim they can remove these accurate items are a scam. They charge big bucks up front and either do nothing or take illegal steps that can get you in trouble. Don't fall for it!

Oregon did. It took her six years to get one of the big three bureaus to remove another woman's atrocious credit history from her file. Judy and her evil financial twin had similar names, the same birth year, and social security numbers that were off by just one digit. Judy even persuaded the other woman to call the people at the credit bureau and alert them that the bad accounts were not Judy's! None of it worked. Judy was eventually awarded $1.3 million in damages by a court.

Advanced Method

Not every case is as alarming as Judy's, but the National Consumer Law Center (NCLC) says it found serious problems when it studied how credit report disputes are handled. The credit bureaus have to deal with vast swaths of data. The NCLC says one way they cope is by boiling information down to numerical codes. So, though you may send in reams of paperwork showing you have always paid your bills on time, your argument can get lost in the automation process. Your detailed dispute might simply be coded "not his/hers."

The bureau then dutifully runs this oversimplified explanation by the creditor who said bad things about you in the first place, and that company stands its ground. It becomes a "you said, the bank said" situation. And remember, the bank is the bureau's customer, its source of revenue. You are not.

What do you do? First, don't use the bureau's online dispute process for serious inaccuracies. The NCLC says that makes it too easy for the bureaus to collate and categorize your complaint.

So go retro. Call the bureau, speak to real human beings (they are required by law to have such people), and keep detailed notes of their names and the dates of your calls.

Next, write a letter. In the letter, state what is wrong with the report and, exactly what you want the bureau to do about it: Delete it? Correct it? Modify it? Reword it? Use the account numbers listed on the credit report, to make it easier for the bureaus to identify which line items you are disputing. This may not be the same account number in your own records, perhaps because the account has been reported (wrongly) to a debt collector who has assigned it a new number. To make yourself crystal clear, also enclose a copy of the actual credit report and circle the items in question.

Send your complaint via snail mail—return receipt requested—with every scrap of proof you can muster. Of course, you will want to attach *copies* (not originals) of any documentation that proves your case.

Mail the whole fat packet to the businesses that furnished the inaccurate information about you, as well. The federal government seems to be moving toward a system in which consumers will be able to challenge companies directly. You are putting those companies on notice that you are ready to fight.

Be sure to keep a copy of this letter for your records. You are starting an old-fashioned paper trail that will help prove the bureau failed to take specific corrective steps. You never know, you may need to show this paper trail to government watchdogs or a jury some day.

Calling Your Creditors May Be a Shortcut

True, the government has set up this circuitous system where you approach the credit bureaus and they approach the creditors, but try calling creditors directly yourself as well. Ask to speak to a supervisor. Explain the situation and fax or e-mail paperwork that proves the negative information the company is reporting about you is wrong. If the supervisor sees the light, ask for a correction and a letter acknowledging the error. Keep that letter forever. Seriously.

Don't forget to send your packet to every bureau that is reporting the erroneous information about you. Solving your problem at one does not help you with the others. They do not routinely share information. I dug up the physical mailing addresses of the big three credit bureaus for you, so you won't be stuck using only their automated online dispute systems. Here they are:

- **Equifax**
  P.O. Box 740256
  Atlanta, GA 30348
  (800) 685-1111
- **Experian**
  P.O. Box 2104
  Allen, TX 75013-2104
  (888) 397-3742
- **TransUnion**
  Consumer Disclosure Center
  P.O. Box 2000
  Chester, PA 19022-2000
  (800) 916-8800 or (800) 888-4213

Taking It to the Next Level

If you get no satisfaction on your own, the Federal Trade Commission (FTC) is the agency tasked with enforcing the Fair Credit Reporting Act and making sure credit bureaus respond to consumer complaints of inaccuracy. Unfortunately, the FTC does not resolve individual consumer matters, but it does collect them and take legal action when it sees a pattern of incompetence or corruption by a company. Here's the FTC's contact information should you need to escalate your complaint to the next level:

- Consumer Response Center
  CRC-240
  Federal Trade Commission
  Washington, DC 20580
  (877) 382-4357
  www.ftc.gov

Why You Should Fight

Here's why it's worth it to fight to the finish and get your credit reports corrected. Errors on your reports—including an identity theft—can, in turn, drag down your credit score. (For more on the relationship between credit reports and credit scores, see Chapter 19.) It happened to Kerry O. of New Jersey. Her financial identity was stolen, the black mark showed up on her credit reports, and that killed her credit score.

When she went to get a $200,000 mortgage, Kerry learned the hard way that negative credit reports cost you money. How much money? Before correcting her credit reports, she could only qualify for a mortgage rate of 8 percent. After correcting them, she qualified for a mortgage at 5 percent. Here's how much money Kerry saved by sticking with it and getting her reports corrected:

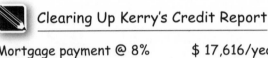

Clearing Up Kerry's Credit Report

Mortgage payment @ 8%	$ 17,616/year
Mortgage payment @ 5%	12,888/year
BIG SAVINGS =	$ 4,728/year

If Kerry had not gotten her report corrected she would have had to pay nearly $5,000 extra a year for her home. Over the life of her 30-year mortgage that would add up to $141,840—a terrible price to pay for things that are not your fault.

Stop the Madness

You can stop those preapproved credit card offers that flood your mailbox. The big three credit bureaus give you the choice of saying "No thank you" for two years or for life. You will have to provide your Social Security number and some other basic information to opt out. I did, and it is dreamy! You can sign up at www.OptOutPrescreen.com or call (888) 567-8688.

Protecting Your File Going Forward

Most credit report errors are the result of accidents or incompetence, but some are intentional, malicious, and criminal. I'm talking about identity theft. If a crook gets your credit card number or your bank account information and makes charges to your *existing* accounts, it is just basic theft. It's like having your wallet stolen. It's a hassle to set the record straight, but the banks will make you whole pretty quickly.

But when crooks create *new* accounts in your name, charge them to the hilt, and then abandon them, *that* is true identity theft and it is devastating. Many victims have a hard time persuading banks that the accounts are not theirs. Often local authorities won't take a police report, believing, wrongly, that it is a civil matter.

Fortunately, the credit bureaus now offer consumers a tool to combat identity theft. It was a long time coming because this tool makes it harder for banks—the credit bureaus' paying customers—to access people's reports, but here it is.

Requesting a Security Freeze

If you really want to safeguard your credit file, consider a security freeze, your right under the Identity Theft Protection Law. Prospective creditors are barred from even *looking* at your file unless you open it for them. They can't get your credit score, either. (Banks and businesses with which you have an existing relationship still have access.) This prevents identity thieves from opening accounts in your name because banks won't establish new accounts without a credit check.

I did a sinister two-part series for *World News with Charles Gibson* in which we went into the Internet underworld where thieves buy and sell people's financial identities. The going rate for a credit card number on the black market was just 40 cents! The underground chat rooms are fast and furious, almost like a stock exchange. I communicated with some identity thieves via instant messaging, and some even sent me free samples to prove they had the goods. Andy G. of California was disbelieving—and devastated—when I called him up to warn him that I had been given *his* credit card number as a free sample.

As you can imagine, I froze my credit reports after doing that scary report. A security freeze is unparalleled protection, but kind of a pain to do. Two of the three credit bureaus made me apply for the freeze via U.S. mail rather than online. And they can charge a small fee, if it's allowed by the state where you live.

Now when I want to refinance my mortgage or apply for a new loan, I have to unfreeze my credit first. That's not been so bad. Each bureau gives you an account number and a secret password to use and then you call a special toll-free number to unfreeze your file. It's instantaneous once you place the call. One bummer: I recently tried to check my own credit reports online and they wanted me to call and order them instead.

To read each bureau's rules and regulations for freezing your credit, go to their websites, listed earlier. I also provide direct links to the security freeze pages of their sites from my website, www.ElisabethLeamy.com. Place a security freeze on your credit reports to protect yourself from identity theft.

BIG TIPS

- Order your credit reports from www.AnnualCreditReport .com.
- Dispute errors ferociously in writing and send via snail mail.
- Mail your dispute to the company that reported the inaccurate information about you, too.
- Place a security freeze on your credit reports to protect yourself from identity theft.

CHAPTER 19

Understanding Your Credit Score

Credit reports are essential, but the mathematical formula derived from them is even more crucial. It is your credit score, a three-digit number that predicts whether you will pay your bills. If you have a good credit score, you will get loans for less and SAVE BIG. A bad score costs you tens of thousands of dollars.

Credit scores now reach into every corner of our financial lives. They used to be just for loans. Then insurance companies discovered a correlation between people with low credit scores and people who make excessive claims. Phone companies use credit scores to decide how big a deposit you have to pay to get service. Your bank may even consider your score when it sets the maximum amount of cash you're allowed to take out at the ATM. Who knows what will be next. That's why a good credit score is so important.

In this chapter, learn to SAVE BIG by:

- Understanding how credit scores are derived and making that work to your advantage.
- Recognizing all the different types of credit scores and which one matters.
- Ordering your credit score from the right source.
- Knowing what score you must have to qualify for the best loans.
- Comprehending how badly a low score can hurt you when you apply for a loan.

How Does a Report Become a Score?

The relationship between a credit *report* and a credit *score* can be confusing. Think of your credit report kind of like a school report card. Instead of listing the classes you took and how you did, it lists the loans you took out and how you did in paying them back. By contrast, your credit *score* is more like an SAT score. It's a three-digit number that sizes up your potential—only it's your potential as a customer rather than as a college student.

So credit *reports* are words. Credit *scores* are numbers. The credit score is derived *from* the credit report. In the 1950s, some pocket-protector types—engineer Bill Fair and mathematician Earl Issac—had the audacity to believe that they could predict human behavior using—get this—*math*. They studied thousands of people, looking at hundreds of factors like late payments, types of credit, how long they'd had a credit card, and their ratio of debt to credit. They figured out which factors were good predictors of whether somebody would pay their bills. Then they assigned numerical values to those factors and created their secret scoring formula. They called this mystery number the FICO score, named after their company, Fair Isaac Corporation.

Today, computer programs analyze a couple dozen different indicators in your credit report and then assign you a score. That's it. That's all a credit score is—a prediction of whether you'll pay. That prediction is usually expressed as a number between 300 and 850 (why the scale doesn't start at zero is beyond me). Like most sports, the higher the number, the better. This is not golf.

Go to the Right Site to Find Unclaimed Money

Is all this talk about your credit score depressing you? Then maybe scoring some unclaimed money would cheer you up.
Unclaimed money accidentally abandoned by citizens is held by each state. You could even use it to improve your credit score. Lots of companies ask for a cut to lead you to the pot of gold. Instead, you can use the website set up by the states to find it for free: www.unclaimed.org.

It all sounds kind of cold, but cold and clinical is *good* in this case. By comparison, when bankers decide your fate on their own, they have the potential to be biased. Scoring applies the same mathematical, methodical standards to everybody. So you don't have to worry or wonder whether some loan officer has preconceived notions about your race, religion, age, gender, and so on.

The statistical models are remarkably predictive, but they're not perfect. Credit scoring models give preference to people who *have* credit, *use* it, and pay it off on time. Ironically, that means if you're so rich that you pay cash for everything, you won't have a high credit score. Additionally, young people—even the really responsible ones—may have low credit scores because of the classic catch-22: You have to have credit to get credit.

How Is Your Credit Score Calculated?

Since I've been harping on how crucial credit scores are, I bet you are wondering how these mysterious numbers are determined. A few years ago, this would have been a very short section, because the FICO scoring model was such a big, sneaky secret. But in 2000, just as legislators were huffing and puffing that something as important as a credit score should be accessible, Fair Isaac went public. It started selling people their scores and explaining roughly how they are calculated.

Credit scoring models are multivariate, a nerdy new vocabulary word I learned, which means that they are sort of three-dimensional sliding scales. No one piece of information can be judged on its own. Each morsel's meaning is reliant on other scraps of information to form the complete picture. The precise details of the elaborate multivariate mess are still murky, but Fair Isaac did release the broad categories it tracks and how important each factor is to your score. Below are the factors that make up your FICO score:

FICO Score Categories

Payment history	35%
Amounts owed	30%
Length of credit history	15%
New credit applications	10%
Mix of credit	10%

Payment History

The fact that your payment history makes up the biggest chunk of your credit score is predictable. I mean, whether you've done a good job of paying your bills in the past is probably a pretty good indicator of whether you'll do a good job paying in the future. Lenders are looking at whether you pay on time, when was the last time—if ever—that you paid late, and how late you were. Collections also fall into this category, and under the classic FICO scoring model, it doesn't matter if the amount was small. The mere presence of a collection action is a huge drag on your score.

Amounts Owed

It's also pretty understandable that the size of your debts would be the second most important factor in determining if you're a good risk and deserve a good score. After all, if you owe a ton of other money already, you may have a hard time paying off a new loan. Surprisingly, your income level is *not* part of your score. Instead the FICO scoring model is really obsessed (not to give a statistical model human emotions!) with how much debt you have compared to how much credit you've been approved for. This is called your credit utilization ratio. In other words, being near your limit, maxed out, is bad.

Length of Credit History

The third largest factor in calculating your credit score is the length of your credit history. This is a frustrating one because you can't exactly control your age and we don't want to start issuing credit cards to two-year-olds. Apparently ol' Bill and Earl discovered a correlation between people who have been banking for a long time and people who bank responsibly. It shows stability. The FICO model weighs how long you've had your oldest account and also the average age of all your accounts.

New Credit Applications

New credit applications are next on the list, and this is where it starts to sound contradictory. It's good to have more credit than you're using. It's good to have a long credit history. But you *shouldn't* apply for *new* accounts? The key is not to apply for a bunch of credit—especially credit cards—all at once. That makes it look like you're about to go on some wild shopping spree, you have a gambling problem, or you're financing an independent film or something. Fortunately, credit scoring models look at mortgage and car loan applications differently. It's understandable that people will shop around for these large loans, and every application you make in a 14- to 45-day time period counts as just one entry.

Mix of Credit

The final factor is your mix of credit. This one is not so intuitive, but apparently Fair Isaac's sociological studies way-back-when revealed that people are better risks if they have a combination of revolving loans and installment loans. In other words, it's best to have a mixture: a home loan, car loans, and credit cards. Mortgage debt is considered good debt since a house can be an investment and is backed up by the piece of property. The thinking on auto loans is that at least the lender vets the borrower more carefully than a credit card company does. Credit card loans get the least respect.

FICO versus Fako Scores

I've spent several pages now talking about your "credit score," but actually there is no such thing—not just one, anyway. You have *multiple* scores, since your credit scores are based on your credit reports and there are three main credit bureaus, each with slightly different information on file about you. Not only that, but your score is constantly changing. It adjusts with every payment you make—or fail to make.

You have multiple scores, but they mostly originate from the same place. Remember the pocket-protector guys? Actually, Bill Fair and Earl Isaac may have been dapper and debonair, for all I know, and they were so far ahead of everybody else that the FICO score is still the only one that really matters. Yet there are other scores out there.

Those other credit scores are sometimes referred to as *Fako* scores! I'll just call them *others*. For years, credit bureaus resisted *telling* people their credit scores, but now they're falling all over themselves *selling* people their credit scores.

In 2006, the big three credit bureaus, Equifax, Experian, and TransUnion, got together and came out with something called a *VantageScore*, which was meant to compete with the FICO score. The VantageScore uses a scale from 501 to 990. Each tier of the VantageScore corresponds to a letter grade. So a score in the 900s is an A, a score in the 800s is a B, and so on. VantageScores were touted as the next big thing that would topple Fair Isaac, but that hasn't happened.

One more detail to add to the madness: Fair Isaac itself has developed several versions of its own FICO score. Just as Microsoft makes Windows '98 and 2000 and so on, Fair Isaac occasionally updates its scoring system. One is called *FICO 08* and another is named *FICO NextGen*. There's also a FICO system for scoring people who don't have much credit yet, called the *Expansion* score. And just as computer customers are still using all the different versions of Windows, different banks use different versions of the FICO score. In fact, some will run your score through multiple FICO scoring editions to see if it makes a difference.

How Do I Get My Score?

How do you get your hands on a gen-u-ine FICO score? Simple: You buy it from Fair Isaac directly. If you want to get your credit score, the only website you need to use is www.MyFICO.com. Many people are under the impression that they are entitled to a free annual credit *score*, when in reality they are only entitled to free annual credit *reports*. The MyFico site charges about $16 for a single bureau score. Just be sure to scroll through all the other stuff Fair Isaac is selling and choose "FICO Standard" if all you want is your score.

If you are just doing a routine check or you're about to make some small credit application, buying one score from MyFICO.com should be enough. But if you are about to buy a house or a car or apply for a small business loan, you should order every FICO score you can get your hands on. Normally, that means purchasing three scores, the ones based on your credit reports at Equifax, Experian, and TransUnion.

Unfortunately, as I write this, Experian has gotten into a tiff with Fair Isaac and isn't allowing Fair Isaac to sell consumers their Experian FICO scores. Yet Experian is still selling those scores to businesses. So your banker can learn your Experian FICO score but you cannot. If this continues, you can always ask your banker for your Experian FICO score. You should also check your Experian credit report, and if it is nearly the same as your other bureau reports, the scores will be very close, too.

What's a Good Score?

After the mortgage meltdown of 2008, a good credit score became more crucial than ever. The threshold for what is considered good moved up. It used to be that anybody with a score of 680 or above could land a great loan with the best possible interest rate. In the fall of 2008, when credit tightened up, lenders started telling me that now only people with scores of 720—maybe even 740—and above could qualify for the best loans.

The definition of subprime changed, too—and engulfed far more people. Subprime borrowers are people with lower credit scores who can't qualify for the best interest rates. People used to be considered subprime prospects, eligible only for more expensive loans, if their scores were 580 or below. That benchmark moved up to 620. Do you know what percentage of the population has a score below 620? Twenty percent. That's a fifth of Americans who can't get a mortgage loan at all, or only one so expensive that it's cost prohibitive.

Want to know where you stand? How your credit score compares to the Joneses? The list below shows what percentage of the population has which score, according to Fair Isaac.

What's Your Score?

Credit Score	Percentage of Population
800–850	13%
750–799	27%
700–749	18%
650–699	15%
600–649	12%
550–599	8%
500–549	5%
300–499	2%

Score Some Forgotten Funds

There are more than $12.5 billion worth of forgotten savings bonds waiting to be claimed. If you have a low credit score, one way to qualify for a mortgage is with a big down payment. Finding a forgotten savings bond in your family's name could be just the ticket! Since savings bonds take so long to mature—20, 30, or 40 years—many families forget they have them. The bonds stop earning interest and just sit there. You can do a simple search online by going to www .TreasuryHunt.gov.

Why Does Your Score Matter?

We've finally come to the point in the chapter where I get to prove to you that your credit score is a big, fat, hairy deal. Consider this: Fair Isaac says somebody with a 550 credit score will always pay about three points more in interest for a mortgage than somebody with a 720 credit score. Interest rates rise and fall with the markets, but that painful point spread remains about the same, and if you have a low credit score it will cost you tens of thousands of dollars.

Let me use myself as an example, because I have a special talent for embarrassing myself more than others! I had some credit problems coming out of college. The usual story: I had three credit cards and zero jobs. I struggled to make the minimum payments. I don't know what my credit score was back then, because FICO scores weren't available to consumers at that time. But thankfully, over the years, I worked diligently to dig myself out of debt. I now have a credit score of 785. That's as of five minutes ago, when I checked online.

So let's look at what kinds of loans I can get with my present, healthy score compared with the mediocre score I must have had when I was young and clueless. Let's say my old self would have had a score of 635 because of a short credit history, debt near my limits, and a couple of late payments. If anything, I'm being too generous to my former self, but that score will prove my point just fine.

We'll start with a four year, $25,000 car loan. With a stellar score of 785, I can qualify for an interest rate of 5 percent. But with a middling score of 635, my interest rate leaps to 11.234 percent.

Let's see how much that is going to cost me over the life of the four-year loan.

Auto Loans: Benefit of High Credit Score

FICO Score	Cost of Loan
635	$31,152
785	27,648
BIG SAVINGS =	**$3,504**

With the 150-point lower credit score, "Bad Eli" would have to pay an extra $3,504 in interest over the life of the loan. If I didn't have to spend that money on interest, it would be a nice chunk of change to put toward paying cash for my *next* car. Even if you break it down into smaller time frames, the additional interest I have to pay because of my mediocre score is significant. It costs me an extra $73 a month, which might well be enough to gas up my car, and $876 a year, which would be plenty to pay for some big, bad repair.

If you think that scenario is bad, you'll feel the real pain when you need a loan for a larger amount over a longer period of time: a mortgage. Let's choose a 30-year fixed-rate mortgage for $250,000. With a score of 635, I can only qualify for a 6.034 percent mortgage rate. With a score of 785, as I write this I would be able to get a mortgage at just 4.46 percent. Here's how that impacts me over the life of the loan:

Mortgages: Benefit of High Credit Score

FICO Score	Cost of Mortgage
635	$541,440
785	453,960
BIG SAVINGS =	**$ 87,480**

As you can see, if I hadn't cleaned up my act and improved my credit score, I would have to pay $87,480 more in interest over the course of that 30-year mortgage. Jeez, that's enough to finance a college education! That amounts to $243 more per month—nearly $3,000 a year—because of a 150-point difference in my score.

BIG TIPS

- Pay for one score if you're applying for minor credit, all of them if you're applying for a big loan.
- Know which credit scores matter.
- Order your score from MyFICO.com for a genuine Fair Isaac score.

CHAPTER

Raising Your Credit Score

If you've looked up your credit score and learned it's not so hot, there is hope. Improving your credit score is kind of like losing weight. It's mostly about the fundamentals. Eating less, exercising more. Spending less, paying bills on time. But in weight loss *and* credit scoring there *are* a few flashy moves you can make to jump-start your progress. They're not substitutes for a healthy diet and prudent payment plan, but they can give you the little boost you need to succeed.

By combining the fundamental strategies with a couple of flashy ones, you can raise your score as much as 100 points in a few months. A hundred points could save you $100,000 or more. A hundred points could be the difference between getting a mortgage or not, becoming a homeowner or not. A hundred points might be just what you need to SAVE BIG.

In this chapter, learn to SAVE BIG by:

- Taking the slow, steady steps on the treadmill that will improve your score.
- Trying some flashy crash-diet moves that can help your score in the short term.
- Requesting a service that is like the gastric bypass surgery of the credit world, where you hire experts to do the hard work for you.

The Fundamentals

With credit scores, it is way easier to lose than it is to gain. That's why, if you have a good score already, you must never let down your guard. Protect it ferociously. You see, a single blunder can cause your credit score to *plunge*, but there is no corresponding single step that will make it rapidly *rise*. Instead, you have to do a bunch of small, slow things right to incrementally improve your score.

The fundamentals of improving your credit score involve a bunch of dos and don'ts. Actions and inactions. And since credit scoring is a multivariate math problem using factors that interact with each other, both are important.

Do This

I like the dos the best because they are positive, affirmative steps you can take to improve your score and SAVE BIG. Some are common sense, others counterintuitive. Here they are.

Do: Pay Down Debt   If you have the funds to pay *down* your debts, you can raise *up* your score. It's the fastest single step you can take. Your score will improve as soon as the new balances are reported to the credit bureaus and factored into your score, which takes about a month. When you order your credit score from www.MyFico.com, you get access to a neat tool called the FICO Score Simulator, which lets you enter different scenarios and see how they would affect your score. I checked the FICO Score Simulator to see how many points I could gain just by paying off the *current* month's charges on my credit cards. I don't even carry a balance, and look at the difference it makes:

Benefit of Paying Down Debt

Eli's score before paying off bills	785
Eli's score after paying off bills	825
BIG GAIN =	**40 points**

Forty points is a significant gain. If you are planning to apply for a mortgage and you need to boost your score, start three to six months in advance. Aggressively pay down your debt so that it is only 10 to 30 percent of your limit. If you can pay it off completely, so much the better. After that, pay cash for everything for three to six months before applying. It will make a substantial difference.

Do: Pay on Time   Don't get mad at me. I'm not insulting your intelligence here. Obviously paying on time will improve your credit score, because payment history makes up 35 percent of it, the single biggest category. But here's the part you may not know: The FICO scoring model gives more weight to recent history than to ancient history. This is good news that you can use to your advantage. It means every positive move you make *now* helps counteract mistakes you made *then*. Just by beginning to pay your bills on time, every time, you will raise your score. It's that simple. But it takes time.

On the flip side, a single late payment—just one—can make your credit score plunge. It's one of the cardinal sins of credit scoring. I just used the Score Simulator at MyFICO.com to see what would happen if I myself make a late payment. Here's what it showed me.

Impact of a Single 30-day Late Payment

Eli's score before late payment	785
Eli's score after late payment	685
BIG LOSS =	**100 points**

Don't think for a second that because you have a high score, you can afford to be tardy. Late payments hurt high scores even more than low ones because they stick out more dramatically. A late payment coming from somebody who *often* pays late is just a sign that their dog ate the bill—again. A late payment on an otherwise *pristine* credit file is like an early-warning flare showing that an individual's financial life may be crumbling.

While we're talking about late payments, you should know that you are responsible for paying your bills on time—even if they don't show up. If a bill is lost in the mail or doesn't make it to you on time because you have moved or are in the hospital or something, it's still your responsibility. Don't blow it.

Paying a bill late is such a big, bad black mark that if you have a dispute with a creditor, I recommend paying the bill anyway while you fight over it. True, you are momentarily out that cash, and it may be a struggle to get it refunded, but if you don't pay, and the merchant reports you as late, the cost to your credit score could be far more expensive. Once the matter is resolved, if the creditor agreed to accept some kind of partial payment, get that agreement in writing, so you'll have proof.

Late Payments Are Not Usually Reported until 30 Days Overdue

Now that I've got you completely freaked out about late payments, I'll fill you in: that three-day slip-up when you couldn't find a stamp shouldn't be a problem. Thirty days is the be-all, end-all benchmark. But don't make it a habit. You don't want to rely on your creditors' goodwill. They could change their practices at any time—and might, in order to make more money.

Do: Pay Automatically   If you have trouble paying your bills on time because you don't have enough money, that's one thing. But if you have trouble paying on time because you're busy or absent-minded, that's another. It can happen if you travel a lot for work, if you have a new baby, if you're struggling with a chronic sickness, or if you're recently divorced and your spouse used to handle the bills. Plenty of people are so disorganized, busy, or frazzled that they pay their bills late even though they have the money.

If you know that you're one of those people, don't *beat* yourself up, *sign* yourself up—for an automatic bill-paying service. By doing so, you arrange for your creditors to automatically zap your checking account each month so you always pay on time. I know, it sounds kind of scary, but they are not allowed to withdraw any more money than you authorize. Automatic bill-pay works best for accounts that are the same every month, like mortgages. It's a wise move that will save you tens of thousands of dollars by protecting your credit score.

Report Thefts Immediately

If you're defrauded via an electronic transaction, your bank might not pay you back. The Federal Reserve's Regulation E says you must report thefts involving online banking, ATM cards, and debit cards within two days to limit your liability to $50. Your liability jumps up to $500 on the third day. And if you don't report the loss for more than 60 days, you are responsible for the entire loss. Another reason to keep an eagle eye on your bank statements.

Do: Keep Ratios Low   The next most important thing you can do to achieve a high credit score is to keep your credit utilization ratio low. The credit utilization ratio compares the amount of debt you have to the amount of credit you've been approved for. All it really means is don't max out your credit cards. I used the FICO Score Simulator to see what would happen if I maxed out my credit cards. Take a look:

 Impact of Maxing Out Credit Cards

Eli's score before running up cards	785
Eli's score after running up cards	675
BIG LOSS =	**110 points**

Ouch, 110 points is devastating. To achieve the best possible credit score, you should not use more than 10 percent of the available credit on your credit cards. However, I think that's unrealistic (and I like to earn rewards with my card), so I'm going to suggest the benchmark that gives you the *next* best credit score: 30 percent. That means if your limit on a card is $1,000, you should never charge more than $300 on that card, even if you pay it off in full. Brutal, huh? Well, amounts owed make up nearly a third of your credit score, so this is critically important.

If you carry balances, then you should make sure that all of those balances are below the 30 percent mark. The 30 percent ideal is applied to each separate card balance and to all your cards when averaged. In other words, even if your *average* is fine because most of your cards have little or no balance, you can still be penalized if one card is near the limit. The scoring model wants you to *have* credit but barely use it. Paradoxical, isn't it?

Do: Apply for a Secured Credit Card   If you are young with a thin credit file, one way to fatten it up is to sign up for a secured credit card. You put down a deposit, say $500, and in exchange you get a credit card with a $500 limit. It sounds like a debit card, but it's not. A secured credit card is reported to the credit bureaus, so by paying it on time and keeping the balance low you will be building a positive credit history that helps your score.

Advance-Fee Loans Are Illegal

BIG SECRET

If somebody says they can guarantee you a loan in exchange for a fee, it's a scam. No bank can guarantee you a loan up front. A real lender might charge a small fee for a credit check, but large fees, especially if they're called *processing fees*, are a telltale sign of a rip-off. If you pay the fee you will get nothing in return.

Don't Do That

I have a two-year-old daughter and I find myself telling her "Don't do that" way more often than I say "Do this." I'm trying to teach her right from wrong, and keep her safe and at this age the don'ts are pretty important. Similarly, the don'ts of credit scoring are as vitally important as the dos.

Don't: Apply for Multiple Credit Cards at Once   When I was working in my first (poorly paid!) TV news job, I got hold of a list of low-interest credit cards. Fearful that I would have trouble qualifying, I applied for every single one of them. Guess what? They all turned me down. The reason? Too many applications for credit!

As I mentioned before, Bill Fair and Earl Isaac discovered a statistical connection that showed that people who apply for a bunch of credit at once are at greater risk of not paying in the next couple of years. In fact, Fair Isaac says a consumer who has applied for six or more loans (mortgages, auto financing, credit cards) in the past year is eight times more likely to declare bankruptcy than someone who has no new credit applications on their record. Fascinating—unless that person is you.

This is a good reason not to open store charge cards when the clerk asks, "Would you like to save an extra ten percent today?" It may sound like a tempting offer, but 10 percent is Small Stuff Savings (unless you're buying something huge.). Plus, the new credit application could drag down your score enough to cancel out the savings you just saw at the register. Don't believe me? Back I go to the FICO Score Simulator to learn the impact of opening a new store card.

Impact of Opening a New Store Credit Card

Credit score before store card application	785
Credit score after store card application	775
BIG LOSS =	**10 points**

You can lose 10 points just for opening a department store card! If you were right on the border between two different FICO score tiers, that 10 points could really cost you when you apply for a big loan. Students of credit scoring swear the ideal number of cards to achieve the optimum score is two. Just two. Fair Isaac isn't saying, but the ideal number certainly isn't 20!

Don't: Close Existing Accounts   On the other hand, if you have gradually opened up a lot of credit card accounts over the years, and you pay them in full or don't even use many of them, let it be. I used to believe that having a lot of open, unused accounts was a strike against you because you could potentially dig deep in your drawer, find those cards, and go crazy with them. According to Liz Pulliam Weston, syndicated MSN Money columnist and author of *Your Credit Score: Your Money and What's at Stake*, this is a myth.

Bottom line: Don't close those accounts. It could hurt that all-important credit utilization ratio by reducing the total amount of credit you are approved for. It's especially bad to close *longstanding* accounts, since length of credit history makes up 15 percent of your score, the third biggest chunk.

When Old Is New Again

Paying off an older collection account may not be a good idea. Why? By law, the credit bureaus are supposed to assign the original delinquency date to every debt. But sometimes when debt collectors make a fresh report about the status of that same debt, it gets re-aged so it looks like a recent problem. This isn't supposed to happen, but it can. As you know, recent activity is weighted more heavily than older activity. So if an unpaid debt is close to the seven-year mark when it will fall off your report, you may want to let it be.

Don't: Consolidate Debts   Many people who are trying to dig out of debt will get a new low-interest credit card and move all their old credit card debt onto it. It's a reasonable choice if your goal is to save time and hassle. But, believe it or not, it can hurt your credit score. How? Because now you have one big balance on a single card, making it closer to the limit. The ratio. The ratio. It's all about the ratio.

Plus, when you remove your balances from those other cards and stop using them, the banks will likely close the accounts for inactivity. That will hurt your length of credit history because you'll have lost older accounts and opened a new one.

Don't: Cosign Loans   If you are trying to shield and protect your credit score, don't agree to be a cosigner on a loan. Sure, you want to help. But it's not just paperwork. That cosigned loan goes on *your* credit report. And if your friend or family member pays it late or doesn't pay it at all, it will ruin your credit score. Worse yet, cosigning means you agree to *pay* that loan if your friend or family member cannot or does not. Are you ready for that? You could lose your good score, your money, and your friendship.

Don't: Go Shopping Until Your Mortgage Closes   After your mortgage application is approved, while you're waiting to close on the house, it's tempting to go on a shopping spree. You want to get nice, new stuff for your dream house, right? Wrong! Many lenders will recheck your credit before the closing to make sure everything is in order. Maxing out your credit cards to buy furniture and knick-knacks could knock 40 or 50 points off your score. That could be enough to get you disqualified or raise your rate.

Don't: Ignore Small Balances   The Classic FICO scoring model holds late payments and collections against you no matter their size. If you once failed to pay a $25 bill, it is just as bad as failing to pay a $25,000 one. FICO, '08 has been reformulated to ignore collections for less than $100, but you can't count on the new formula because lenders use all different editions of the scoring software.

Flashy Moves

Now you know about the fundamentals, the nutrition and exercise part of improving your credit score. So its time for some flashy moves—the equivalent of fasting—for your credit score! Promise me you will layer them on top of the healthy habits like paying your bills on time and keeping your balances low. If you try to use these exciting strategies on their own, you won't be addressing the core problem: that you spend more money than you have. Think of it this way: Crash dieters always gain the weight back plus a few pounds. That can happen to crash credit card customers, too.

Try This

These days we know enough about credit scoring models that we can work the system a little bit. Since we know credit scores are based on credit reports, there are perfectly legitimate ways to get more positives and fewer negatives listed on your report. It's also possible to tweak the all-important credit utilization ratio somewhat. Here are some tactics you can try.

Move Your Money Around   Remember how important it is that you keep your credit card balances low? And remember that the score takes into account the average ratio but also each card's individual utilization ratio? Well—insert devilish grin here—you can manipulate the system a bit if you have some cards that are near the limit and others that are not. All you have to do is move your balances around, so that the charges on every card are below 30 percent. Ten percent is even better.

A word of caution: This is only a short-term solution. If you have a problem paying off your credit cards, it will catch up with you. But it's certainly fair game to move your money around to goose your score a little and then start paying down the cards for a more long-term improvement.

Request a Higher Limit   Since a ratio consists of two numbers, if you can't move one, try to move the other. How? Call up your bank and request a higher credit limit. In the post-2008 economic climate, you may not have as much luck as you used to, but it's worth a try. All you have to lose is some time listening to elevator music.

One caution: Ideally the phone operator will raise your credit limit without checking your credit report, because inquiries on your credit report hurt your score and we don't want that to offset the gains made by raising your limit. So ask the operator how much she can raise your score without checking your credit report. Got that? I know it's mind-numbing.

Debit Cards Can Be Dangerous

A debit card is a great alternative to a credit card because the money comes straight out of your bank account so you can't overspend. But if thieves get hold of it, they are taking *your* money instead of the credit card company's money. Visa and MasterCard limit your liability to $50 if you report the theft promptly. But it can take days before your bank restores the money to your account, jeopardizing your ability to pay your bills.

Ask Creditors to Report Positive Information   While you're on the phone with your new call center friend, ask her why she isn't reporting positive information about your account that could help your score. Some card companies don't report credit card limits. Others only report to one of the three credit bureaus. If your account is in good standing, it would be a tremendous benefit to your score if that bank reports the account to all three bureaus. Some of the bureaus may not even know it exists! Scan your three credit reports for discrepancies like this and politely ask—on the phone and in writing—if the bank will report the positives.

Ask Creditors to Delete Single Sins   If your overall payment history with a company is good and you make one glaring mistake, you may be able to get the bank or credit card company to delete it. Your chances are best if you're a longstanding customer and it's clear that the late payment or other blunder was out of character. All you do is call up the company and ask. If the first low-level operator says no, ask for a supervisor.

Simply explain that your overall history with the company is good, point out that you are a loyal customer (especially if they make a lot of money off of you), and ask if they would do you the courtesy of removing the offending item from your three credit reports. Creditors have the leeway under the law to perform favors like this.

Pay before the Closing Date   This next tip is like a magic trick. Sleight of hand. I love it. Look at each credit card bill and find where it tells you the *closing date* for the account. The closing date balance is what the bank reports to the bureaus. And that's what they use to calculate how close you are to your limit. It's the old utilization ratio thing again. So make sure there is a low—or no— balance on that date! Just go online and pay the bill a couple days before the closing date. If your bank uses the same closing date each month, you could even automate this early payment to idiot- proof it.

One footnote: You must also pay any charges you make in the couple of days *after* the closing date, to avoid interest charges. It's even possible your bank could blow it and report you as late if you don't pay the charges incurred after you made your early payment.

Become an Authorized User   Another way to establish or improve credit is to be added as an authorized user to another person's account. This may sound a little slippery, but it's perfectly legitimate if the other person is a family member or close associate. Many par- ents do this for their kids. Even though the authorized user is not responsible for paying the bill, the account—and all its history— will show up on their credit report. Of course, you must make sure you are added by somebody with a good credit record of their own or this move will hurt instead of helping you.

As you can imagine, some opportunists have latched onto this helpful practice and twisted it around. Shady websites have been offering to sell people a spot on a stranger's good credit card. Some people were renting out their authorized user slots to dozens of people at a time. This is unacceptable and could get you prosecuted for fraud.

Get a Credit Union Installment Loan   Credit scoring models look on personal loans from banks and credit unions more favorably than they do credit card loans. That means another possibility is to see if you can get a personal installment loan—credit unions often have the best rates—and use it to pay off your credit cards. That way you can wipe out all those considerations about how close you are to the limit on your credit cards.

Hired Help: Rapid Rescoring

Now it's time to reveal the gastric bypass—the weight-loss surgery—of the credit scoring world, where you hire professionals to do the hard work for you. The process is called credit rescoring or rapid rescoring. Professionals with special access to the big three credit bureaus will correct errors on your credit report that are dragging your score down.

The service is offered by local credit bureaus, who work in cooperation with the big three credit bureaus. These rapid rescoring experts alert Equifax, Experian, and TransUnion if there is a mistake in your credit file that is unfairly hurting your score. They have access to dedicated phone and fax lines at the big three, so they can bypass all the bureaucracy that makes correcting your own credit report so time consuming. If you are a good candidate, they can get an error corrected in 24 to 72 hours. Presto!

The results can be dramatic. Valerie B. of Maryland saw her score rise from 598 to 790 after rescoring. Her credit reports erroneously stated that she had failed to pay off her car loan. What really happened is that her bank had been bought by another bank just as she made her final payment, and the records were lost in the shuffle. Rescoring to correct the mistake allowed Valerie to qualify for a 6 percent mortgage interest rate instead of 8 percent. Here's how much the improved interest rate saved her over the life of her 30-year mortgage:

Difference Made by Rapid Rescoring

FICO Score	Cost of Loan
598	$393,480
790	321,480
BIG SAVINGS =	$ 72,000

Credit rescoring is only available when you are applying for a mortgage, because there's a recognition that that's when an improved score is most critical. If your score needs a boost, your mortgage lender or broker can send your file in for rapid rescoring. Unfortunately, it's not available directly to consumers.

To be clear, credit rescoring experts can only correct legitimate errors on your report. If there's an unflattering entry and it's *true*, they can't help you. To help them fight true errors, you will want to support their efforts by poring over your credit reports, searching for mistakes, and providing documentation that proves your case.

The Power of 100 Points

At the beginning of this chapter, I promised to show you some fundamentals and some flashy moves that could boost your credit score by 100 points in just a few months. Now let's see how that effort helps you SAVE BIG. Suppose you started out with a credit score of 620, the lowest score you can have and still get a mortgage. If you raised that score up to 720, you would qualify for a mortgage at 5.093 percent interest instead of 6.46 percent interest. Here's how much that saves you each year on a $300,000 mortgage:

Power of 100 Points: Mortgage

FICO Score	Cost of Loan
620	$22,656/year
720	19,536/year
BIG SAVINGS =	$ 3,120/year

So the savings is $3,120 a year. If you kept the loan for 30 years, your total savings would be $93,600 thanks to that 100-point boost.

Now let's look at a car loan. In this case, raising your score from 620 to 720 lowers your interest rate from 12.780 percent to 6.348 percent. Amazing. If it's a three-year auto loan for $25,000, here's your savings:

Power of 100 Points: Auto Loan

FICO Score	Cost of Loan
620	$30,240/three years
720	27,504/three years
BIG SAVINGS =	**$ 2,736/three years**

That's $2,736 that you can put toward your next car. Nice. Here's my favorite part about raising and then maintaining your credit score: It's free. All you have to do is use your current credit responsibly and you will save thousands on your future credit. You will SAVE BIG.

BIG TIPS

- Pay your bills on time, every time by setting up automated payments.
- Keep your debt-to-credit ratios low by paying down cards and redistributing money among your cards.
- Don't apply for a lot of credit at once, but don't close existing accounts, either.
- Ask creditors to delete isolated negative entries that are out of character.
- Ask about rapid rescoring if you are applying for a mortgage and inaccurate credit reports are dragging your score down.

CHAPTER

Cut Credit Card Debt

If your debts are high and your credit score is low, chances are credit cards are the culprit. The Federal Reserve says the average amount of credit card debt among families that carry a balance was $7,300 in 2007, the latest year for which numbers are available. The average credit card interest rate is 15 percent. Put those two together and it's clear credit cards are pricey products. If you charged nothing more (which is unlikely!), you would owe about $1,000 in interest over the course of a year.

Since our goal in this book is to attack your biggest expenses, we're going to go after credit card debt. Just as it's possible to buy a home or a car for less, it's possible to pay off a credit card for less. There are better-smarter-faster ways to pay off credit card debt that can help you SAVE BIG.

In this chapter, learn to SAVE BIG by:

- Freezing your credit cards—literally *and* figuratively.
- Using your savings account to pay your credit card debt.
- Choosing the right order to pay off your debts.
- Paying your credit card bills not more, but more *often*, to retire them faster.

The Minimum Payment Mess

If you want to SAVE BIG, credit card debt is the enemy. Pure evil, especially if you are making only the minimum payment. Vanessa J. of New York is pregnant. Suppose she were to spend $3,000 on furniture to make her new house perfect for the new arrival. Now, say she were to charge the fabulous furniture on her credit card with a 30 percent interest rate, a rate that is not uncommon these days. Then, what if Vanessa and her husband ended up making just the minimum payments on that credit card? Brace yourself. Here's how much the credit would cost them:

The Minimum Payment Mess

Original price of furniture	$ 3,000
Interest over 27 years	11,814
TRUE COST of furniture =	**$14,814**

In this scenario, Vanessa and her husband end up paying five times more for their furniture than they originally intended. And—get this—by making only the minimum payment, it would take them 27 years to retire the debt—*if* they never charged another thing on their card, which is unlikely. That is the terrible trap of making only the minimum payment.

I know you've heard about the minimum payment mess before, but what's a personal finance book without a rant about credit card debt? It had to be done. Besides, I've got the chops since I've been there. I dug myself out of debt one dollar at a time. If you have credit card debt, no other advice in this book matters until you pay it off. Okay. I hereby proclaim the lecture over. Read on for creative, constructive ways to become debt-free and SAVE BIG.

To Stop Collectors from Calling, Just Write Them a Letter

This is my favorite consumer tip of all time. All you have to do is ask the collector for their company name and address. Then write them a letter—send it certified—telling them you do not wish to be contacted anymore. Under the Fair Debt Collection Practices Act, they must obey. The debt doesn't go away, but the upsetting phone calls do. After that, the collector can only contact you to inform you of a specific legal action it is taking against you.

Old-Fashioned Discipline

If you carry credit card debt, I want you to put down this book for a sec, go to your wallet, get out all your credit cards, grab a pair of scissors, and cut up your cards. All but one.

Are you feeling the withdrawal symptoms yet?

Have you broken out in a cold sweat?

Well, I have news for you—you're about to get even colder.

I want you to take the remaining card, stick it in a one-gallon plastic zipper bag, fill the bag with water, and freeze it. Yes, freeze your credit card in a block of ice. You are putting your excessive spending on ice. You can chip the card out of there if you have a true emergency, but the effort it takes should prevent impulse buys.

Speaking of freezing, now I want you to go on a spending freeze. You are only allowed to spend money on the essentials that keep you alive. In my debtor days, my weaknesses were clothes, decorating, and dining out. I eliminated those categories and only spent money on housing, gas, and food. It sounds like a drag, but actually a spending freeze knocks tons of things off your to-do list and helps you focus on the things that matter, like friends and family.

The real key to reducing credit card debt is *sending* more instead of spending more. If you follow the preceding advice, you'll stop *spending* more. Next you need to figure out a way to start *sending* more—making bigger payments to your credit card company. I did this by sending money when I had it, even if I didn't have a bill due. Cash in my hand had a way of turning into shoes on my feet, so I had to get rid of that cash fast.

I'm dating myself, but what I did was preaddress and stamp several envelopes so I had them ready. Anytime I had extra money in my checking account, I popped it in an envelope and kissed it goodbye. You can do the same thing if you bank online. In fact, it will be out of your sticky little fingers even faster when you click that mouse.

Beware Debt Settlement Companies

Their persuasive pitch is that they can help you retire your debts for pennies on the dollar. But often they charge a huge fee up front that could be going toward your debts.

Many debt settlement companies tell people not to pay their bills while they build up a lump sum to offer to their creditors as a settlement. Stopping payment on your bills is devastating to your credit score. Plus you could be hounded by collection agents or even sued. Many people drop out of these programs before the company settles a single debt for them and they never get their money back. Meanwhile, penalties and fees have accrued and they owe more than ever.

Credit Counseling

If you are too overwhelmed to reduce your debts on your own, don't delay. Get credit counseling. Scratch that. Get *legitimate* credit counseling. Seek out a nonprofit company that provides counseling for free or charges no more than $25 to $75 a month for its services. For-profit credit counselors have been known to charge hundreds or thousands up front and do nothing to help you. Others have promised to forward people's payments to their creditors, then run off with the money instead.

You can find a legitimate credit counselor through the National Foundation for Credit Counseling, www.NFCC.org, or the Association of Independent Consumer Credit Counseling Agencies, www.AICCCA.org.

The granddaddy of them all is Consumer Credit Counseling Service (CCCS). A CCCS counselor can negotiate with your credit card companies to lower your interest rate and maybe your monthly payments, so you can get your credit cards under control. In one type of program, you send a lump sum to CCCS, which divides it up and forwards it to your creditors. Meanwhile, CCCS gives you an earful of education about how not to get into debt again.

Credit Counseling Does Not Hurt Your Credit Score

The FICO scoring model does not consider credit counseling one way or another. It is a neutral entry on your credit report. It is possible, however, that you will have a hard time getting a mortgage loan while you are in credit counseling. That's because human bankers review your actual credit report, in addition to your credit score, when you apply for a big loan like a mortgage. If you're in credit counseling, you're not quite ready for a house yet anyway. Usually entries about credit counseling are dropped from your report as soon as you pay off the debts you needed counseling about.

Newfangled Strategies

Back when I was teetering under credit card debt, I wish I had known that there are some nifty tricks for knocking your debts down. I have since learned all sorts of newfangled strategies that will help you reduce your debt level, improve your credit score, and SAVE BIG on your future purchases. Here they are.

Negotiate Your Rate

You can often negotiate for a lower interest rate, which will help you pay off your debt more quickly and cheaply. All you do is call up your credit card company and politely ask them to lower your interest rate. Naturally, you will also mention that other card companies have offered you a lower rate, so if this company doesn't help you, you will take your business elsewhere.

We tried this with a bunch of young *Good Morning America* employees and it was a grand success. We showed off their results live on the show. Here's what a few five-minute phone calls accomplished:

 Benefit of Asking for a Lower Credit Card Rate

Cardholder	Before	After
Cardholder 1	14.99%	8.99%
Cardholder 2	17.49%	10%
Cardholder 3	23.65%	16.25%

Those simple phone calls can make a big difference in how much and how long it takes to pay off your credit cards. Let's say you have $15,000 in credit card debt (I see it all the time) and you want to pay it off in two years. How much would negotiating for a lower rate help you? Let's use the numbers from cardholder 2 since it's a real interest rate reduction I've seen with my own eyes. Here's the math:

 Negotiating a Lower Rate on a $15,000 Balance

Interest Rate	Amount Due
17.49%	$2,885
10%	1,613
BIG SAVINGS =	**$1,272**

Wow! By simply negotiating a lower interest rate, you would be able to save $1,272 over two years.

In the post-crisis economy, you may not be able to achieve as big an interest rate cut, but the fact remains that it is easier for a bank to keep a current customer than to get a new one, so the bank will probably work with you.

Get a Different Card

If your current card company is unsympathetic, several websites list low-interest credit cards you can apply for instead. Just be sure to apply for them one at a time with some space between applications to keep hits to your credit score to a minimum. Check www.CreditCards.com, www.Cardtrak.com, and www.LowCards.com.

Use Savings to Pay Debt

I know lots of smart people who have a good-size savings account *and* credit card debt. That is just dumb. Oh, did I say that out loud? I know, I know, people feel it's important to save for emergencies. Trust me, credit card debt *is* an emergency. It is sapping your financial strength. You can instantly make a profit by using low-interest savings to pay off high-interest credit card debt.

If your savings account yields 2 percent interest and your credit card charges 17 percent interest, you make a 15 percent profit by using the savings to pay off the debt. Money managers would kill to make that kind of gain in the stock market! Here's how the numbers would play out with a balance of $10,000:

Using Savings to Pay $10,000 Debt

Rate	Interest
Credit card debt @ 17%	$1,700 charged
Savings account @ 2%	$ 200 earned
BIG SAVINGS =	**$1,500**

If these numbers didn't convince you and you are clinging to the idea that you need a large savings account in case of an emergency, then think of it this way: Take the *sure* savings and gamble on the *possible* costs. You are guaranteed to save money by using your savings to pay your debt. You may or may *not* have a future emergency. If you do, you can use your credit card to pay for it. Still squeamish? Let's compromise. Keep $1,000 in your savings account. Send the rest to your credit card company and start to SAVE BIG.

To be clear, I am not talking about tapping into a 401(k) or IRA here. If you already have money in one of these retirement accounts, don't withdraw it because the penalties could well be worse than the credit card interest. If you are contributing to one of those while you have credit card debt, stop and pay the debt first. The one exception is if your employer makes a match, in which case you should contribute just the amount that is matched to get the free money.

You Can Get a Higher Interest Rate on Your Bank Account

The website www.Money-Rates.com lists the highest savings account interest rates at any given time. There are even checking accounts that offer interest rates as high as 6 percent. For that, check the website www.CheckingFinder.com.

Pay in the Right Order

Another strategy that helps you retire debt faster is to pay your credit cards in the most beneficial order. People always ask me, should I go after the highest interest rate first or the highest balance first? There are different answers for different circumstances, but this is a book about saving money, and the way to SAVE BIG is to move from highest to lowest interest rate. Why? Because the debt with the highest interest rate is costing you the most money. The less time you are carrying a balance on that card, the less time you will be paying that onerous interest rate. When that balance is wiped out, move on to the next highest.

Many experts argue that people should pay off the cards with the smallest balances first, for the psychological boost of finishing off an entire debt. That's insulting. Since this book is specifically about saving money, I'm going to stick to my guns. Fire on the highest-interest debts first.

You May Be Able to Negotiate up to 60 Percent off Your Debts

When the recession hit, credit card companies became much more open to the possibility of allowing people to settle their debts for less than they actually owe. In other words, if you owe $10,000, you will only pay $4,000 and the creditor will write the rest off as a loss. But only do this if your credit score is already a wreck and you don't plan to apply for a big loan any time soon.

Pay More Often

Instead of paying your credit card bill once a month, when it's due, try making a half payment every two weeks. Many of us are paid biweekly, so this evens out your cash flow. More importantly, it results in making more payments per year, since there are more than four weeks in most months. I mentioned this strategy for paying mortgages off early. Well, it works for credit cards too. The reason is basic: There are two months of the year that you end up making three payments instead of two.

I'm going to use a real whopper of a debt for this example, to show what a difference this strategy can make. Let's say you owe $20,000 at 24.99 percent interest. A typical minimum payment would be $800 a month. So instead you send $400 every two weeks. Here's how this will help you SAVE BIG:

Benefit of Paying Biweekly Instead of Monthly

Schedule	Interest Owed
Monthly	$8,539
Biweekly	$7,539
BIG SAVINGS =	$1,000

It's amazing! Not only do you save $1,000 in interest, you cut four months off of your 3-year repayment schedule by paying biweekly! The upshot of paying biweekly is that you end up sending in just $67 a month extra. Of course, I don't encourage anybody to make just the minimum payment. This strategy works even better if you pay more. The best plan of all is to keep making the same size payment even as the minimum payment required goes down.

There's another factor at work here that I haven't even included in the math. You are short-circuiting some of the credit card company's interest charges by making one of your payments earlier in the billing cycle. That's because when you carry a balance, you are charged interest every day of the cycle. By paying some principal early in the cycle, you are reducing the average daily balance that interest is based on.

Make Money by Spending Money

When your credit card debt is dead, it's time to make a card work for you instead of you working for it. The website www.BillShrink.com can help you identify the ideal card for your lifestyle, the key to earning maximum points. Keep in mind that credit card companies are often more generous with travel points than shopping points. If you want a cash-back card, don't settle for one that pays less than 1 percent. More possibilities: Swap points with other individuals at www.Points .com. Donate miles converted from credit card points to injured service members and their families at www.HeroMiles.org. Donate points to charity at www .ThankYou.com.

Using the 14-day payment method is easy with online, automated banking. Just make sure your bank won't fine you for not paying the entire minimum balance on the due date, since that's what banks are used to. Some people send small amounts even more often. If you do that, check to see if your bank limits the number of payments you can make per month. The website www.CreditCards. com keeps track of these rules in its section on "Micropayments." I will link you to the specific page you need from my website, www .ElisabethLeamy.com.

BIG TIPS

- Cut up and freeze your credit cards so you begin to send more money than you spend.
- Negotiate with your credit card company for a lower interest rate.
- Use savings to pay your credit card debt, if you have it.
- Pay the card with the highest interest rate first.
- Pay biweekly instead of monthly.

IV

GROCERIES

Guerrilla Grocery Shopping

Groceries are our fourth largest expense, even though it can feel like you don't have much to show for all that money. The grocery category includes food, personal care products, and household supplies. Groceries cost an average of $10,692 a year for a family of four, according to the IRS. It makes perfect sense. We need food to live, and some would say we can't survive without deodorant and dishwasher soap, either!

The usual advice to save on food is to pack your own lunch. Yawn . . . Yes, that will save you about $7 a day, but it's a pain. When I pack my lunch and take it to work, my body goes into some sort of freak starvation mode and I inevitably wolf down my sack lunch at 11 A.M. Then I'm famished again at 3 P.M. and end up going out and buying *another* lunch. I soon get tired of packing a limp lunch and buying a late lunch and I give up. Besides, that's Small Stuff Savings.

By contrast, my four Guerrilla Grocery Shopping weapons will have you paying pennies on the dollar for your groceries. You could choose any one tactic and cut your bills significantly. Layer them together and you'll do even better. How much better? I will demonstrate $21,051 worth of grocery savings here in Part IV. If you wanted

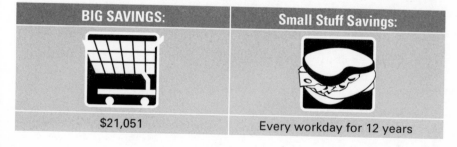

BIG SAVINGS:	Small Stuff Savings:
$21,051	Every workday for 12 years

G uerrilla Grocery Shopping is using your wits and the weapons available to outsmart the system and SAVE BIG on groceries.

to achieve the BIG SAVINGS I ring up in the coming chapters, you would have to pack your lunch every workday for the next 12 years!

Surprised that groceries can bring such BIG SAVINGS? They can—and the great thing about them is that they are universal. Not everybody owns a house or a car, but we all have to eat and bathe and do laundry. And if we can learn to do those little things for less, we'll be able to afford the big things. If you are struggling with my advice to buy a house ASAP and pay cash for your car, this is the part of the book that will make it possible.

How? Guerrilla Grocery Shopping is using your wits and the weapons available to outsmart the system and SAVE BIG on groceries. It's you versus the store, and I'm going to show you how to win!

- **Chapter 22:** The first Guerrilla Grocery Shopping weapon is price matching, where you find a store that will match other stores' sale prices so you don't have to run all over town to bag bargains. This trick of knowing *where* to shop can save you 45 percent.
- **Chapter 23:** Stockpiling is the second weapon in the Guerrilla Grocery arsenal and it means stocking up on groceries when they're deeply discounted instead of buying them as you need them. Just by knowing *when* to buy and then stocking up, you can save more than 50 percent.
- **Chapter 24:** Knowing *how* to shop is Guerrilla Grocery weapon number three: Creative Couponing. The key here is never to use a coupon by itself. Instead pull off Coupon Combos, where you layer different discounts on top of each other and you can save 80 percent—even get many groceries for free. Yes, free.
- **Chapter 25:** In the final grocery chapter, I share my wild card weapons for Guerrilla Grocery Shopping, from forming a grocery buying club to bidding for groceries at a grocery auction. If my BIGGEST, best advice is still too time-consuming for you, then fast forward to the end of the grocery section

where I share the Not-Shopping method, which requires you to do nothing. Literally nothing—yet it can still save you up to 24 percent!

Are you ready for battle, Guerrilla Grocery Shoppers? Great! You are going to eat this advice up. Let's turn the page and learn how to save $21,051.

CHAPTER

Price Matching

Our first Guerrilla Grocery Shopping weapon is price matching. Rather than rushing around to all the stores in the area to buy the items they have on sale for the week, you go to one store that honors other stores' sale prices and get everything there. That's price matching. Generally, there is at least one grocery store in an area that will honor its competitors' sale prices as a way of drawing business.

Most grocery stores have a few sale items each week that are so cheap the store loses money on them. They offer them because they figure while you're there buying ultra cheap bread, you'll also buy high-priced peanut butter and jelly to go on that bread. The trick of price matching is to pick off the most deeply discounted sale items of the week all at one store. That way, you save time, you save gas, and you save money.

In this chapter, learn to SAVE BIG by:

- Finding out if your local grocery stores price-match.
- Looking up sale prices online so you don't have to slog through store circulars.
- Trying out big national chains that price-match.
- Getting store brands on sale at a *different* store!

How to Price-Match

Here we go. Guerrilla Grocery Shopping 101. The first step to price matching is to find a store that does it. How do you do that? This is low-tech: You *ask*. Many stores have a "Don't tell unless they ask" policy. In other words, they offer price matching but they don't advertise it. So call around. You may find that the policy varies within chains, so be sure to check with the local store you plan to frequent. Most will only price-match close competitors within a certain mile radius.

Once you find a store that price-matches, it's important for you to get a grip on its policy. Some stores require you to hand over their competitor's circular—from a newspaper, a direct mail flyer or the Internet—as proof of a lower price available elsewhere. Other stores will take your word for it. A few have competitors' circulars at the cash register for the clerk to reference, so all you have to do is ask. Find out which level of proof your store requires and be ready to rumble.

Try for One-Time Price Matching

Even stores without a price-matching policy will sometimes do it on a one-time basis. Let's say you're having a frantic week and you notice the store across town is having a once-in-a-lifetime sale on Cheerios, but you just can't make it there. A Guerrilla Grocery Shopper will check to see if their local store will price-match this one item this one time. Be sure to ask the store manager (not a cashier) and be pleasant and polite.

When you get to the store that price-matches, it's a good idea to put all your price-match items in one area of your cart, then load them on the belt together. When that merchandise comes up on the belt, explain that you are price-matching and the clerk will know just what to do.

If you have more than one choice of stores that price-match, try to shop at one that matches *and* has consistently low prices overall. You will inevitably need some items that aren't on sale anywhere and can't be price-matched, so it's helpful if your chosen store has low everyday prices across the board.

A Word about Walmart

The mother of all price-matchers is Walmart, which has groceries at many of its stores now. Walmart will match the price of any store in your local market. (No wonder mom-and-pop stores hate this monolith.) The megastore doesn't offer deep weekly discounts like traditional grocery stores, but it will honor *their* weekly discounts. Often, Guerrilla Grocery Shoppers don't even have to bring the competitor's circular as proof. Walmart will honor not only advertised specials but also club card savings. And Walmart's own prices are typically low, for those items you need that aren't on sale anywhere.

A few important things to keep in mind when price-matching at Walmart:

1. **Same brand, same size.** You need to find the same brand and size to get the match. If you see a sale ad that does not specify a brand, Walmart will match that price, as long as you find the same type and size of product.

2. **You need a specific price.** Walmart honors sales in which a specific price is named, like "Campbell's Soup: $1." It doesn't honor percentage-off sales where the ad just says "Campbell's Soup: 40% off" because its original prices are already lower on a daily basis. Walmart also will not price-match buy-one-get-one-free deals being offered at other stores.

3. **Store brand for store brand.** If some other chain is having a sale on its store brand, Walmart will honor it with its own store brand as long as it is the same size and type of product.

4. **Coupons.,** Walmart takes coupons but does not match other chains' double or triple coupon offers.

5. **Know your geography.** Check with your local Walmart, because different stores use a different radius as their cut-off. For instance, one Walmart may match every competitor within 25 miles whereas another may limit it to 10 miles.

Target Matches Walmart Move for Move

In an effort to compete with its archrival, Walmart, Target now carries groceries and is starting to price-match in its Super-Target stores. Even regular Targets offer some foods and many personal care and household items. Be sure to ask the details of the local price-matching policy, so you'll know how to use it and abuse it to the max.

An Easier Way to Price-Match

I know what you're thinking. Who has time to flip through a zillion circulars, then bring the whole unwieldy pile to the store and browbeat some clerk into giving you the match? You don't have to. All hail the Internet! There is a better way! Read on, Guerrilla Grocery Shoppers.

Set up an Online Shopping E-Mail Address

I have a separate e-mail address I use just for online shopping. Most Internet service providers allow you to have multiple screen names. This way all the advertisements and coupons that stores send won't clog up your main e-mail account. But you can still check your shopping account whenever you want to make sure you don't miss out on any great offers.

All you do is go to the groundbreaking website www.CouponMom. com, developed by my sweet and savvy friend Stephanie Nelson. Stephanie's ideas for organizing and automating grocery deals were so innovative that they earned her a spot first on *Good Morning America* and later appearances on the *Today Show*. I'll tell you how to use her site to SAVE BIG with coupons in Chapter 24, but you can also use it just for price matching.

CouponMom.com is a free service. To sign up, all you have to do is provide an e-mail address and create a password. Once you have registered, click on "Grocery Deals by State" and you will see a list of grocery and drugstores in 44 states. (If your state or store is not listed, read Stephanie's instructions for how to use her site to create your own best buys list.) Then click on your state and store.

Voila! It's like looking at the store circular, only better because the list is organized alphabetically by brand name, and the far right column tells you what percent discount you're getting off the regular price! I love that, because when you see $1.49 for Skippy peanut butter, you may not know how good a deal that is. The CouponMom website tells you it's 57 percent off! Guerrilla Grocery Shoppers scoop up deals like that!

Price Beating Beats Price Matching

Some stores will do better than price-match. When you're asking around about price-matching policies, be sure to look for stores that *beat* their competitor's prices rather than just matching them. For example, Lowe's and Home Depot both promise to beat each other's prices by 10 percent. Price-beating is a particularly valuable tool when stores carry many of the same items.

The CouponMom website has little boxes you can check next to the products you want. Repeat the process, looking at the sales lists for every store in your area, until you've found all the biggest bargains. When you're done, you can print out a shopping list with just those items on it. Then take your handy list of the week's big sale items from multiple stores and march into one store that price-matches. Quickly find all your items and head to the register.

See if your store will accept the CouponMom list as your proof of other stores' sale prices. Many stores do not even require you to provide proof, so this should work. If your store is a stickler about having store circulars in hand, then get in the habit of keeping the circulars that come in the mail and the newspaper every week. Just have them with you. You don't even have to look at them unless the clerk asks you at the register.

Alternatively, you can go high-tech and print out the circular from the store's website. You may also like the website www .MyGroceryDeals.com, which aggregates hundreds of store circulars all in one place. A final resource is www.ShopLocal.com, where you can search by product, find the store circular with the lowest price, and print out the page you need.

Price Matching to the Rescue

I once tried out this online price-matching strategy on behalf of a Dallas mom named Tawawna B. All the *Good Morning America* financial experts were trying to help her find ways to manage her money because right after she finally pursued her dream and went back to graduate school, her husband got laid off.

To show her the potential of price matching, I chose five items Tawawna's family buys every week and used CouponMom.com to shop the sales at three different Dallas-area grocery stores. After I found the best deals, I sent her off for one-stop-shopping at Walmart to snag them. Here's how we did:

The Power of Price Matching

Regular cost for five grocery items at Walmart	$20.69
Price-matching cost for five grocery items	10.77
Dollar savings	$ 9.92
BIG SAVINGS =	**48%**

That's a $9.92 savings on just five items. More importantly, Guerrilla Grocery Shoppers, it's 48 percent. Imagine if I had price-matched her entire list. Imagine if I had done it all year!

But I'm reading your mind again. You're glad that I *saved* Tawawna 48 percent, but you want to know how much time I had to *spend* to do it. I'll tell you: about half an hour. It was actually my first time using the CouponMom site, so it took me a little extra time to familiarize myself with the layout. I'm confident I could go back now and do the same thing for even more items in 15 minutes or less. In fact, I'm going to do just that.

Price Matching on Black Friday

You know how people get up at 4 A.M. and go stand in line in the cold to get those door-buster deals the day after Thanksgiving? Instead of going to the stores that offer those amazing deals, go to Walmart. Walmart doesn't do deep Black Friday discounts because its strategy is to offer low everyday prices. But it will honor other stores' Black Friday sales! This Big Secret is courtesy of Chrissy Pate of www.BeCentsAble.net.

How Much Can You Save?

Okay, Guerrilla Grocery Shoppers, I just went back to CouponMom. com to see how much money I could save you if I price-matched 50 items. I chose a well-balanced variety of food, personal care, and household products that a typical family of four would buy. By price-matching, I was able to spend $111 instead of $200! Let's say you buy those same 50 grocery items every week. Here's how the savings would add up in a year:

 Benefit of Price Matching

50 items at regular price	$10,400/year
Same 50 at price-match price	5,772/year
BIG SAVINGS =	**$ 4,628/year**

It comes to $4,628 saved over the course of a year! That's a 45 percent discount. Price matching is Guerrilla Grocery Shopping weapon number one because it works—and it's easy.

 ## BIG TIPS

- Ask local stores if they price-match.
- Try to price-match at a store that also has low everyday prices.
- Use CouponMom.com to search for the best store sales.
- Keep your store circulars in case you need proof.
- Go to the price-matching store and cash in.

Stockpiling

What if you were to take the great Guerrilla Grocery savings you achieved by price-matching and multiply it to the nth degree? What you would have then is a strategy called stockpiling. Stockpiling is Guerrilla Grocery Shopping weapon number two. Instead of just saving by buying deeply discounted sale items each week, you stock up on them so you have enough to last you until those products go on sale again.

Personal care products, household supplies, dry goods, and canned foods are the easiest items to stockpile because they have a longer shelf life than perishable items. But if you have an extra freezer, you can also stockpile frozen foods, breads, meats—even cheeses and milk. The philosophy is simple yet counterintuitive: Don't buy groceries when you need them. Buy groceries when they are on sale. How much will stockpiling save you? It can cut your grocery bills by more than half. For a family of four, that's thousands of dollars a year.

In this chapter, learn to SAVE BIG by:

- Knowing what your favorite groceries cost—*really* knowing.
- Copying experienced stockpilers who share their deepest discounts online.
- Predicting when your favorite products will go on sale.

Know the Cost

Since the object of stockpiling is to buy a bunch of groceries when they're at their cheapest, Guerrilla Grocery Shoppers first need to know the cost of things they buy.

Quick: How much does a gallon of organic milk cost?

If your answer is "I have no clue," you just flunked my pop quiz. Don't be embarrassed. I wasn't sure, either. I had to check to see that a gallon of organic milk normally costs about $6.39. Here's the problem: If I were to see a big, bold, red sign advertising organic milk on sale for $5.89 a gallon, I might go for it. But that's only an 8 percent discount! Not good enough!

If you don't know a product's *regular* price, you're not a great judge of whether the *sale* price is low enough to make stockpiling worthwhile. I just studied a bunch of grocery circulars, and most of them hype their deals without doing a great job of telling you the actual percentage you're saving. Grocery prices can easily fluctuate 60 percent over six months, and you want to buy things at the bottom. To buy at the bottom, you need to recognize the top.

Get a Cell Phone with a Price-Check Feature!

The software is called Shop Savvy and it's available on iPhones and some T-Mobile phones. The phone's camera reads the bar code on any grocery product. Then the software displays all the prices for that product at local stores and online stores. The process takes just seconds. It's a high-tech way to know the cost.

Make a Top 20 List

You don't have to become some sort of grocery savant with hundreds of prices memorized. Just make a top 20 list. It should be a combination of the top 20 things you *buy* the most and those that *cost* the most.

Write the prices down. Use an index card, a notebook, your PDA, an Excel spreadsheet, a tattoo, whatever. If you're the type who saves receipts, dig up three months' worth and highlight your most frequent and most expensive grocery purchases. If you don't have your old receipts, peer into your fridge and cabinets to figure out what your top 20 buys are and then track the prices the next few times you shop.

When There's a Limit, That's the Bottom

When a store advertises "Limit three per customer," that's a great indication the price is near the bottom of the cycle! The management doesn't want a handful of savvy shoppers to clean the store out of its super-duper supermarket deal. They want to share the wealth with as many customers as possible to build loyalty. Well, your spouse is a customer and so are your kids. If it's a great deal on something you need, stockpile it!

Here's an example of how much it helps to know the prices of what you purchase most. Joan D. of Florida loves Diet Coke. Her big, friendly extended family loves it too. It's in their top 20. Surprised? Don't be. According to the federal government, beverages make up an amazing 16 percent of the typical grocery budget. One way to SAVE BIG would be to cut out all store-bought beverages and just drink free tap water. But that's a drag! So instead, read on.

Joan and her visitors drink about six cans of Diet Coke a day. She's seen the price fluctuate wildly from $2.40 to $3.97 per 12-pack. So if she stocks up only when Diet Coke is at its bottom price, here's how much she can save:

The Power of Knowing the Price

Top price for Diet Coke	$3.97 per 12-pack	$727 per year
Bottom price for Diet Coke	2.40 per 12-pack	439 per year
Dollar savings	$1.57 per 12-pack	$288 per year
BIG SAVINGS =	**40%**	**40%**

A savings of $288 is 40 percent off, but it's just the beginning. Remember, Guerrilla Grocery Shoppers, you are going to multiply savings like this out over your entire grocery list.

Decide Your Discounting Goals

One way to decide when the time is right to stockpile an item is to come up with your own discounting goals. You can use either dollar amounts or percentages or both. I like the percentage method, especially for packaged goods. For example, I have decided that I am only interested in products I can get for at least 50 percent off. I'm greedy. If I stick to those, then I know that stockpiling is cutting my grocery bill in half!

Alternatively, you can get in a groove where you know what good prices are for certain items. In *Shop Smart, Save More*, author Teri Gault encourages consumers to "buy more than you need when you don't need it." Here's how she uses dollar amounts to decide when to stockpile. Gault says she will buy skinless meat only if it is $2 a pound or less. She likes to stock up on bone-in beef or pork if it's less than $1.50 a pound and bone-in chicken if it is less than $1 a pound.

Sell-By Dates Are Your Buy-By Dates

Meat on sale is a good deal. Sale meat that's on clearance because it's close to the sell-by date is a *great* deal. It's perfectly safe. There's a time cushion with a sell-by date because it's not a use-by date. Then, when you freeze that meat, you are stopping it in time.

Let Somebody Else Do the Work

If you just can't get a handle on what things cost at the top and at the bottom, there are websites that will do the work for you. As I mentioned previously, www.CouponMom.com shows you the best sales of the week at hundreds of stores nationwide. You can do what I do and pick a percentage—like 50 percent—and only buy items that are discounted at least that much.

Another helpful site that identifies the best grocery sales is www.TheGroceryGame.com. This site takes it one step further and tells you when a deal is so good that you ought to stock up. (Note: TheGroceryGame.com offers a month-long free trial and then charges a monthly fee, which should pay for itself.)

There are also free blogs where veteran stockpilers show off their best bargains. All you have to do is copy their most inspired moves! One great one is run by two women I interviewed for *Good Morning America*, Chrissy Pate and Kristin McKee. These two

Missouri moms were feeling the financial pinch after they quit their jobs to stay home with their kids. They realized that the one expense they had control of was their groceries.

Hungry for ideas, they hunted around for information about how to save. It was hard at first, but they eventually cut their grocery bills in half. They then started www.BeCentsAble.net to make it easier for other people to do the same. I highly recommend their grocery savings workshops, available around the country and as an online tutorial on their website.

If a Store Is Out of a Sale Item, Ask for a Rain Check

Many stores have rain check policies, so that if one customer (a Guerrilla Grocery shopper like you!) cleans out the shelves during a super sale, other customers won't miss out. Often it's a formal rain check policy, where you actually get a little receipt that shows you are entitled to the sale price when the item is restocked. Ask for this paper proof if it's a product you really want to stockpile.

BeCentsAble.net provides a forum for dozens of savvy savers from all over the country, who post the best deals they see in the circulars and the stores. They do it as a public service—and to show off! (If your local store isn't covered on BeCentsAble.net, just Google the store and location, and you are likely to find a blogger who covers it independently.) Here are some examples from a savvy shopper called Nova Thrifty who posted the deals she found at a store in the Washington, D.C., area, where I live.

Nova Thrifty's Finds	Special Price	Regular Price
Chicken breasts	$8.95/5 pounds	$22.45/5 pounds
Porterhouse steak	$4.99/pound	$9.99/pound
Milk	$5/two 1-gal. jugs	$5.98/two 1-gal. jugs
85% lean ground beef	$3.98/2 pounds	$7.98/2 pounds

(continued)

Nova Thrifty's Finds	Special Price	Regular Price
Light and Fit yogurt	$4 for 10	$7 for 10
Canada Dry Ginger Ale	$10/five 12-packs	$29.95/five 12-packs
Stouffer's entrees	$10 for 5	$14.95 for 5
Tropicana Pure Premium	$1.88 each	$3.99 each
Breyer's ice cream	$1.88/quart	$4.99/quart
Pepsi	$1.99/6-pack	$4.29/6-pack

As you can see, some of the deals this savvy, selfless shopper shared are phenomenal! Like $8.95 instead of $22.45 for five pounds of chicken. That's 60 percent off! Five 12-packs of ginger ale for $10 instead of $29.95 is 67 percent off! Now let's see how the savings add up:

Savings If You Copy the Savvy Shopper

10 grocery items at regular price	$111.57
10 grocery items at special price	52.67
Dollar savings	$ 58.90
BIG SAVINGS =	**53%**

A total of 53 percent off—I'll take it. If we were being truly strategic stockpilers, we would have done even better by skipping the milk, which wasn't a huge discount, and purchasing extra of the chicken breasts and ginger ale, which were. Are you starting to see how this can work? And how it doesn't have to be hard? One way to be a Guerrilla Grocery Shopper is to be a copycat!

Learn to See Sales Coming

Successful stockpiling is mostly a matter of knowing what things normally cost, then spotting killer sales and cleaning out the shelves. But it's also possible to predict sales in advance. Yes, you can gaze into your crystal ball and see prices falling in the future. Here's how.

Seasonal Savings

One way to predict when sales will be at their lowest point is to pay attention to the seasons. Certain grocery products always go on sale at the same time of year. Some are obvious, like ketchup and mustard around the 4th of July, and pie crust and potatoes around Thanksgiving. But others are more mysterious. For instance, I bet you didn't know that Quaker puts all its products on sale in January. Or that March is National Frozen Foods Month. And Prego and Ragu have sauce wars in September.

Here's a list of reliable seasonal savings. Some are predictable because of holidays and the weather. Others are tied to obscure promotional months like National Fiber Month. You'll want to be on the lookout for these stockpiling opportunities.

January

Bread	Hot tea	Rubbermaid totes
Cereal	Pepsi	Side dishes
Chili	Planners	Shelf organizers
Cold-weather meals	Prunes	Tostitos
Diet foods	Quaker products	Weight-loss products

February

Candy	Chinese food	Heart-healthy foods
Canned foods	Chocolate	Snack foods

March

Beverages	Frozen foods	Kraft products
Cleaning supplies	Ham	Paper products
Eggs		

April

Asparagus	Ham	Soy products
Cookware	Kosher foods	Vacuum cleaners

(continued)

Eggs

Leafy greens

Lamb

Whole grain foods

May

Baked beans

Barbecue sauce

Bottled water

Bug repellent

Cleaning supplies

Condiments

Frozen vegetables

Ground beef

Home maintenance

Hot dogs

Lemonade mix

Paper goods

Plastic plates and cups

Ribs

Soda

Small appliances

Strawberries

Sunscreen

June

Building materials

Cheese

Hardware

Ice cream/yogurt

Tools

July

Condiments

Pickles

Computers

Hamburgers

Hot dogs

Soda

August

Cereal

Cold cuts

Fresh fish

Fresh fruit

Fresh vegetables

Juice

Peaches

School supplies

Waffles

September

School supplies

Breakfast foods

Capri Suns

Campbell's soups

Canned goods

Cereal

Fruit snacks

Gardening supplies

Housewares

Jelly

Lunchables

Peanut butter

Prego spaghetti sauce

Ragu spaghetti sauce

October

Baking products	Instant potatoes	Pudding
Candy	Kraft foods	Stovetop stuffing
Cheese	Marshmallows	Turkey
Chicken broth	Nuts	Vanilla/corn syrup
Chocolate chips	Pasta	Whipped cream
Crackers	Pie shells	Wine
Cranberries	Pizza	

November

Baking ingredients	Cookies	Plants
Candy	Cranberries	Sweet potatoes
Canned goods	Creamed soup	Thanksgiving foods
Chicken broth	Flour	Turkey
Condensed milk	Frozen pies	Yams

December

Baking supplies	Champagne	Meat
Canned goods	Party foods	

Sale Cycles

In addition to seasonal savings, Guerrilla Grocery Shoppers can take advantage of sale cycles when stockpiling. Grocery products go on sale at predictable intervals. Lauren A. of Pennsylvania noticed that the cheese she likes is discounted every 12 weeks and the chicken breasts her fiancé enjoys go on sale every four weeks. There's no across-the-board rule, but if you pay attention you, too, will begin to see how frequently the items on your top 20 list are discounted.

Lauren is very careful with her money, and she also noticed that often the same product is on sale at one grocery store this week and another one next week. That's because product manufacturers provide store-specific incentives to goose sales of their merchandise, and they move from one store to the next. Remember, if the sale is not at your preferred store, you can price-match it!

The key is to buy enough of your favorite products when they are discounted to get you through to the next sale cycle. Once the sale cycle has passed, you may not see any discounts on that item for a couple of months or more. That's why it's important to stock up when you can. It's kind of like when one airline lowers fares and the rest scramble to follow. Grocery manufacturers are competitive that way, too. But it's more subtle because peanut butter doesn't cost as much as a plane ticket.

Watch Out for Scanner Errors

Scanner errors are especially common on sale items. Grocery stores contain an average of about 47,000 different products, according to the Food Marketing Institute. It's easy for employees to miss some when they're programming new sales into the register. Studies have shown scanner errors are 3 to 1 in favor of the store—overcharging instead of undercharging. I did a *Good Morning America* investigation myself, and 5 of the 12 stores we tested made mistakes at the register, some overcharging us by as much as 40 to 60 percent.

Practical Considerations

Okay, this all sounds like grocery greatness, but you probably have a few questions about how much it's going to cost to build a stockpile, and how much stuff to buy. Fair enough. Here we go.

How Much Does It Cost?

Building a stockpile may sound expensive. After all, we're talking about hoarding up to six months worth of food, personal care products, and household supplies. But actually, you will not be buying any more of these products than you normally do. You will just be buying them at different times. Remember, instead of purchasing groceries when you need them, you will be purchasing groceries when they are on sale.

Each shopping trip, you will still buy eggs and a few fresh fruits and veggies, but you will also buy whatever categories of groceries are deeply discounted at that time. Some parts of your stockpile will be growing while others are shrinking. You will cook accordingly. It can be a little awkward at first before your stockpile is well-rounded. But you will have everything you need within a couple of months.

How Much Should You Buy?

Some stockpilers believe in hoarding three to six weeks' worth; others say three to six *months'* worth is more like it. I would hate to see you run out of something, rush to the 24-hour store at midnight, and pay a premium for it. So I suggest you try for a two-month stockpile at first, then expand it to four to six months if the strategy is working for you. Storage space can also help you decide the size of your stockpile. Here's how to think about the three grocery categories:

1. **Food.** This is where analyzing your receipts could really come in handy. Look at three months' worth of receipts. Add up the number of chicken breasts, boxes of spaghetti, canned soups, granola bars—whatever stockpileable items your family likes. That will give you a feel for how much to keep on hand.
2. **Personal care products.** Teri Gault of TheGroceryGame.com has a strategy I like for determining how many personal care products you should stockpile. She suggests keeping the same number of products on hand as there are members of your family. So if you are a family of four, always have four new tubes of toothpaste, four bottles of shampoo, and so on, in your home.
3. **Household Supplies.** The amount of cleaners, paper towels, sponges, and so on that you should stockpile is less of a concern because they have a very long shelf life. If you miscalculate and buy two years' worth, who cares? Think of it as cleaning supplies in the bank. You'll be clean . . . and rich.

This all boils down to one simple concept: To be a truly stellar stockpiler, you should buy what your family likes, what they will use, and whatever is most deeply discounted at any given time. That's the whole point. Otherwise the effort—and the products—will go to waste.

Bigger Is Not Always Cheaper

People assume you get a better price if you buy chicken broth in humongous cans instead of little ones. Or chips in big bags instead of snack size. Or diapers by the hundreds instead of by the dozens. But I have done several stories over the years where we showed that these very products are sometimes less expensive in smaller packages. It pays to pay attention to unit pricing to avoid this trap.

Stockpile of Savings

When you pile up groceries, you will pile up savings. To show you, I shopped for 50 different grocery products that people typically use. I won't bore you with a list of every single one, but I will tell you that I included a few products from every key category: meat, dairy, canned goods, frozen foods, grains, bread, house cleaning, personal care, and so on.

Then I compared what it would cost to buy these items for top price versus bottom price. My balanced 50-item list cost $204 at the top price. But it cost just $93 if I stockpiled every product when it was at its lowest—all by doing something that seems crazy and counterintuitive! Now, here's how those savings look on an annual basis:

 Benefit of Stockpiling

Top price	$ 10,608/year
Bottom price	4,836/year
BIG SAVINGS =	**$ 5,772/year**

Woo-hoo, $5,772 is serious savings! And it's 54 percent off! That's why stockpiling is Guerrilla Grocery Shopping weapon number two.

BIG TIPS

- Buy groceries when they are on sale, not when you need them.
- Know the cost of your top 20 products.
- Resolve to pay a certain price or a certain percentage off for your groceries.
- Monitor seasonal savings and sale cycles.
- Use websites like CouponMom.com, TheGroceryGame.com, and BeCentsAble.net to find the bargains you will stockpile.

CHAPTER

Creative Couponing

Every word in the grocery section has been leading to this one: *coupons.* Price matching and stockpiling get even better with coupons. That's why Creative Couponing is Guerrilla Grocery Shopping weapon number three. The key to Creative Couponing is never to use a coupon by itself. Always layer it with some other strategy. The other key is to use online tools to make couponing easy—and lucrative. The old-fashioned way of clipping coupons in advance is too time consuming.

I used to make fun of couponers. It seemed like the ultimate example of Small Stuff Savings, but then *Good Morning America* sent me to interview some women who have cut their grocery bills in *half* by using and abusing coupons in the most clever ways. The savings cannot be ignored. Guerrilla Grocery shoppers who take advantage of Creative Couponing save as much as 80 percent and even get some groceries for free.

In this chapter, learn to SAVE BIG by:

- Using a website that makes it possible for you to use coupons without really clipping coupons.
- Waiting to use coupons instead of using them right when they come out.
- Combining coupons with other offers.
- Looking up Target coupons after Target has stopped providing them.

Clicking Not Clipping

Is your scissor finger breaking out in hives just from the thought of clipping coupons? Don't worry. I'm going to show you how to *use* coupons without really *clipping* coupons. I define *clipping* coupons as spending Sundays poring over coupon circulars, painstakingly cutting out coupons in *advance* that you *might* be able to use. I don't do that and you shouldn't, either. The key is to click, not clip.

Thanks to Stephanie Nelson, aka "The Coupon Mom," you can still use coupons from the Sunday circulars, but you'll only have to spend five minutes cutting them right before you shop. You'll cut instead of clip. Here's how it works. The CouponMom website (www .CouponMom.com) tracks every coupon in most every Sunday circular. Instead of blindly clipping coupons and hoping you will be able to use them, you just save all the circulars without cutting them. Then, *when you need something,* you search for the product on CouponMom.com and the site tells you if there is a coupon for it in a recent circular.

CouponMom.com has flipped the entire process over so that it is easy and productive. First the need, then the coupon, instead of vice versa. It makes so much more sense. Here's a step-by-step tutorial on the simple, money-saving process:

1. **Know the main circulars.** You can see the names of the circulars on the front or in tiny print on the binding. Couponers refer to them by their initials. They are:
   - Red Plum (RP).
   - Smart Source (SS).
   - General Mills (GM).
   - Procter & Gamble (PG).
2. **Save your circulars.** Save all of your circulars—whole, *without* cutting—for two months. Most coupons expire after 10 weeks, so you can toss the circulars at that point. A few individual coupons are good for 15 weeks. It's up to you if you have space to keep them that long.
3. **Label them.** Scrawl the name and date of each circular on the cover in magic marker to make it easier to identify them quickly.
4. **Organize them.** Organize your stash of circulars in whatever way works for you—a stack, a box, a binder, or an accordion file. This way you have *all* the current coupons at your disposal when you need them.

5. **Search CouponMom.com.** Before shopping, go to the "Grocery Coupon Database" on CouponMom.com. You can search by brand name or product type. If you were looking for chocolate chips, you could type in "Nestle" or "chocolate chips" to find them.

6. **View results.** The CouponMom website will then list the date and source of every coupon for chocolate chips. Circulars are identified by their initials, as shown in step 1.

7. **Cut and go.** Now you can go directly to the circulars that contain coupons for the products you need.

It's brilliant! No more clipping coupons in advance and hoping the tiny scraps don't fall out of your wallet before you manage to use them. On the CouponMom site, as you see deals you want, you can check a box next to them to create a customized shopping list. Using that list, you cut out or print out *only* the coupons you *need*. Then you're off to the store. Easy-peasy.

Sign up for Free, Customized Deal Alerts at www.CouponMom.com

This is a handy offer, because you get to create your own list of products you want to receive alerts about. The alert feature lets you list a whole bunch of items, so one smart thing would be to enter everything on your top 20 list.

Where to Find Your Coupons

Approximately 88 percent of coupons people make use of come from the Sunday circulars. Many Creative Couponers get at least two newspapers a week to maximize their coupon opportunities. Local newspapers often offer great deals on a Sunday-only subscription. Another option: Some grocery and convenience stores sell the Sunday paper later in the day for half price. Alternatively, especially if you plan to use coupons as a means to donate to charity, it's easy to rationalize asking friends and neighbors to give you their unused circulars.

You Don't Have to Use the Coupon for the Product in the Picture

Often a coupon will say "any variety" or words to that effect. But the picture on the coupon will be of the newest, most expensive product in that product line. Don't fall for it! You can use the coupon for anything in the line, and the best deal is to use it on the cheapest product.

Increasingly, there are valuable Internet coupons, called bricks, online. CouponMom.com indexes some of them. Another website, www.HotCouponWorld.com, also has a searchable coupon database. It's maintained by members and indexes some sources that CouponMom.com does not. If you would like to search coupon sites on your own, here are some good ones:

- http://CoolSavings.com
- http://Coupons.com
- www.RedPlum.com
- http://SmartSource.com

Coupon Combos

When a manufacturer puts a coupon in the Sunday paper, it's hoping you will rush out and use it that week. Don't do it! Instead, lie in wait like the Guerrilla Grocery Shopper that you are. As I mentioned, most coupons are good for about 10 weeks, sometimes up to 15. That means you don't have to use them when they are new. Waiting can present some golden opportunities.

Remember, the premise of Creative Couponing is that you should never use a coupon by itself. You should always combine it with some other savings strategy. I call those Coupon Combos.

Manufacturers often promote their products in waves, first with coupons, then with sales in specific stores, and finally with mail-in rebates. Sure, you could use the coupon right away and save some money. But if you keep your coupon until the sale starts or the rebate is offered, then you can take advantage of *both* forms of discounts and SAVE BIG. That's the most basic Coupon Combo and I'm about to share many more.

Sale + Manufacturer's Coupon

Matching up store sales with manufacturer coupons is easy because websites like CouponMom.com, HotCouponWorld.com and www. BeCentsAble.net, do it for you. The CouponMom site is the easiest to use. Here are the three easy steps:

1. Go to CouponMom.com and click on "Grocery Deals by State," just as we discussed in Chapter 22.
2. Choose a store and you will see a list of the best sale items organized by brand name.
3. If there's a coupon available for a product, you will see the dollar value of the coupon and the name and date of the circular where you can find it.

I just spent 30 seconds online and found a current example that shows that sales are good, but sales plus coupons are better. Check it out:

Hot Shot Ant Spray

Regular price	$2.99
Coupon	1.50
Final price	$1.49
BIG SAVINGS =	**50%**

Okay, normally I'd be crowing about how that's half off— 50 percent! A purchase worthy of stockpiling. But check out what happens when you do a Coupon Combo, combining a coupon with a sale:

Hot Shot Ant Spray

Regular price	$2.99
Sale price	1.49
Coupon	1.50
Final price	Free!
BIGGER SAVINGS =	**100%!**

Yes, that's right, there was a coupon for Hot Shot Ant Spray in the July 19 Smart Source circular. And by waiting to use it until there was a sale, I could "buy" Ant spray for free. This is not some freak occurrence. If you pair sales with coupons you will *routinely* get groceries for pennies on the dollar or for free. If you see low cost or no cost opportunities like this for products your family doesn't use, you can donate them to a local food bank.

How to Get Extra Internet Coupons

There is a way to print more than one e-coupon or brick at a time. Photocopying e-coupons is not allowed. It's considered fraud. But most manufacturers allow you to print two coupons at a time from their site. After you print your first coupon, all you do is hit the "back" arrow on your computer until the coupon is sent to your printer again. If you wait a couple weeks, the website may reset and allow you to print two more coupons. New e-coupons usually come out the first day of the month, so it's a good idea to check that day, so you have more opportunities over the course of the month for the site to reset, allowing you to print additional coupons.

Coupon + Doubled or Tripled

Sales are one way to use a store's incentives in combination with coupons. Double and triple coupon offers are another. For example, if you have a $.50 coupon, the manufacturer kicks in $.50 off of your purchase and the store matches it with another $.50 of its own money. Nice!

Although the double or triple discount is usually automatic at the register, you will need to know, in advance, which stores double or triple coupons so you can double or triple the amount of business you give them! My neighborhood grocery store has a huge banner out front that proclaims "We Double Coupons." Since not all stores are so brassy about this generous policy, don't be shy— just ask at the courtesy desk. There are also two online guides to grocery stores that double coupons, which can be found at www.GroceryCouponGuide.com and www.Couponing.About.com.

I'll link you to the precise pages of those sites that you need from my site, www.ElisabethLeamy.com.

Once you have determined which stores double or triple coupons, here are a few key questions to ask the manager:

- Do you double coupons only on certain days or every day of the week?
- To what amount do you double coupons? (The most common policy is $.50 and below, followed by $.99 and below.)
- Do you limit the number of coupons for the same product that you will double in a single shopping trip? (If they only double the first one, you can wait and buy more of that product in a separate trip to the store.)
- Are there special times when you double or triple coupons up to a higher amount?

Many Stores Now Accept Expired Coupons

Some stores accept expired coupons to hold on to loyal customers. Guerrilla Grocery Shoppers can take advantage of this, because many manufacturers alternate between offering coupons and offering sale prices. If you can use an expired coupon, you have even more opportunity to match it up with a sale.

With a thorough understanding of your store's coupon doubling or tripling policy, you now have to get your head around some new math so that you can use your coupons wisely. For example, if your store doubles coupons up to $.99, that means a $1 coupon is only worth $1 but a $.75 coupon is worth . . . $1.50! Odd. It doesn't take a rocket scientist to realize a $.75 coupon is suddenly more valuable than a $1 one at this store.

Coupon doubling and tripling policies are little gold mines. Seek out the stores that do this—especially for stockpiling—and you will SAVE BIG. Here's an example. HotCouponWorld.com has a forum where new couponers can brag about their best bargains. A newbie named J.J. Rogers wrote in that she had several $.35 coupons for C&H sugar, which the store honored at triple value. Here's the deal she got:

 Sweet C&H Sugar Deal

Regular price	$3.05
Sale price	1.50
Triple coupons	1.05
Final price	$ .50
BIG SAVINGS =	**84%**

Wow, 84 percent off? Sweet! Literally. So what did J.J. the newbie do? She acted like a Guerrilla Grocery Shopper and bought 15 five-pound bags. Whoa. That's 75 pounds of sugar! Instead of paying $45.75 for it, she spent only $7.50. Her kids will be wired for life!

BIG SECRET
You Can Use Manufacturer Coupons from One Store at Another Store

If you see a coupon printed on a store flyer, look closely: Does it say "store coupon" or "manufacturer coupon?" If it's the latter, it's the manufacturer who is paying for your discount, so you are free to use that coupon at a different store!

Manufacturer's Coupon + Store Coupon

Up to this point we've been talking about coupons the manufacturer offers to get you to try its products. But stores also offer their *own* coupons, to get you to come in. This is another Coupon Combo that will help you SAVE BIG. I know, I know, you're scared by the familiar phrase "Cannot be combined with other offers." True, you cannot combine two different manufacturer coupons, but you *can* combine a manufacturer coupon with a store coupon because the money is coming from two different sources. Yippee!

For some reason drugstores, like CVS and Walgreens, offer far more store coupons than grocery stores do. That means drugstores can often be a great source not only of personal care and household goods, but also of food. They may not have much variety, but you can SAVE BIG on things like cereal and soup if you combine a store coupon with a manufacturer coupon at a drugstore. Look for store coupons in flyers on racks in the drugstores and also in direct mail and Sunday circular ads. Here are some more sources of store coupons:

- Store Sunday circulars. (Look for the words "Store Coupon" across the top.)
- Single-page store newspaper ads.
- Direct mail ads sent to your home.
- Store magazines.
- Store websites.
- Store e-mails. (Joining the store loyalty program could be your best source of store coupons.)
- In-store flyers on a stand at the front or back of the store.
- The price-check box at CVS stores. Scan your loyalty card to print coupons.
- Store clubs like baby clubs or pet clubs.
- Fund-raising books sold by nonprofits for about $5.
- Websites like HotCouponWorld.com and www.AFullCup.com.

Look for Stores That Accept Competitors' Coupons

Often stores don't advertise that they accept competitors' coupons. You'll probably have to ask. It can be essential for those situations where stores promote the same products one after another. So while one store is offering coupons for a product, another may be offering sales on that product. Combine these two opportunities and SAVE BIG!

Targeting Target Coupons You can hit the bull's-eye at Target if you're looking for manufacturer plus store Coupon Combos. Target offers extensive coupons on its website and it accepts manufacturer coupons, too, though it does not double them. Plus, Target allows you to use coupons on sale items.

Here's the trick: Target posts its coupons online for only two weeks, but they are typically good for *six* weeks. And by that time, many of the items in the coupons have gone on sale, so you can combine a store coupon with the sale price to SAVE BIG.

Make **Money with Rebates and Rewards**

Rebates are refunds you have to apply for. Rewards are store credits you get automatically. Drugstores are the hotbeds for these hot offers. You can now apply for Walgreen's EasySaver rebates on the chain's website, which takes all the annoyance out. Ask for your rebate on a gift card and Walgreen's gives you an extra 10 percent. Walgreen's Register Rewards and CVS's Extra Care Bucks are store credits that the register spits out when you make a purchase. Guerrilla Grocery Shoppers learn to roll this month's rewards over to next month's purchases and get many products for free!

So how do you get those coupons after Target takes them down? There are websites that are known as Target coupon generators. It's perfectly legal. HotCouponWorld.com and AFullCup.com are two of them. They have big buttons on their home pages that say "Target." Sign up and print. It's a cinch. Here's one example of a Target Coupon Combo that I just found.

 Morningstar Farms Veggie Burgers

Regular price	$3.79
Manufacturer coupon	1.00
Target coupon	2.00
Final price	$0.79
BIG SAVINGS =	**79%**

A 79 percent savings is fabulous! And here's the best part: I didn't actually do the hard work of figuring out whether there were manufacturer coupons and store coupons available. I just went to BeCentsAble.net's forum where smarter Guerrilla Grocery Shoppers than I regularly post their finds. Marcy, who writes a blog called "Stretching a Buck," spotted the meatless burger offer. And I'm free to poach it—or grill it or fry it!

Buy-one-get-one-free + Two Coupons

Another Guerrilla Grocery Shopping strategy that helps you SAVE BIG is combining buy-one-get-one-free offers with coupons. Did you know that when a store advertises that something is "Buy one, get one free," or "BOGO," it usually means that both products are actually half price? That means that if you really only need one of the product, you don't have to buy both. Ordinarily that would be a hot little savings tip in itself, but we're not into getting just what we need. We're into SAVING BIG!

So here's the real revelation: If you see something on sale as a buy-one-get-one free offer, that means you can do a Coupon Combo where you use two coupons on top of the BOGO deal. There are thousands of opportunities like this. A dad who calls himself HopOnCouponPop—a play on the popular children's book title— found a great deal on dish detergent by using this strategy. Here's how his deal worked:

Cascade Dishwasher Powder

Buy-one-get-one-free price	$6.00
Two coupons for $3.00 off a box	6.00
Final price	Free!
BIG SAVINGS =	**100%**

But wait—there's also another buy-one-get-one-free trick. If a store offers a product on a BOGO basis, and you also have a manufacturer coupon to get the product on a BOGO basis, you can do both. It's another way to get two items free. Why do they allow it? Because buy-one-get-one-free deals are really half-price-on-each deals and because one discount comes from the store and the other comes from the manufacturer.

Keep Coupons for Services a Secret

If you have a coupon that offers $100 off your next paint job, gutter cleaning, or another negotiable service, you can't tell if you're really getting a discount unless you know the company's usual price. So call and get a quote first and *then* reveal that you have a coupon. That way, you know the company didn't mark the price *up* first before applying the coupon to it.

X Off of Y Purchase + Other Coupons

I'm sure you've seen those coupons where you get *X* dollars off if you spend more than *Y* amount. For example, spend $40 and receive $10 off of your purchase. By itself, that's a 25 percent savings, which is mediocre. But many stores will honor the *X* off of *Y* offer *on top of* all your other store and manufacturer coupons. Here's a deal on baby formula cobbled together by Terri4548, who posted her first brag on HotCouponWorld.com.

Enfamil Baby Formula

Regular price	$25.99
$5 off of $20 coupon	5.00
Walgreens store coupon	2.00
Enfamil manufacturer coupon	2.00
Enfamil check	5.00
Final price	$11.99
BIG SAVINGS =	**54%**

Getting 54 percent off is not bad for a Guerrilla Grocery Shopper-in-training, right? Here's the crucial key: You must hand the coupons to the clerk in the right order. First, present the *X* off of *Y* coupon so that the total is still high enough for it to count. In this example, the offer required a purchase of at least $20 to get $5 off so if she had used all her other coupons first, her total amount would have been under $20 and the *X* off of *Y* offer wouldn't have worked. To get the most out of *X* off of *Y* coupons, try to spend as close to the minimum required as possible.

Beware of Counterfeit Coupons

You should never pay for coupons. (The one exception: charity coupon books.) The point is to save money, not spend money, so avoid the cheaters selling coupons on auction sites. If you download e-coupons from the manufacturer's website or reputable websites, you will know they are real. Genuine coupon sites require you to download a small program that lets your printer create barcodes. This is how stores—and you—know your coupon is legit.

Coupon Combo Coaching

I've given you the nuts and bolts for using coupons to buy your soup to nuts, but for further coaching and coaxing, there is wonderful support out there on the internet.

- **BeCentsAble.net.** Take the inexpensive online tutorial or find an in-person class taught by a BeCentsAble educator in your area. Check out the forums where Guerrilla Grocery Shoppers share their best deals. Kristin McKee and Chrissy Pate are writing a book called *Be CentsAble* which will be packed with additional savings information.
- **CouponMom.com.** In addition to her indispensable Grocery Deals by State and Grocery Coupon Database, Stephanie Nelson has written a new book entitled *The Coupon Mom's Guide to Cutting Your Grocery Bills in Half.*
- **HotCouponWorld.com.** This site, run by volunteers, is full of articles to get you started, forums to ask questions, a great coupon database, plus links to printable coupons.
- **TheGroceryGame.com.** This website preaches and teaches stockpiling and matches coupons to sales for maximum impact. It also lists store coupon policies. There is a fee, which cuts into your savings, but it should pay for itself.

How BIG Are Our SAVINGS?

How much can you save through Creative Couponing, our third Guerrilla Grocery Shopping weapon? Man, this is gonna be great!

I can't wait to tell you! Once again, I assembled a balanced list of 50 products from every category that a typical American family of four purchases regularly. Every product had an accompanying coupon. The before price was $191. The after price was—get this—$39! Now check out the yearly savings:

Creative Couponing Annual Savings

Regular price	$9,932/year
Price using coupons	2,028/year
BIG SAVINGS =	**$7,904/year**

Look at that—$7,904! Folks, that is quite simply a life-changing amount of savings! Price matching alone saved us 44 percent. Stockpiling ratcheted the game up to 54 percent. By adding Creative Couponing as the final layer of savings we have reached an 80 percent discount—80 percent! This $7,904 is the kind of savings that will have you on your way to other BIG moves, like paying cash for a car or making a substantial down payment on a house. I love it.

BIG TIPS

- Don't use your coupons right away. Wait until you can do a Coupon Combo.
- Use CouponMom.com and other sites to match coupons to stores' sales.
- Find out which stores in your area double or triple coupons.
- Use store coupons and manufacturer coupons together.
- Print Target coupons from other websites if Target has taken them down.
- Hand X off of Y coupons to the cashier first.

CHAPTER

Wild Cards

Price matching, stockpiling, and Creative Couponing are the most well-tested weapons of Guerrilla Grocery Shopping. But I am always pushing myself to find new and creative ways to help people save on their groceries. After all, what could be more essential to our families?

My bosses at *Good Morning America* are obsessed with grocery savings techniques, too, so they have sent me all over the country to meet Americans with unusual savings strategies to share. We've looked into clubs and farms and auctions and peeked into people's pantries. The one requirement has always been that I find ways to SAVE BIG. Now I want to show you some of the more offbeat ideas I have gathered.

In this chapter, learn to SAVE BIG by:

- Starting a grocery buying club to qualify to buy wholesale.
- Bidding your way to bargains at a grocery auction.
- Not shopping. That's right—doing *nothing*.

Grocery Buying Clubs

One way you can SAVE BIG is to form a grocery buying club, also sometimes called a co-op. When multiple families band together they can qualify to buy groceries wholesale. I'm not talking Costco or Sam's Club. I'm talking Jeanne, Janet, Linda, and Ann's club. Buying wholesale means you're buying your groceries from the same distributors who usually sell to grocery stores. You're cutting out the middleman. A refrigerated 18-wheeler literally pulls up and makes a delivery (so you save gas, too!)

The typical savings achieved by forming a grocery buying club is about 25 percent. Jen W. of New Hampshire says she saves her family of three about $200 a month. Larger families report saving as much as $500 a month.

Wholesalers who sell to grocery buying clubs recommend having 7 to 10 families in your club. But it's really up to you to determine how many families you need in order to meet the minimum order required by your wholesaler. Jen's wholesaler requires a minimum order of $350 and she finds she can easily meet that with just three families in her club.

You Can Often Use Regular Coupons to Buy Organic Foods

Finding organics for less is always a challenge, but here's a hot tip. Many manufacturers will let you use a regular product coupon to buy the organic version of that same product. Just look for wording that says something like "good for any ABC product." You would be amazed how many mainstream foods are now available in special organic versions—from crackers to soup to spaghetti sauce.

Grocery wholesalers can typically supply anything except fresh fruits, vegetables, and dairy. The best buys are on bulk products like pasta, rice, flour, and sugar. Club members purchase jumbo sizes of these products and divide them up for maximum savings. Organics and environmentally friendly items are the other highlight because many of the wholesalers that serve clubs specialize in natural products. Grocery wholesalers list their products in catalogs or on their websites.

Usually members of the club divide up the responsibilities. One member compiles the order; in the age of e-mail, it's easy to cobble together a collective list with a few round-robin messages. Then somebody faxes or e-mails the order to the wholesaler. Another member collects the money, either in advance or on delivery day. Somebody else volunteers their home to receive the delivery. The final step is getting together to gossip and divide up the loot.

When we did our *Good Morning America* story we wanted to verify that the wholesale prices were really worthwhile. We priced five products offered by a wholesaler. We chose natural products since they are so popular now. Here's our shopping list:

- ✔ Annie's Bunny Crackers
- ✔ Envirokids cereal
- ✔ Spectrum olive oil
- ✔ Seventh Generation baby wipes
- ✔ Cascadian Farms frozen corn

Now, here's the savings you could get buying just those five items wholesale:

 Benefit of Starting a Buying Club

Retail price	$36.65
Wholesale price	28.04
Dollar savings	$ 8.61
BIG SAVINGS =	**23%**

A 23 percent discount is really respectable for natural, organic, and green products. It is always more difficult to find savings on those because they are pricier to begin with, the profit margins are slimmer, and they are in high demand. So grocery buying club members are happy to get such a healthy savings on healthy products! And remember, that savings will be multiplied times an entire shopping list.

Intrigued about starting a grocery buying club? There are wholesalers in all parts of the country who sell to buying clubs. Here's a website that lists many of them: http://CoopDirectory.org.

While You're Starting Clubs, Form a Cooking Club

Cooking clubs work well with five families. Once a week you cook dinner for your family and the four others and deliver it to them. The other four days they cook and deliver to you. You save time by cooking only one night a week. You save money by buying in bulk. Ginny B. of Virginia says she cut her grocery bills in half this way. It's possible you could save so much that you can dine out on weekends guilt-free!

Grocery Auctions

Another wild card Guerilla Grocery Shopping strategy is to attend a grocery auction. You heard me right—a grocery auction, where an auctioneer is auctioning off . . . groceries. It sounds weird, doesn't it? You've got the same fast-talking auctioneer, but he's hawking apples instead of antiques. Amazing!

For yet another *GMA* story—we are obsessed with groceries—we attended a grocery auction in New Haven, Indiana. There were about 500 people at the Indiana auction, all there through word-of-mouth, and they were loving it.

A grandmother named Donna M. told us she was grateful for the food auction because she's on a fixed income and it has allowed her to eat a healthier variety of foods and SAVE BIG. David T., who had just been laid off, echoed these comments saying that he only spent $150 dollars on items that would normally cost $450. Everybody we met said food auctions have a buzzing, social atmosphere that's way more exciting than a trip to the grocery store!

It works just like a regular auction, with one key difference. Since there's more than one of each product; everyone who wants an item walks away with it in hand. The auctioneer gets people bidding on an item, say frozen French fries. Once the price will go no higher, that's the price everybody who wants that product pays.

Most food auctions offer hundreds of different foods and household supplies. Some are surplus goods, like you'd get at a discount store such as MacFrugal's or Big Lots. There are also a lot of dinged and damaged packages, with perfectly good products inside. You will also see items close to their expiration dates.

Expired Food Is Legal

Selling expired foods is not only legal but perfectly safe. The FDA explains that the products may lose some taste quality and nutritional value, but they are not dangerous. The one exception is infant formula because babies count on it for all their nutrition.

By bidding for groceries instead of buying them, you can save 50 to 90 percent! But bidder beware! In the excitement of an auction atmosphere, it's also easy to overpay, so it's essential that you know what your favorite foods normally cost so you'll know whether you're really bagging a bargain.

I put the auction prices to the test by comparing them with prices at a grocery store. I picked a random cross section of products. Here's our shopping list:

✔ Lysol disinfectant spray
✔ Swanson's chicken broth
✔ Horizon organic milk
✔ Triscuits
✔ Six-pack of V-8 juice
✔ Six-pack of Odwalla smoothies

Robin Roberts was oohing and ahing when I revealed the results to her on the *Good Morning America* set in New York, because, the auction yielded a 66 percent savings!

Benefit of Buying at a Grocery Auction

Store price for six items on list	$34.12
Auction price for six items on list	11.50
Dollar savings	$22.62
BIG SAVINGS =	66%

Two-thirds off! Remember, earlier in the grocery section, we talked about how expensive organic milk is at about $6.49 a gallon? At this auction people were getting it near the expiration date for just $2.75 a gallon. They would then freeze it, which makes the expiration date meaningless. (It is perfectly fine to freeze milk.) The best bargain of all was the Odwalla juice, which turned out to be a whopping 88 percent savings!

To find a grocery auction near you, check out the website of the National Auctioneers Association: www.Auctioneers.org. The site has a tool you can use to search for auctions and auctioneers by zip code.

Don't Assume Going-Out-of-Business Sales Are Great Deals

Many going-out-of-business sales are run by professional liquidators who make a business out of going out of business. They usually raise prices up to the full manufacturer suggested retail price and *then* discount from there, so you could be paying more than you would have when the store *wasn't* going out of business. There are some bargains, but you need to shop and compare just like you always do.

Couch Potato Shopping

And now, the moment some of you have been waiting for. I am about to reveal how you can save 8 to 24 percent by doing . . . nothing. Literally nothing. This one's for those who think price matching, stockpiling, Creative Couponing, starting a club, and bidding at an auction are just . . . too . . . much . . . effort.

Okay, couch potatoes, here's how to save on potatoes. Don't buy any. Once a quarter or once a month, skip a regular shopping trip and subsist on what's in your freezer, fridge, and pantry. I have coined an oh-so-clever term for this. I call it the "Not-Shopping" method. I got the idea from Steven Shaw, an award-winning New York food writer. Steven normally shops every Sunday. One week he couldn't go, and he realized that, with a little creativity, he could easily feed his family all week with the food already in his home. (He lives in a New York City apartment, so imagine how much more food many of us have hoarded in our sprawling, suburban homes!)

Steven thought he could go even longer than a week, and he taunted others on his foodie website to take up the cause. The idea took off. We at *GMA* challenged a woman on the opposite coast to try Not-Shopping. Amanda, a mother of two, told us she usually went to the grocery store twice a week and spent a total of $200. She admitted it was easier to go pick up brand-new ingredients rather than root around for supplies in her own home. We asked Amanda to make do with just what she had for a week. Oh, and we asked her to do it on a week that she had out-of-town guests!

She went for it and served meals like tortellini with ground beef and asparagus, spiced chicken skewers with brown rice, and spaghetti with meat sauce. Amanda even baked a cake from scratch for her guests. Later, she said the experience was a "piece of cake," and that it had changed her habits forever.

Let's say you normally shop 50 weeks a year, because you vacation the other two weeks. Here's how much you can save if you cut out just one shopping trip per quarter:

Benefit of Not-Shopping Quarterly

Shopping every week	$7,500
Skipping one trip a quarter	6,900
Dollar savings	$ 600
BIG SAVINGS =	**8%**

That's 8 percent! Impressive, given that you don't have to choose a certain store or clip a single coupon. In fact, you get to choose *not* to go to the store and *forget* all about coupons!

But as a Guerrilla Grocery Shopper in the couch potato class, I know you can do better! I bet you have more food languishing in your cupboard than that! After all, *Shop Smart* magazine reports that the average mom with kids spends about $150 a week on groceries and throws out 14 percent of the food she buys for her family. So, how about Not-Shopping once a *month* instead of once a quarter? Here's what would happen:

Benefit of Not-Shopping Monthly

Shopping every week	$7,500
Skipping one trip a month	5,700
Dollar savings	$1,800
BIG SAVINGS =	**24%**

Now we're talking! That's a 24 percent savings! Woo-hoo! Of course, if you choose to Not-Shop too often, your wasteful extra supply of foods will dwindle, so it's up to you to find the right Not-Shopping frequency. That's your *one* task: figuring out how often *not* to shop. I think you can handle it.

BIG TIPS

- Start a grocery buying club and you could save 25 percent.
- Bid for groceries at a food auction and you could save 66 percent.
- Try the Not-Shopping method and save up to 24 percent.

PART V

HEALTHCARE
Curing High Costs

Medical costs are the fifth largest annual expense for most Americans—$3,452 per person, more than 5 percent of the average income, according to the Agency for Healthcare Research and Quality. The costs add up fast, what with health insurance, copayments, dental care, doctor visits, eyeglasses, prescription drugs, over-the-counter medicines and supplements, plus hospital bills. The expense can be a bitter pill to swallow—so some people don't, and they're getting even sicker.

So how can we cut costs? I guess you could cancel all your magazine subscriptions and swipe them from your doctor's office instead. That would be *one* way to save on medical expenses! Okay, okay, it was hard to come up with a Small Stuff Savings example for healthcare. But one of the most common money-saving tips is to cancel your magazine subscriptions. Monthly savings: $6.25 for somebody with three subscriptions.

Not good enough! In the coming pages, I will show you how to SAVE BIG on healthcare. My grand total is $44,578. You would have to give up 1,783 magazine subscriptions to save that amount of money!

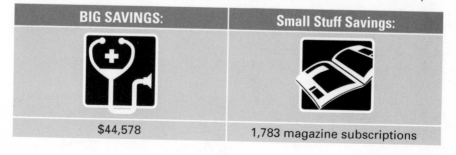

BIG SAVINGS:	Small Stuff Savings:
$44,578	1,783 magazine subscriptions

> To SAVE BIG on healthcare we need to behave like consumers instead of patients. Healthcare is a business.

Even with something sensitive like healthcare, it's possible to cut costs. You may be thinking, healthcare costs are somebody *else's* problem because you have access to the "platinum plan" through your work. Watch your bad back! Even people with work-based health insurance spend an average of $3,354 for a family plan these days, because most employers now require you to pay part of your own premium. Furthermore, according to the Kaiser Family Foundation's latest annual survey, 40 percent of companies plan to increase the amount their workers contribute in the next few years.

Here's the bottom line: To SAVE BIG on healthcare we need to behave like consumers instead of patients. Yes, healthcare is a business. That's why this section is laid out in the order you usually *consume* healthcare—from choosing a health plan, to seeing the doctor, to filling a prescription and going to the hospital.

- **Chapter 26:** We begin with health insurance. If you currently have one of those health plans in which you make just a tiny copayment when you see a doctor or go to the hospital, don't be smug. You are probably wasting thousands of dollars a year. I'll show you two cheaper ways: higher deductibles and paying as you go. Uninsured? We'll unearth surprising sources of coverage.
- **Chapter 27:** I'll teach you how to negotiate with your doctor, politely and professionally, and get as much as half off of your bill. If you're willing to tell your doctor about your arm and your leg, but not that he is *charging* you an arm and a leg, then you're going to need a cast—for your wallet. Negotiating is not that hard when you learn where to find comparative costs.
- **Chapter 28:** Prescription drugs come next. When you get a prescription, do you head straight to the nearest pharmacy to fill it so you can start feeling better? Don't! I uncover more than $20,000 worth of savings achieved through going

generic, switching meds, pill splitting, shopping around, and more. There are even programs that provide medications at *no* cost.

- **Chapter 29:** Experts say 80 percent of hospital bills contain inaccuracies. This is where you really need to cure high costs. Have you ever compared your hospital *bill* to your hospital *record* to find overcharges? You should. Better yet, get an expert to do it for you—for free. I'll tell you how to find help before or after you're hospitalized and even cut your costs in half.

Learn how to SAVE BIG on healthcare and you're sure to feel better right away—$44,578 better! The doctor will see you now.

CHAPTER

Choosing a Health Insurance Plan

What's in a word? A lot, when it comes to healthcare. There it is right there, the crux of the issue in that one modern, made-up word: *healthcare.* When did we stop calling it health *insurance* and start calling it health*care?* If you want to save money, don't ask huge conglomerate companies to *care* for you. Take good care of yourself and pay them to *insure* you. Cutting the cost of health insurance is the first way to SAVE BIG in this category.

What I mean is this: True health *insurance* is for the BIG stuff that is out of our control. Catastrophic care. It's more cost effective to pay for the little things like checkups and preventive maintenance yourself if you can afford it. I mean, we don't expect our car insurance policy to buy us new tires, do we? And our homeowner's insurance doesn't cover leaky faucets. We take care of those ourselves. If our car and house policies *did* cover all the little things, they would be prohibitively expensive. *Just* like so many healthcare policies are today.

In this chapter, learn to SAVE BIG by:

- Raising your deductible as high as you can afford to.
- Opening a tax-free Health Savings Account, a much better tool than a Flexible Spending Account.
- Choosing a health plan that costs less up front but more when you go to the doctor.
- Getting a group rate on health insurance through some surprising sources.

Raise Your Deductible

If we're going to start thinking of health insurance as just that—*insurance*—then what's the first thing people do when they want to save money on their insurance? They raise their deductible. The deductible is the amount you have to pay out of pocket for your care before the insurance kicks in. The higher your deductible, the lower your premiums will be, because the insurance company gives you a sizable discount for paying for your low-level care yourself. Raise your deductible, lower your premiums and you will SAVE BIG.

I learned about high deductibles when I started my first on-air television news job at age 23. I was a freelancer and didn't have health insurance. I was also making just $21,000 a year and didn't think I could afford healthcare coverage. (Wouldn't the people of Bakersfield, California, have been surprised to learn that their new weekend anchor wasn't a staffer and was struggling with this common dilemma!)

I called my dear old Dad to ask for advice and his wise words have never left me. He pointed out that insurance is not for routine stuff. Rather, it's meant to protect you and your family from catastrophic financial loss. Daddy suggested I skip all the fancy plans that paid for lots of preventive care and instead choose an inexpensive one with a high deductible that would give me excellent protection if something awful happened, like a car accident or a major disease diagnosis. Sure enough, once I looked at plans with high deductibles, I could easily afford the premiums.

There May Be an Insurance File on You

A little-known company called MIB Group, Inc., keeps records on people who have applied for life, health, disability, or long-term care insurance. This file contains the information you have previously divulged about your health. When you apply for a new policy, the insurance company may check this file to see if you are hiding any conditions. There will only be a file on you if you have previously applied for private insurance. If so, you can request a copy of your file to assure that it is accurate before applying for a new policy: www.mib.com.

Most families can muddle through even $10,000 worth of medical expenses, if that's the size of their deductible. It's not pretty, but it's possible. But the $250,000 bill from the family member who has a heart attack and needs critical care can bankrupt you. How do you recover from that? That's why the best way to SAVE BIG is to pick a plan that has a high deductible but offers generous coverage once you meet that deductible.

According to an annual Mercer Survey, the median health insurance deductible chosen by people with workplace coverage in 2007 was $500. That's way too low! The median that workers chose in 2008 was $1,000. That's a step in the right direction, but not as dramatic as what I have in mind.

Who Should—and Shouldn't—Do This

A high deductible is not for everybody. Raising your deductible works best for younger, healthier people who don't need much medical care. However, anybody who takes good care of themselves or makes a comfortable living should consider it. A high deductible worked for me when I was 23 and even works now that I'm in my 40s because I am blessed with good health.

If, however, you have a chronic medical condition that requires continuous care, or you live financially close to the edge, this advice is not for you. For people with chronic illnesses, an employer-based plan with a low deductible and generous benefits is best. If you have a low income and a high deductible would ruin you financially, you may be better off in an HMO plan with no unexpected costs. If you fall into either of these categories, don't be discouraged. There are still tens of thousands of dollars worth of savings for you in my next three chapters on doctors, prescriptions, and hospitals.

The Most Important Part of Healthcare Is Free!

What could this free mystery treatment be? Lifestyle: choosing a healthy diet and exercising regularly. In the United States, we spend the largest amount of healthcare dollars on hospitalization and nursing care, the middle amount on doctor visits and drugs, and the least of all on prevention. We need to flip our priorities over, and this mission starts with each of us.

How (Well) It Works

To show you how you can SAVE BIG by raising your deductible, let me give you an example. I just spent a couple of hours analyzing health insurance choices for Stephanie F. of Oregon. Stephanie is a healthy 41-year-old woman with a sense of adventure. She and her husband, Keith, recently spent a year backpacking around Southeast Asia. Now that they've returned, Keith and Stephanie are determined to take some time to find their dream jobs, so they need health insurance in the meantime.

I found five possible plans for Stephanie, all with one company, where every aspect of the coverage is the same except for the deductible. This makes for a nice clean comparison. Check it out:

Possible Health Plans for Stephanie

Deductible	Premium
$ 500	$4,236/year
$ 1,500	$2,808/year
$ 2,500	$2,352/year
$ 5,000	$1,536/year
$10,000	$1,164/year

Which policy should Stephanie choose? Let me take you through my thought process—point by point, price by price—before we make that decision.

- **$500 deductible.** Yes, it would be nice for Stephanie to have health insurance that kicked in after just $500, but she would pay dearly for the privilege—$4,236 a year! Imagine how many doctor visits that money would cover if she paid cash. Actually, I'll tell you: about 34 15-minute appointments at $125 each!
- **$1,500 deductible.** If Stephanie chooses the $1,500 deductible instead of the $500 one, she can save 33 percent. It's a *sure* savings of $1,428 a year in exchange for a *possible* cost of $1,000. She could set the $1,428 aside and use it to cover the $1,000 difference, and still have money left over.
- **$2,500 deductible.** This doesn't seem like a good deal, because the deductible is a full $1,000 higher than the $1,500 one, but the savings is only $456 more.

- **$5,000 deductible.** This is a hefty deductible that Stephanie might not even meet in a year. But remember, the goal with *true* insurance is not to use it. Nobody wants to get in a car accident or have their house broken into in order to use their car and homeowner policies. With this option, Stephanie is risking $5,000, but if she doesn't have many healthcare needs, she will never have to pay that much. And she will save $2,700 a year in premiums.
- **$10,000 deductible.** At this level the savings are substantial— $3,072 a year or 71 percent compared to the $500 deductible. Yes, Stephanie is risking $10,000 but the savings she receives will pay for that in three years. If she starts a policy like this while she is still young, she could have money in the bank to pay for a pricier policy when she is older and wants more coverage.

How low can you go? Or should I ask, how *high* can you go? I would recommend the $10,000 deductible plan for Stephanie because she's healthy, she has solid finances, and she will SAVE BIG.

This particular comparison was of private health insurance plans, because Stephanie is not working, but you have similar choices when you enroll in your work-based health plan. Choose a higher deductible and you will SAVE BIG. It's that simple.

It's up to you how far you are willing to take this concept, depending on your comfort level. As you saw in this example, there are benefits at every price point. It's an individual choice based on your unique situation. Bottom line: I don't care how high you raise your deductible. I just want you to raise it.

Protection for those with Preexisting Conditions

You've probably heard of the HIPAA law as it relates to your privacy rights, but it actually stands for the Health Insurance Portability and Accountability Act, and it protects people with preexisting conditions. As long as you were covered for at least a year at your previous employer and as long as you haven't had a gap in coverage of more than 63 days, insurance companies cannot discriminate against you. Your former employer is required to provide you with a "certificate of creditable coverage" that you can present to insurance companies when you apply.

High Deductible Health Plans with Health Savings Accounts

In 2003, the federal government acted like it had just invented something new and coined the term High Deductible Health Plan (HDHP). Just by capitalizing some words (and passing a law), Congress created a new tool for you. A High Deductible Health Plan is . . . a health plan with a high deductible. Duh! Specifically, to qualify as an official High Deductible Health Plan, an HDHP must have a deductible of at least $1,200 a year for individuals or $2,400 for families as of 2010. The required deductible is adjusted every year for inflation. The HDHP itself isn't that exciting, but when you sign up for one you are then eligible to open a Health Savings account—which *is* exciting. In fact, it's the only way to open one!

Health Savings Accounts (HSAs) are accounts in which you can save money for healthcare costs tax-free. HSAs are something so great that I can't believe there's not more noise about them. (In fact, they're so great that I worry the government will do away with them and High Deductible Health Plans.) HSAs are much better than the older Flexible Spending Accounts (FSAs).

In the old, obnoxious Flexible Spending Account system you have to guess how much you will spend on healthcare each year and then set aside that amount. If you guess wrong and don't spend all the money, you forfeit the balance of your account. Oops! You lose! (Did you know your employer gets to keep that money?) Dr. Marie Savard, medical contributor for *Good Morning America*, tells me that when she was in private practice, toward the end of the year, patients used to request all sorts of expensive, premature tests in a desperate bid to use up their FSA dollars.

By contrast, the new Health Savings Accounts are so much saner. Here's what makes them appealing:

- HSAs roll over from year to year. You don't forfeit the money.
- They are portable, so you can take them with you to another job.
- Employers typically contribute to HSAs.
- HSAs earn interest or can be invested (carefully!) in the market.
- You can cash in your HSA for any use after age 65.

Here's the grand vision for High Deductible Health Plans paired with Health Savings Accounts. Say somebody like Stephanie chooses the $5,000 deductible health insurance policy I showed you earlier. She will save $2,700 a year compared to the cost of the $500 deductible plan. She can then put that savings into her Health Savings Account. It's a pretax account, so she saves even *more* money because of that. Stephanie can then use those funds to pay cash for her entry-level care, since it's not covered by her high-deductible insurance. If she is fortunate, healthwise, she may have money left over in her HSA, and at age 65 she can withdraw it for any purpose she desires. Maybe she'll use it to take another backpacking trip with her husband, Keith. I wouldn't put it past them!

Many Colleges Charge for Healthcare, Even Though Students Are Covered under Their Parents' Plans

You may be paying twice for healthcare coverage if you have college-aged kids. Buried in the reams of enrollment and tuition paperwork could be a clause about the student health service on campus. It can cost thousands of dollars. If your son or daughter can access your own insurance company's doctors and hospitals in the area where the college is located, you could forego this double coverage. Most policies cover dependent children until they are age 22 if they are enrolled in college.

Pay As You Go

The second way to SAVE BIG on health insurance is to pay more of your own medical costs as you go. Unfortunately, most people these days do not. Here's a stunning statistic: In 1970, Americans paid 40 percent of their own medical costs—their doctor visits, lab tests, and so on—out of pocket. Today, we pay just 15 percent, according to the Kaiser Family Foundation. We pay a lot more in insurance premiums but a lot less of our own actual medical costs. That's a money mistake because it's always more expensive to run costs through a middleman, in this case an insurance company.

Why do people make that mistake again and again? There seems to be a mentality in this country that a good health plan is one in which you only have to make a modest copayment when you go to the doctor or land in the hospital. When I set out to write this book, I was telling one of my girlfriends about it. She was pregnant, so I bragged that one of the sections would help her drastically cut her hospital costs when she went to deliver her baby. She sort of tittered and said, "That won't be necessary. My insurance takes care of all that. I don't have to pay a thing."

Man, is she wrong! I guarantee you my friend is paying a pretty penny in monthly premiums for her so-called "free" coverage. But she is paying in advance and the money is automatically deducted from her paycheck, so it doesn't *feel* like she's spending money. That's the trap! For healthy people, it's almost always more economical to pay a lower monthly premium up front and then pay a higher percentage of your healthcare as you go. Why pay in advance for medical services and visits you may never use?

You Pay for Your Insurance, So Make It Pay for You

One way to SAVE BIG is to make sure your health insurer doesn't deny eligible claims. According to a Harris Interactive poll, 45 percent of people who appeal are able to get some sort of satisfaction. So take the following steps:

- Send your appeal quickly. Often there is a 30- to 40-day time limit by which it must be received.
- Mail it certified so you have proof it arrived.
- Request a detailed written denial so you can prepare a strong counterargument.
- Ask the benefits administrator at your work for help. The insurer wants to keep your company's business.
- Get your state insurance commissioner involved. Find yours at www.naic .org.

I didn't figure out the beauty of paying more for healthcare as you go on my own. My husband, Kris, the financial planner, taught me. When we got the fat packet of healthcare choices from my employer, we sat down, went through the options, and then ran the numbers to figure out how to SAVE BIG.

We had about a half dozen choices. The Kaiser Family Foundation says 58 percent of people these days go with a preferred provider organization (PPO), and we chose that option, too. But then we had three more choices to make within that matrix: Should we opt for the plan where we pay 10 percent, 20 percent, or 30 percent of our medical costs when we actually see a doctor? Certainly 10 percent and 20 percent *sound* better, but they come with much higher premiums in advance. Here's the breakdown:

Kris and Elisabeth's Health Insurance Dilemma

Pay-as-You-Go Percentage	Premium
10% plan	$8,580/year
20% plan	$3,952/year
30% plan	$1,872/year

We really wanted to SAVE BIG, so here is, step-by-step, how we thought things through:

- **The 10% plan.** This plan is out of the question. Paying only 10 percent of healthcare costs down the road is a false comfort because the yearly premium is so enormous: $8,580! Ugh. Even if you *knew* you were going to have open heart surgery *and* chemotherapy next year, it's a bad deal. My husband Kris did the math, factoring in the premium and deductible, and this plan would *never* pay for itself. It's impossible for us to spend enough money for the 10 percent plan to be worthwhile.
- **The 20% plan.** An 80/20 plan, where your insurance company pays 80 percent of your costs and you pay the other 20 percent, is the most popular form of PPO by far, including at my company. So is it worth it for you? Here's a mental test you can do to figure it out. The premium for the 20 percent plan is $3,952. That would buy us a whopping 32 15-minute doctor visits at $125 each if we paid cash for them. Do the members of your family go to the doctor 32 times a year? We certainly don't. So that's a sign this plan charges us for services we won't use. In fact, the 20 percent plan begins to pay for itself only after you have spent $15,000 in a single year on healthcare! If you know you have expensive medical

conditions, this could be right for you. For us, no way. We are blessed with good health. Knock wood.

- **The 30% plan.** The premiums for this plan cost about half as much as for the 80/20 plan. Yes! But we have to contribute a significant amount, 30 percent, to our healthcare costs as we incur them. That may sound intimidating, but we will actually save money all the way up until the $15,000 mark by paying doctors, labs, and hospitals as we go instead of paying an insurance company up front. And so far we have never spent anywhere *close* to that amount, even the year we had birthing costs for our daughter. Let's say we spend about $3,000 a year for our three-person family. $1,000 each. Here's our savings at that level, if you factor in premiums and deductibles:

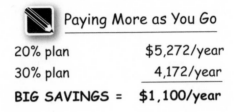

Paying More as You Go	
20% plan	$5,272/year
30% plan	4,172/year
BIG SAVINGS =	**$1,100/year**

For us, the 30 percent plan works best and we SAVE BIG: $1,100 a year. For those who buy health insurance privately, the same principles apply. I'll say it one more time: If you're willing to pay more of your own healthcare costs as you go to the doctor, the premiums that you pay in advance will be so much lower that you will SAVE BIG. If you *do* have a bad healthcare year, you will have saved so much money in other years that you'll be able to cover the costs of the expensive year yourself. Paying more as you go is less expensive for healthy people. Period.

Pay Less with Private Insurance

It may sound surprising, but sometimes private insurance is cheaper than group insurance. That's right, if you're young and healthy, an individual health insurance plan may be less expensive than the one offered at work. Why? Because the work plan must accept everyone, so it is priced to cover the insurance company's broad risk. Amy S. of Illinois discovered she could get a private policy for herself for $115 a month. Adding herself to her husband Craig's plan would have cost $350 a month!

If You're Uninsured

If you don't have health insurance, finding an affordable plan is not nearly as daunting if you use the principles I have already laid out: high deductibles and paying as you go. Once again, I offer the caveat that these cost-saving strategies work best for healthy people with decent incomes.

If you're searching for health insurance, you can look online to get a rough idea, but keep in mind that the nifty quotes you get in five minutes on the Internet are only rough estimates. The insurance company must go through an underwriting process before it gives you final approval and a final price.

That's why you will eventually want to turn to an insurance agent or broker for help. You want somebody who can shop multiple companies and myriad plans to get you the best deal. A good source for this is an independent insurance broker with the ability to sell policies from many companies. You can find one at http:// TrustedChoice.org, the website of the Independent Insurance Agents and Brokers of America. Another source is the National Association of Health Underwriters, www.NAHU.org.

Take the Health Coverage Eligibility Quiz

The Foundation for Health Coverage Education can help you figure out what kinds of health insurance are available to you. Take the Foundation's excellent, easy Health Coverage Eligibility Quiz at http://CoverageForAll.org to learn your public and private options. You might be surprised. For example, in 2008 it was possible for a pregnant woman making $63,000 a year to get free health coverage through the state of California.

The fact that most group plans in this country are offered by employers is an accident of history. During World War II, there were wage freezes, so companies offered health insurance as a form of payment instead. You should explore whether you can qualify for group insurance through some group other than an employer.

There are increasingly clever ways to do this. Here's a list of possibilities to get you started:

- **Alliance for Affordable Services.** This organization serves small businesses and offers healthcare plans. Visit it at www. AffordableServices.org.
- **Alumni association.** Does your college or university send you "partnership offers" all the time? Read them because there might be a decent health plan in the pile.
- **AARP.** If you are over age 50, you can purchase health insurance through the American Association of Retired Persons— www.AARPHealthcare.com.
- **Chamber of commerce.** Yes, your local Chamber might offer health insurance to members, especially small business owners. Call and ask.
- **College plans.** If you have a college-age child who is covered by a commercial health plan—not just the campus health service—offered by the university, your child might be able to add *you* as an additional insured. Consult the policy paperwork.

Form Your Own Group

Some states let you form your own insurance group, with as few as two people! Different states have different standards. For example, one state stipulates that each employee in the group must work at least 25 hours a week. Another requires the group to submit tax forms to verify it is actually connected to a business. Check with your state insurance commissioner to see if this is possible in your state. Go to www.naic.org for links to every state insurance commissioner.

- **Credit card companies.** Yes, we love to hate them, but you might learn to love your card company if it offers you affordable health insurance. Call the customer service number to find out.
- **Farm bureau.** You don't have to be a farmer to join your state's farm bureau. Membership fees are minimal and the bureaus have negotiated discounted rates with health insurers.

- **National Association for the Self-Employed.** This loose federation of folks has a health plan through one insurance company. For more information visit www.nase.org.
- **National Association of Female Executives.** Here's yet another association with insurance benefits. You can find out the criteria at www.nafe.com.
- **Part-time job.** Many large employers offer healthcare benefits even to part-time workers. You may have to pay more, but you'll be covered.
- **Religious organization.** Some religious groups offer health plans, so check with your church, mosque, synagogue, and so on, for information.
- **Small Business Service Bureau.** This small business trade group has health plans. To find out more, visit www.sbsb.com.
- **Trade associations.** Go to the website of any trade group you belong to—or could belong to—and see if it offers a group health insurance plan.

BIG TIPS

- Raise your deductible as far as you comfortably can.
- See if you can get an official High Deductible Health Plan with Health Savings Account.
- Choose a pay-as-you go structure instead of one where you pay higher premiums up front.
- Use an independent broker to shop for private insurance.
- See if you can creatively qualify for group insurance if you are uninsured.

CHAPTER

Negotiating with Your Doctor

After you choose a health insurance plan, you go to the doctor, right? Doctor visits are the second place where you can SAVE BIG on healthcare. Doctors are the most important part of our healthcare team, and I think they should be paid fairly for their services, but if you want or need to SAVE BIG at the doctor's office, it is definitely doable.

You may be thinking, "I don't need to save money at the doctor's office—my insurance pays for that." So let me ask you a few questions. Do you have to pay a deductible before your insurance pays the doctor? Then it matters to you. Do you ever go out of network? Then it matters to you. Do you pay a percentage of your doctor visits, called coinsurance, rather than a copay? Then it matters to you. Does your policy have a lifetime limit that charges you if you go over that threshold? Then it matters to you, too.

In this chapter, learn to SAVE BIG by:

- Negotiating with your doctor for lower fees.
- Suggesting you pay the Medicare rate instead of the market rate.
- Asking to pay the insurance company rate even if you're uninsured.

Approaching Your Doctor

If the thought of negotiating with your doctor gives you heart palpitations, perfect. You can go to the doctor for those, and you'll be right where you need to be to start negotiating! Seriously, though, there's nothing to be nervous about. In a Harris Interactive poll, 61 percent of people who negotiated with a doctor were successful in getting a lower fee. But here's the problem: Only 12 percent of people surveyed had ever even tried. So you can be one of the few. Since most people *aren't* asking for a lower price, the doctor has more leeway to offer *you* a lower price!

Find Doctors You Love and Then Avoid Them Like the Plague—Unless You Have the Plague

If you have what feels like a routine illness, especially one that you've had before, call or e-mail your doctor and describe your symptoms to find out if you need to be seen. You can often avoid the cost of a full-fledged appointment. Also question whether follow up appointments are truly needed. Doctors sometimes tell you to come back out of habit. A variation: Avoid costly specialist visits by asking if your primary care physician can provide your maintenance care for a chronic condition like asthma or diabetes.

Are you surprised that doctors are so willing to give discounts? Actually, it makes sense. After all, every doctor in a preferred provider organization (PPO) gives the insurance company a discount off their regular rate. And doctors give the government a discount when they treat Medicare patients. So why shouldn't they give a break to the actual patient with the break in their leg? When I gave this advice on the air during a *Good Morning America* story, the most wonderful thing happened. We got the following e-mail from a woman who saw my story right before heading to a doctor's appointment:

> After hearing the cost-saving tips on your show, I asked my doctor if he could reduce his fee. Without hesitation, he agreed. I am applying my fee reduction savings towards the purchase of hats and mittens for children in an inner-city Philadelphia school.

I contacted the school's principal who said these items are always needed.

— Joni S., Pennsylvania

How to Ask

If you're going to ask for a discount, you need to figure out the best way to go about it so you'll succeed. Some experts say you should get the care you need and *then* ask for a price break. I'm not crazy about that idea. Seems sneaky. I guess I would understand it if you are seriously ill and have reason to worry the doctor is going to say no. But I think the better course of action would be to schedule your appointment as usual and then bring up price, in person, at the beginning of the appointment. It's hard for anybody to refuse somebody who asks them for a favor face-to-face.

Yes, I did say face-to-face. You need to negotiate with your doctor directly. Not the nurse, not the front desk, certainly not the billing department. Most doctors got into the field because they want to help people. Mostly they help them physically, but occasionally financially. Your case will be particularly sympathetic if your household income is a factor. For example, if you point out that the procedure you need costs $5,000 while your annual income is $25,000, the doctor will probably understand how important this is to you.

It also helps to offer to pay in advance. Since doctors spend thousands of dollars chasing after patients who don't pay their bills, somebody who is willing to pay up front is a very attractive prospect. According to the website www.Bills.com, doctors have been known to discount their rate by 20 to 50 percent for patients who pay cash in advance. Even at 50 percent off, your payment may be attractive to a doctor who is accustomed to discounting even more for health insurers that don't pay up front.

Thank Your Doctor

Have you ever called your doctor's office or sent a thank-you note to show your appreciation that they helped you get well? Me neither, but I'm going to start. Think about it. Doctors listen to people complain all the time. Expressing gratitude will make their day and they, in turn, may make your day sometime in the future when you need a price break or time-consuming help fighting with your insurance company. This warm and wonderful advice is courtesy of Michelle Katz.

Paying the Medicare Rate

Since doctors are accustomed to discounting their fees for Medicare patients, one tactic is to ask to pay the Medicare rate or the Medicare rate plus 20 percent. This is less practical for a simple office visit but well worth it if you need a significant procedure.

How do you find out the Medicare rate? Ask the doctor's office for the CPT code or Current Procedural Terminology code. CPT codes are the five-digit codes that identify the test or procedure you need; they are different from diagnosis codes. These CPT codes are developed by the American Medical Association to describe every medical service. Type that code into the CPT search section of the AMA's website, www.ama-assn.org. It's a little hard to find, so I will link you to it from my site, www.ElisabethLeamy.com. You must search the correct code plus the city and state where your doctor is located to get an accurate price, as Medicare prices vary regionally.

Here's how paying the Medicare rate helps you SAVE BIG. Anthony D., 56, of northern Virginia needed a quadruple bypass operation. Anthony was laid off a while ago and let his COBRA health benefits lapse because he simply couldn't afford them. He looked up the Medicare reimbursement rate for the heart surgeon's fee and discovered that 33536 is the CPT code for the surgeon's portion of the operation. Once he knew the Medicare rate for the surgeon's services, he compared that to the price he had been quoted. Here are the numbers:

 Getting the Medicare Rate

Quadruple bypass market rate	$5,558
Quadruple bypass Medicare rate	2,839
BIG SAVINGS =	**$2,719**

Yikes! Paying full fare of $5,558 was out of the question for Anthony. Fortunately, he was able to take this information about the Medicare rate and use it to negotiate a deal with his doctor. He had his surgery and says he feels like a new man. He's out power walking for the first time in years and says his two-year-old dog doesn't know what to make of it because she had never been on a real walk before.

If you are uninsured, or are going out of network, or have the type of insurance plan in which you pay a percentage of each medical bill, persuading your doctor to accept the Medicare rate would be a significant savings for you.

Book Physicals for December

If you schedule your physical for December, if your insurance benefits have run out, you can move the appointment to January. You'll have a new slate of benefits, but you won't have put off checking up on your health for too long. This trick can also work for dental work you need. Schedule half for December, the other half for January when your new benefits kick in.

Paying the Insurance Company Rate

If the Medicare rate doesn't resonate with your doctor, then you can ask to pay the contracted rate or allowed amount that insurance companies pay. It's one insurance company perk that even uninsured people can get and it works for anybody who is paying part or all of their own doctor bill.

The contracted rate is the discounted price doctors agree to accept when they join an insurance company's PPO. According to the independent medical pricing website www.HealthcareBlueBook. com, this rate can be two to five times less than the doctor's regular rate. (One reason doctors' regular rates are so high is so that they can charge insurance companies a percentage of that rate and still get a decent payment for their services.)

In order to learn the insurance company rate for services, you can look up the procedures you need on HealthcareBlueBook.com by key word or category. The site lists what it considers fair prices for hundreds of procedures. These prices are based on the average amount insurance companies pay for each procedure. HealthcareBluebook. com says you should be able to get the service you need for its quoted price if you pay in full at the time of treatment. Be sure to input your zip code for an accurate price in your area.

Present the HealthcareBluebook.com price to your doctor and see what happens. It's a great starting point for discussion—and negotiation. For that same quadruple bypass surgery, here's how much somebody like Anthony could save by paying the insurance company rate.

If Anthony Pays the Insurance Rate

Quadruple bypass market rate	$5,558
Quadruple bypass insurance rate	2,779
BIG SAVINGS =	**$2,779**

Wow, $2,779 is half off. Your results will vary, but there's one thing that won't change: If you don't ask for a discount, you won't get one.

Ask for a Payment Plan

If you're struggling with health concerns, you don't need the extra burden of struggling with financial concerns, too. So don't be shy—negotiate the cost of your procedure with your doctor by asking her to honor the Medicare or insurance company rate.

If none of this works, there is a fallback position. If you can't convince your doctor to give you a discount, then ask for a payment plan. Some doctors will insist on earning their full fee, but will allow you to pay it gradually over time.

BIG TIPS

- Try negotiating the cost with your doctor—especially for major procedures.
- Use the Medicare rate or the contracted insurance rate as a pricing guide.
- Offer cash up front.
- Your backup plan is to ask for a payment plan.

CHAPTER

Picking Your
Prescriptions

According to the Agency for Healthcare Research and Quality, the average American spends $1,191 a year on prescription medicines—and that includes people *with* insurance. But that average really doesn't tell the true story because young, healthy people who take next to no medications keep the numbers down. The unlucky folks with multiple medical conditions can quite literally go bankrupt trying to pay for the myriad drugs they need. I'm here to tell you that there is hope. Cutting the cost of prescriptions is the third way to SAVE BIG on healthcare costs and—better yet—it's *easy!*

Of course, the information to come is particularly valuable to people with no health insurance. But if you take a medicine that your insurance company refuses to cover, I can help *you*, too. Or if you take a drug that is covered but comes with a higher copay, I can help. In fact, there's even money-saving advice for people whose generous insurance plans cover all their meds and have all low copayments, because if you take a lot of different drugs, those copays still add up. Say you take five medications and each has a $10 copay. That's $50 a month, $600 a year. I can help with that, too.

In this chapter, learn to SAVE BIG by:

- Sticking to the medications on your insurance company's approved list.
- Avoiding name-brand drugs whenever possible.
- Cutting pills or growing pills to exploit the way pills are priced.

- Substituting over-the-counter meds for prescription ones.
- Paying cash even if you have insurance.
- Shopping around because prices vary dramatically among stores.
- Getting free prescription drugs from the pharmaceutical industry.
- Shopping around for medical tests too.

What Medications to Take

You may be puzzled by the title of this section, because most of us take what our doctors tell us to take. End of story. But the truth is, many doctors aren't in touch with the cost of different drugs. They just *write* the prescriptions. They don't have to fill them. So the first step in saving on prescriptions is to alert your doctor that you want to cut costs. Once your doc is on board, you can SAVE BIG by deciding, together, which meds you should take and in what strength.

Follow the Formulary

If you have health insurance, the first step on the road to savings is to try to take medications that are on your insurance company's preferred list. This list is called a formulary. You can probably print the formulary from your insurance company's website. Print an updated one before every doctor's appointment and take it with you.

Ask your doctor to look at the list when prescribing a medication to treat your condition. Ideally, your doctor can identify more than one drug that is appropriate for you. There are usually a few, sometimes dozens of medications that can be used for any one condition. But wait! Don't let your doctor write a prescription just yet.

Get Two Prescriptions for the Same Medication

Just in case a new medicine doesn't agree with you, you don't want to waste money on several months' worth. Prescription meds are not returnable. So instead, ask your doctor to write you two prescriptions: one that will last a couple of days or weeks and another, longer one that you can fill after that if the medication agrees with you and helps you.

Next step, go home and get online to research the prices of the different drugs on your short list. Two helpful websites are http://RXaminer.com and http://DestinationRX.com. I like them both because they're easy to use and packed with money-saving info. All you have to do is type in the name of the drug and up pops a list of prices at various pharmacies, generics you could take instead, and even similar drugs made by different manufacturers that you could consider substituting.

This chore is less worthwhile for medicines you will just be taking for a short time. But for maintenance meds you need for a chronic condition, it is well worth it. Once you have found the least expensive medication, *then* call your doctor's office and ask her to phone in a prescription.

If your doctor really wants you to take a prescription that is not on the formulary, you have two choices.

1. You can ask to try a different drug in the same class first to see if it works for you.
2. You can appeal to your insurance company—with your doctor's help—and make the case that this one medication is uniquely suited to help you.

Go Generic

When a pharmaceutical company develops a new drug, it is rewarded with a patent that lasts up to 20 years, so it can make money on its invention and recoup the costs of developing it. But when the 20 years or so are up, other companies are allowed to manufacture generic versions of the drug. The philosophy is that medications that improve lives should be as broadly available as possible. This is the moment in time when you can start to SAVE BIG. In fact, going generic will save you more money on prescriptions than any other move.

Let's get to an example right away. As I write this, antidepressants are the most prescribed drugs in America. (That's a book in itself!) The most famous of all is Prozac. I bet you've never heard of Fluoxetine. It should be famous, too—for being cheap. Fluoxetine is the generic for Prozac. Look what happens if you buy this generic medication instead of the name brand:

Going Generic

Name-brand Prozac	$8,290/year
Generic Fluoxetine	1,940/year
BIG SAVINGS =	**$6,350/year**

Whoa! You can save $6,350 a year if you buy generic. I feel the depression lifting already. That's a phenomenal savings—77 percent—for somebody without insurance. And if you *are* insured, you can see why your insurance company would want to nudge (shove?) you toward the generic drug to save itself money.

It makes you wonder why doctors write prescriptions for brand names at all when they could save their patients a lot of money by specifying a generic. The answer is that there are nearly 6,000 medications on the market, making it impossible for doctors to keep track of them all and when patents expire and generics become available. Plus, name-brand drug company reps make the rounds daily, dropping off free samples to keep their drug's names in the doctor's memory. Generic drug makers don't do that.

Are Generics As Good?   There's a misperception that generic drugs aren't as good as name-brand drugs. That's baloney. Here are the facts. The Food and Drug Administration (FDA) requires generic medicines to contain the exact same active ingredient in the same amount as the name-brand med.

The only difference is in the *inactive* ingredients used to bind the generic pill together. These inactive ingredients can affect how the body absorbs the active ingredient, which could make a generic medication slightly more or less effective than a brand medication for a particular individual. It's also possible for individuals to have negative reactions to the inactive filler ingredients themselves, like perhaps a dye. (To be fair, your body could also react *better* to the filler ingredients in a generic than in the original name-brand drug.)

The one time that generics may not be an option is with drugs that have what's called a narrow therapeutic index. That gobbledygook term means too little of the medication is not effective and too much is toxic. The effective dose must be very precise and differences in the inactive ingredients of a generic could bother sensitive patients. A handful of antiseizure medications, asthma drugs, blood thinners, heart medications, psychiatric drugs and thyroid meds have narrow therapeutic indexes. Ask your doctor and pharmacist for guidance.

Amy D. of Ohio wishes she had known. She discovered she had epilepsy in her early twenties, later than most, which made it particularly terrifying. Amy and her doctor worked hard to find just the right medication to control her seizures. And then a pharmacy, following the requirements of her insurance company, switched her to the generic version of the drug without alerting her. Amy suffered a seizure while riding her bike and broke her leg and fractured her eye socket. Today her doctor, her insurance company, and her pharmacist all know that, for her, taking a particular medicine—in this case, a name brand—is necessary.

Beware of Prescription Drugs that End in *ER, CD* and, *XR*

These and other initials stand for *extended release* and *continuous delivery.* They are often trumped-up variations of medications that were big moneymakers for the manufacturer but lost their patent. Manufacturers sometimes invent slightly new versions of their biggest blockbusters and patent them in an attempt to keep the dollars flowing. That's their right. And it's *your* right to ask if older, cheaper, generic drugs will work just as well for you.

For the vast majority of people, generics are a life-saving, cost-saving option. Since doctors won't necessarily tell you about them, you need to ask. One option is to request to start out on a generic drug and see if it works for you. If it's not effective, *then* you can try the name brand—or another generic! If you want the generic option, make sure your doctor does not write or check the box that says "Dispense As Written" or "Do Not Substitute" on your prescription form. These words are usually meant to instruct the pharmacist to use a name brand only.

You should be aware of one complexity when you go generic. You might not always get the same generic! For example, there are about a dozen different manufacturers who make generic versions of the sleep aid Ambien. To cut their own costs, pharmacies may switch from one manufacturer to another, depending which one currently offers the best price. So from month to month your pills could look different. To make sure you are just getting a new generic and not the wrong medicine, you can look up a picture of the medicine at DestinationRX.com.

Old Can Be Gold

As I mentioned before, pharmaceutical companies give up exclusive rights to their own medications when the patent expires. For that reason, drug companies try to make as much money as possible off of their medicines when they are new. That means older medicines can be golden—for you!—whether generic *or* name brand. For example, when *Consumer Reports* rated diabetes drugs, it named an older drug called Metformin a best buy because it's quite effective for most patients, yet it's a lot less expensive than a newer name-brand drug called Avandia. Take a look at the cost difference in these two prescriptions over the course of a year:

Benefit of Using Older Drugs

Avandia	$1,872/year
Metformin	270/year
BIG SAVINGS =	**$1,602/year**

That $1,602 is a savings worth striving for! Ask your doctor if there are older medicines you can try before resorting to more expensive new ones.

Over-the-Counter   Sometimes older drugs become so tried-and-true that they can even be converted into over-the-counter medicines. This is another way to SAVE BIG. For example, Prilosec for heartburn is now available as an over-the-counter medicine right at the store in a 20-milligram dose. Yet it's still possible to purchase it in the same strength as a prescription, too. Crazy, I know, especially when you see the cost difference:

 Same Drug Over-the-Counter

Prilosec prescription	$ 1,997/year
Prilosec over-the-counter	234/year
BIG SAVINGS =	**$1,763/year**

Isn't that bizarre? I have no idea why the same drug costs two different prices depending where you get it, but you can exploit irrational pharmaceutical price points like that for your own benefit.

BIG SECRET

Just Say No to Drugs— Brand-New Ones, That Is

If your doctor offers you free samples of a medication for a chronic condition, you might want to pass. Pharmaceutical reps usually distribute freebies of the newest, most expensive medicines in their collection. If there is a less expensive, older drug, you don't want to get started on a pricey new one that you will have to pay for once the samples run out. However, if your doc can provide free samples for a brief, acute illness like a sinus infection, go for it.

Different Drug, Same Class

If your doctor recommends a newer drug that has not yet gone generic or over-the-counter, before you swallow the huge cost, you may be able to swallow an alternate pill instead. Ask about a different drug in the same class. In other words, another company's version of a similar drug. It's called therapeutic substitution. Certainly, there are times when one manufacturer comes up with a medicine that is uniquely effective. But often the various drugs in a class are quite close and the only reason your doctor has chosen one over another is habit.

The real trick is to switch to a different drug in the same class that is old enough to have gone generic. That's when this strategy can make all the difference.

Why do drug companies charge such varied prices for medications that do basically the same thing? Because they can. It's a free-market economy and they can—and should—charge as much as they can get. But *you* can—and should—pay as little as *you* can! Of course, you will want to check back with your doctor to make sure that a substitution like this is working for you. If he clears it, then prepare to SAVE BIG.

Let's use another heartburn example—since prescription drug costs can cause just that—to prove my point. Nexium won't be available as a generic until 2014, so it's still pretty pricey. But its competitor cousin, our familiar friend Prilosec, *is* available as a generic, called Omeprazole. So here's how substituting could save you money:

Different Drug in the Same Class

Nexium	$2,066
Omeprazole	186
BIG SAVINGS =	**$1,880**

Hallelujah, $1,880 saved! That's a whopping 91 percent!

Size Matters

With a title like "Size Matters" in a chapter on pharmaceuticals, you may think this is a special section about Viagra, but it's not. Sorry to disappoint. But I'm going to show you some sexy savings instead.

Pill Splitting   I don't know why, but many medications cost roughly the same regardless of the number of milligrams in each tablet. I don't get it. The pharmaceutical company is giving you more, sometimes twice as much, of its prized compound, but doesn't charge you much—if any—extra for it.

Take Lipitor, the popular cholesterol drug. A 30-day supply of 20-milligram pills costs $127. But a 30-day supply of 40-milligram pills *also* costs $127. Let's say your prescription is to take one tablet twice a day. Instead of buying twice as many 20-milligram tablets, you can buy the 40-milligram ones and cut them in half. You may have heard of pill splitting before, but has anybody ever shown you how much this simple trick can save you? Look:

 Pill Splitting

Two 20-milligram tablets	$ 3,066/year
One 40-milligram tablet	1,545/year
BIG SAVINGS =	**$1,521/year**

Now $1,521 is fantastic, but it's important to check with your doctor and pharmacist before splitting pills. Some medications, like extended release formulas, should not be split. An easy way to tell if a pill is safe to split is if it is scored along the top for this very purpose. It also helps to get a little $10 gadget at the pharmacy that splits pills neatly and evenly.

Still nervous about uneven doses? I have a great resource for you. In his indispensable book, *How to Save on Prescription Drugs*, Dr. Edward Jardini, a practicing physician, says that he tells his patients to "take the 'big half' now and the 'small half' next dose" so that things even out. In the book, and on his website, http://HowToSaveOnDrugs .com, Jardini has created a great table he calls the "Expensive Drug Survival Index." It indicates whether drugs are suitable for splitting as well as other ways to save on different name brands.

BIG SECRET

Save Not Just by What's Written But How It's Written

Ask your doctor to write "Use as directed" instead of detailed dosing instructions if you want to split pills.

Some insurance companies don't allow you to get more than a month's supply of medicine at a time. If your strategy is to get 30 higher-dose pills and split them so they last two months, that could be a problem. Exactly how you take those pills can be a private matter between you and your doctor. Ask your doctor to explain the pill-splitting protocol during your office visit instead of on the prescription pad.

Pill Growing   Don't worry, I am not going to tell you to plant your pills and water them in hopes that they will sprout little baby pills and save you money. I coined the term pill growing to describe another practice that can help you SAVE BIG on prescriptions—namely, taking one big pill instead of a bunch of little pills. Since many pills cost the same amount, regardless of the actual milligram strength, this concept works in reverse, too.

Often, a doctor will start you on a low dose of a medicine and then ramp up the dosage as your needs become clear. At first, it might make sense to just take more of the tablets you already have, to use them up. But if you keep doing it that way, you are wasting money. Say you are on the antidepressant Celexa. A single 10-milligram pill costs $3.30. A single 40-milligram pill costs $3.60. So if you take four of the 10-milligram pills, you are paying nearly four times as much as if you take one 40-milligram pill! *Grow* your pills and check out the savings on an annual basis:

 Pill Growing

Four 10-milligram pills/day	$ 4,820
One 40-milligram pill/day	1,314
BIG SAVINGS =	**$3,506**

Believe it or not, many doctors don't think of this idea. I can remember swallowing a whole handful of the same pill years ago because a doc didn't think it through. In five minutes you can research the cost of different strengths of pills at a website like RXaminer.com or DestinationRX.com. The two sites are corporate relatives, but organized differently. Choose the one that makes sense to you.

Pill Counting   It's possible to save yet more money by craftily choosing the count—how many pills you get dispensed at one time. Apparently, pharmacies have their own tipping points—the numbers of pills that are convenient and cost effective for them to dole out. So, for example, the price per pill at one pharmacy may be way lower if you get 90 at a time than if you get 30 at a time. While at another pharmacy, the ideal number could be 120 pills. Thanks to Internet cost comparison websites, it's easy to check this out. They usually list the price for 30, 60, 90, or 120 days' worth of pills. Just do the math to figure out the price per pill and ask your doctor to prescribe that amount.

Where to Get Your Medications

Once you've straightened out *which* medications you're going to take in *what* strength, the next layer of savings is *where* you get them. If you are one of those people who drive straight from the doctor's office to the closest pharmacy to fill your prescription, hold up! That may be fine if it's a prescription you won't be taking for long and if you have insurance, but if you take some medicines regularly, it pays to shop around.

Brick-and-Mortar Stores

Consumer Reports did an admirable study in which researchers called around to 163 stores around the country and asked the prices of four popular prescription drugs. They found fascinating—and expensive—differences. A store in Billings, Montana, was charging $257 for a common osteoporosis medicine. The identical drug was just $160 in Omaha, Nebraska, at a store in the *same* chain! *Consumer Reports* found a difference of 26 percent between the most expensive chain and the least expensive one in its study.

Clearly, shopping around is worth it, and I have good news! You can shop around without leaving the house. The website DestinationRX.com lists prices at both online pharmacies and brick-and-mortar pharmacies. Just watch for occasional notices saying the prices are not guaranteed. In that case you will want to call the pharmacy to confirm.

The big players in the pharmacy world are able to pass their bulk discounts on to consumers. Here's a look at some specific chains and how you can take advantage of what they have to offer.

Costco   I'll tell you right now, the least expensive pharmacy in the *Consumer Reports* study was Costco. And here's a nifty secret: You don't have to be a Costco club member to buy prescriptions at the warehouse store! You just march right up, and when the employee at the entrance asks for your membership card, explain that you are going to the pharmacy. You can also purchase prescriptions at www.Costco.com, which seems to have very competitive Web prices.

Walmart When Walmart announced it would sell nearly 300 of the most common generic prescriptions for just $4, it rocked the pharmacy world. I did more than one story for *Good Morning America* exploring the news. Walmart has now expanded the list to nearly 350 medications. The mega chain was able to do this because of its tremendous buying power. And that gives *you* some buying power. It's always worth checking to see if a medication you take is on the magic list.

Walmart's move even upended people's expectations about insurance! Suddenly, you could get many prescriptions at Walmart for $4, which is less than the average copay of close to $13. Can you imagine? Skipping your insurance and paying *cash* for medicine? I now recommend checking exactly that for every prescription you fill regularly. Which is cheaper, the $4 Walmart price or your copay?

Many other stores have now matched Walmart's bold move. Archrival Target is one of them. Kroger is another. Kmart offers $5 generic prescriptions. Some Kmart locations also match the prices of competitor pharmacies within a certain radius. So if Walmart is not convenient for you, you have other options. Ask or they won't tell.

Look into Drug Discount Cards

Drug discount cards allow you to purchase approved drugs for 15 to 40 percent off. The Together RX Access card is the broadest, offering close to 300 brand-name meds plus a pile of generics from several different manufacturers. To qualify, you must not be eligible for Medicare. For more information, visit www.TogetherRXAccess .com. Medical manufacturers, who do not participate in this discount card, may have others of their own.

Online Pharmacies

Don't discount online pharmacies as a place to fill your prescriptions because boy, can they discount for you! I'm a little creeped out by the idea of ordering medications over the Internet, but there is a way to scope out the legitimate online pharmacies. The National Association of Boards of Pharmacy (NABP) developed an accreditation program for them. Look for the VIPPS seal on the site, which stands for "Verified Internet Pharmacy Practice Site." If you click on the seal, you should be linked to the NABP for verification. This designation assures that the online pharmacy complies with the licensing and inspection requirements of the state where it is located.

If you're still not comfortable with an online pharmacy you've never heard of, consider the cyber arm of a brick-and-mortar retailer you already know. CVS, Eckerd, Walgreens, Rite Aid, and others have websites where prices are often lower than at their *own* stores.

Once you are comfortable that you have found some legitimate online pharmacies, go one step further and compare prices among them. I used a pharmacy comparison website just now to search for the blood pressure medicine Verapamil HCL. I found broad differences in price. Check it out:

Shopping around for Verapamil HCL Online

Highest-priced online pharmacy	$569/year
Lowest-priced online pharmacy	40/year
Dollar savings	$529/year
BIG SAVINGS =	**93%**

So if you spend an extra five minutes you can save $500 and 93 percent? That's worth doing!

Mail-Order Pharmacies

Don't forget about the mail-order pharmacies that many insurance companies provide for their clients. The insurance company execs aren't doing it out of the goodness of their hearts. They steer you to mail-order pharmacies to save their companies money. But it can save *you* money too. For insurance companies, mail-order pharmacies are cheaper because they deal in large volumes, don't have to pay rent for a bunch of retail stores, and don't spend much time counseling patients.

For you, mail-order pharmacies are often cheaper for the same reasons *and* because you can have your doctor write a 90-day prescription and only make one copayment for it. I think this was originally allowed because it takes a while for mail to arrive, so patients needed an ample supply so they wouldn't run out before the next shipment. Whatever the history, if you take multiple meds, this adds up. Let's say your usual copay is $25 and you take five different medications because you have a cluster of related conditions like high cholesterol, high blood pressure, and diabetes. Here's how much even a person with insurance could save per year:

Getting a 90-Day Prescription via Mail Order

Making copayment every 30 days	$1,500
Making copayment every 90 days	500
BIG SAVINGS =	**$1,000**

Not everybody takes that many meds regularly, so consider the percentage saved: 66 percent. Two-thirds. Very helpful.

Pharmaceutical Assistance Programs

The only thing better than getting your prescriptions for the 66 to 93 percent discounts that I have been showing you is getting them for free. That, too, is possible, thanks to pharmaceutical companies that want to help people out—and maybe burnish their reputations a little in the process. The biggest pharmaceutical companies each give away more than $200 million worth of medicine every year, according to Pharmaceutical Research and Manufacturers of America (PhRMA), a trade group.

Beware of Companies That Charge You for Free Medicine

BIG SECRET

Whenever somebody tries to do good, bad guys will piggyback on the cause and try to make some money for themselves. I first heard about pharmaceutical assistance programs when I investigated a crooked company that was pretending to have special connections to the big drug companies and was charging people $200 a month to process their free pharmaceutical assistance program applications. Please! There are a few legitimate outfits that help people with this paperwork, but they charge one-time fees of $5 to $25.

People love to complain about drug companies, but here's an example of how they sometimes help people. Veronica W. of Kentucky was one of the nation's first female truck drivers. She loved the freedom of the road—and the solid income. But then, one day while she was taking a break at a truck stop, she had a serious stroke. She couldn't drive anymore and eventually lost her insurance. Thanks to drug company assistance programs, she is able to get about $600 worth of crucial medications for free every month.

Nearly every pharmaceutical company offers such a program. Some come with fairly easy paperwork, others are more complicated. These programs are typically only extended to people with no health insurance or at least no prescription drug coverage. To that point, some companies require extensive proof that you are unable to afford the medications on your own. Other companies allow you to join the program even if you have a decent-size income, as long as you are able to prove that the medications are a hardship for you. Once you have qualified, the pharmaceutical company sends the meds to your doctor or pharmacy for you to pick up.

PhRMA, the trade organization for the pharmaceutical industry, has a great clearinghouse service called the Partnership for Prescription Assistance (PPA). This program will link you with the maker of your drug. Go to http://Pparx.org for access to more than 475 different assistance programs. The site is easy to use and will give you a great starting point.

BIG SECRET

Pharmaceutical Company Websites Can Be Sources of Freebies and Discounts

The more commercialized prescription drugs have gotten, the more drug companies have borrowed pages from more common products' playbooks. So figure out who makes the medicines you take routinely and check out their sites. You may see coupons for discounts or even free samples. You then work through your doctor and pharmacy to take advantage of these offers.

Medical Tests Are Prescriptions, Too!

When you go to get an MRI or a blood test, you get a prescription for that, too. So guess what? Some of the same savings principles that I discussed earlier in this chapter apply to medical tests: shopping around and going online. If you are uninsured or are insured but have to make a substantial coinsurance payment, it's worth it to shop around for medical tests. Members of Medical Billing Advocates of America say the difference in price from one facility to another could be 20 to 60 percent.

Shopping Around for Tests

Ingrid C. of California had tried everything to relieve shooting sciatic pain that started when she was pregnant. Acupuncture. Massage. Medications. But that singular pain that starts in the base of your spine and then shoots down your leg continued. No fun. Ingrid needed an MRI to determine if she had a ruptured disk or if something else was causing her sciatic pain. Her doctor gave her a prescription for the precise type of MRI she needed. Since she's a shopper by nature, this beautiful, brilliant woman decided to shop around. Why not for an MRI? Here's what Ingrid encountered:

> ### Shopping Around for an MRI
>
> | | |
> |---|---|
> | Top price | $4,000 |
> | Bottom price | 1,500 |
> | **BIG SAVINGS =** | **$2,500** |

By shopping around for an MRI, Ingrid was able to save $2,500, which is 63 percent. That's even more than the experts promised!

Get Help Estimating Healthcare Costs

The website www.HealthProponent.com offers a service called "Health Cost Estimator." The service helps you shop around for medical procedures. Health Advocate, parent of Health Proponent, says common medical procedures like colonoscopies can vary in price by as much as 100 percent. You can call around on your own or get help from a service like this.

Going to an Online Lab

I know it sounds weird, but you can save money on lab tests by using an online lab. No, you don't have to bleed (or worse) on your computer. You go to a local facility to have blood drawn or give a urine sample and then the vials are sent to the online lab for analysis. These services are available direct to consumers, so you can even opt to get testing done privately and then share it with your doctor when and if you choose to.

The website www.MyMedLab.com claims it can save customers up to 75 percent off of regular lab prices. Another online lab with a high Better Business Bureau rating as of this writing is http://PrivateMDLabs.com. You can check the reputations of other online businesses by going to www.BBB.org.

BIG TIPS

- Take the insurance company formulary to your appointment.
- Research drug prices online, then have your doctor phone in a prescription.
- Go generic to save the most money of all.
- Ask for old drugs instead of new ones, including those that are now over-the-counter.
- Split, grow, and count pills.
- Shop around among brick-and-mortar and online pharmacies.
- Fill a 90-day prescription through your insurance company's mail order pharmacy for a single copay.
- Tap into free pharmaceutical industry prescription programs at Pparx.org.
- Shop around for medical tests and lab tests, too.

CHAPTER 29

Haggling with Hospitals

Even if you've picked a good health plan, negotiated with your doctor, and navigated your prescriptions, you could still land in the hospital. The bad news is that it's going to cost a lot of money. The good news is you can save a lot of money. Hospital bills are your fourth and final opportunity to save on healthcare. After all, they are legendarily inaccurate. According to Medical Billing Advocates of America, as many as 80 percent of patients' bills contain errors. It's not that hospitals are crooked. It's that their bills are *complicated*. It may sound daunting to deal with, but I'm going to explain where to get professional help—for free.

If you think high hospital bills don't affect you because you have a great insurance plan, let me make my little speech again. Because of deductibles and lifetime limits, *your* money is at stake. A serious surgery and recovery can easily run $200,000. If you owe a coinsurance payment of 20 percent, that's $40,000. Big bucks. More philosophically, when hospitals overcharge insurance companies, everybody's premiums go up. But if you pay attention—before, during, and after your trip to the hospital—you can SAVE BIG.

In this chapter, learn to SAVE BIG by:

- Shopping for hospitals and negotiating a discount in advance.
- Comparing your medical *bill* with your medical *record* and demanding corrections.
- Enlisting the patient advocate to help you fight her own hospital.
- Hiring a professional bill-fighter who will help you—for nothing.

Before You Go

Have you ever been hospitalized? If it was an emergency, you get a free pass. But if you knew in advance that you were going to the hospital, did you ask for an itemized estimate of the charges? Me neither. Yet when I retiled my bathroom, I insisted on a written estimate. When I got the tie rod ends in my car replaced I demanded one (not that I understood it). We need to do the same before we head to the hospital. This is what I mean when I say we should behave as consumers, not as patients. No more blindly following "doctor's orders."

Hospital Fees

When you learn you need to be hospitalized for a procedure, find out if your doctor has privileges at multiple hospitals and could perform this procedure at any of them. If so, you can shop around and see which facility has the lowest charges for all the support your doctor needs when treating you: the operating theater, the recovery room, the nurses, and so on. Often community hospitals are less expensive than university teaching hospitals.

Next, make sure the hospital with the lowest costs accepts your insurance, if you have it. Then ask the hospital what is included in its fee. Speak to the medical professionals, not the billing department. Get a detailed breakdown in writing, complete with CPT codes. Remember, those are the codes that identify different medical procedures. As we discussed in Chapter 27, you can use those CPT codes to look up what Medicare charges for a service. Add up the Medicare charges and keep them in mind as you broach the subject of price with the hospital.

The Best Way to Save on Hospital Costs Is to Not Go to the Hospital

According to the Kaiser Family Foundation, 31 percent of all healthcare costs are hospital costs. Many procedures can be safely performed at outpatient facilities or surgery centers these days. Ask whether this is a possibility for you. The surgery center may even be run by a hospital, but it's still bound to be cheaper.

Now ask the hospital if it's willing to offer you a flat fee or a percentage discount for the procedure you need. A Harris Interactive poll showed that 70 percent of people who ask a hospital for a break do get a discount. So go for it!

Michelle Katz, author of *Healthcare for Less*—and a person who's had some harrowing personal experiences in hospitals—says flat fees are usually a better deal because then your rate is locked in. A flat fee may even include anesthesia, if needed. Lastly, compare the flat fee or percentage discount to the Medicare rate to decide whether to bargain further. If you need to bring the price down some more, offer to pay cash in advance if you can.

Insurance Precautions

Once you feel you've done all you can with the price, you need to take two more steps regarding insurance. It's not enough to know that your main doctor and the hospital are on your plan. You will also need to make sure that everybody treating you accepts your insurance. Here's a list of other professionals you could encounter who must be on your plan in order for you to receive full coverage.

- Anesthesiologist.
- Radiologist (many hospitals now use a specialist to read X-rays).
- Psychiatrist (if you have a psychiatric consultation for any reason).
- Dermatologist (if you get bedsores while at the hospital, you might see one).
- Infectious diseases specialist (if you develop an infection while hospitalized).
- Laboratory (if your materials are sent to an outside lab).
- Physical therapist.
- Occupational therapist.

Most insurance companies require you to get their permission before being hospitalized for a nonemergency procedure. Get this precertification in writing! E-mail will do. In his book *Get Clark Smart*, radio host and consumer advocate Clark Howard says, "You almost need to complete a checklist to avoid financial disaster." To prove his point, he recounts the frequent complaints he gets from patients who got verbal authorization for a procedure, only to have the insurance company renege later. He tells the story of a woman who thought she had her insurance company's approval before having a hysterectomy. She didn't—and ended up owing $3,500 out of pocket instead of $200. Ouch! Remember, the proof is in the paperwork.

While You're There

Once you're at the hospital, there's more work to be done to SAVE BIG. Hospitals often bill for services that weren't actually rendered. Part of the problem is that the data goes into the bill when a doctor enters an order, not when the service is actually delivered. If tests are canceled or meds refused, the information may not make it back to the billing department.

To avoid this problem, I recommend that you keep a log of events while you're at the hospital—doctors who visit, meds you're given, meals you eat or don't eat. If you're not up to keeping your own log, this is a good, constructive task for family and friends who are there to support you. Don't rely on your memory. Hospital bills can take months to arrive.

Bring Your Own Supplies to the Hospital

You've heard of the $30,000 hammer? Well, just like the government, hospitals can have expensive supplies. So if you take medications routinely, ask your doctor if you can bring your own home supply rather than buying them from the hospital. Also bring things like your own toothbrush and slippers. Medical devices like crutches and support garments are often cheaper on the outside, too. You may meet resistance from hospitals worried about liability, but bring everything that you can from home.

Since we're on the subject of the written word, while you're at the hospital, check to make sure that every teeny, tiny detail of your admission paperwork is accurate. One wrong digit in a Social Security number, one wrong letter in a name, and your insurance company will deny that you exist and refuse to pay.

You should also put in a request for a copy of your complete medical records. This is the minute-by-minute documentation of everything that was done to treat you. The substantial copying cost is worth it because it will help you SAVE BIG later.

Along with that, ask for an itemized bill. They are separate. All states now require hospitals to provide an itemized bill upon request. You wouldn't pay your credit card bill if the bank just sent you the total, would you? You need a pages-long bill that spells out what each step in your treatment cost. You—or preferably a professional whom you hire—will then compare and contrast the medical *record* with the medical *bill* to look for expensive errors.

Which brings me to the final to-do for your hospital stay—besides getting better! Ask to be introduced to the patient advocate or ombudsman. This could be an individual or a team. Most hospitals now have people in place who help patients navigate the hospital. You want to meet this person and tell them how much you value what they do, because you might desperately need their assistance soon.

Apply for Free-Care Funds

If you are uninsured, and you end up in the hospital, inquire about free-care funds. Private individuals make donations for this very purpose. Not all hospitals have them but many do. There is also something called the Hill-Burton program, in which the federal government provides money for certain hospitals to give free or low-cost care. You can find out about Hill-Burton programs at www.hrsa.gov/hillburton.

Hospital Billing Errors

You've heard the scary news about medical mistakes that harm patients, but for the purposes of *this* book what I find scary are medical *billing* mistakes that harm patients. Let me tell you more about Michelle Katz, who I mentioned earlier. I profiled Michelle for a *Good Morning America* story. Michelle is a hotshot healthcare savings author with a master's degree in nursing. Little did she know she was one day going to have to use her expertise to help her own husband.

One day, as the couple sat and talked, Michelle noticed her husband's face turning gray and his skin going cold. Then he went stiff.

Her nurse's training flooded back and she started CPR. She thrust so hard that she cracked her husband's ribs—necessary force that let her compressions reach his heart. For 16 minutes Michelle pumped life into his body until, finally, the ambulance came and took him to the hospital, where he would stay for more than a week and get critical care.

It was a rare type of heart attack that few people survive, but against all odds, he lived. Michelle had saved his life. Now she turned to saving on his medical bills. She felt a duty to fight the mistakes and overcharges that she teaches her readers about in her books *Healthcare for Less* and *101 Health Insurance Tips*. Here are the mistakes Michelle found, some of the most classic hospital billing blunders:

- **Incorrect admission and release dates.** The hospital staff had billed Michelle's husband for a bunch of procedures the day *before* the heart attack happened. What are they, psychic?
- **Misplaced decimals.** At the hospital, he had been given a medication that normally costs about $87.40, but he was billed $874 for it! Often billing clerks just hit an extra digit by mistake or misplace a decimal.
- **Fat fingers.** This is what they call it when a data entry clerk hits the "Enter" key too many times. In this case, Michelle spotted a medication that was listed seven times even though it's supposed to be given a maximum of four times daily. Any more than that would have been an overdose.
- **Erroneous medications.** Michelle noticed that her husband's bill included a charge for pills. But he had a breathing tube in his mouth and couldn't take pills. All meds were given intravenously.
- **Medical mistakes.** The hospital caused an IV infection in her husband's arm, and then charged for the extra day he was forced to stay because of it. Patients shouldn't have to pay for the care required to undo medical mistakes, but it happens frequently.

The Rest of the Worst

Those were just the billing errors experienced by one patient in one hospital in one week. Here are other common mistakes, as reported by medical billing experts who help patients fight inflated hospital bills.

- **Charges for things that are supposed to be included.** Supplies like syringes, IV tubing, and gauze are usually included in the cost of the room.
- **Up-coding.** This is where a hospital bumps a procedure up to the next code level and charges for something more complicated which costs more.
- **Wrong ICD-9 code.** This stands for International Classification of Diseases. It's a diagnosis and it needs to be right or an insurance company will deny coverage. For example, the hospital may list the code for "tumor" when your record should show "cancer," which is more serious.
- **Wrong operating room time.** It's common for hospitals to claim you were in the operating room longer than you actually were.
- **Private room charge.** Sometimes patients are charged for a private room when they were really in a shared room or when they were placed in a private room only because all shared rooms were full.
- **Room fee on the day of discharge.** Traditionally, since discharge day is not a full day, there should be no room charge, same as a hotel.
- **Inaccurate personal information.** Hospitals often misspell names or transpose Social Security numbers, and then the insurance company refuses to pay.
- **Wrong patient ID number.** This is the number you're assigned during your hospital stay. It's usually on your wristband. If they put the wrong one on your bill, it's trouble.
- **Unauthorized procedures.** Things the doctor didn't order.
- **Phantom services.** Services the patient did not receive.
- **Canceled work.** The doctor's orders are entered immediately, but if those orders are canceled, the cancellation may not make it into the record.
- **Duplicate claims.** If the hospital doesn't get paid quickly, it may resubmit the claim and then the insurance company may reject both claims because they are duplicates.
- **Doctor's ID number missing.** Insurance companies often reject bills if the doctor's official federal ID number is missing or hard to find.

- **Place of service missing.** Insurance companies want to know where you were treated and whether it was a hospital or out-patient facility.
- **Meals.** You are typically charged for every meal even if you refuse it. Record meals in your log.

Fighting Back

Back to Michelle Katz's story. Her husband's bill was $200,000. The first headache was when the insurance company refused to cover it because the hospital had misspelled his name. Once that was straightened out, the couple still owed 10 percent of the bill. That's $20,000. Ouch. Michelle went to work. First she attacked the five billing errors she had spotted. Then she negotiated a discount for her husband's care. Here's an approximation of what she managed to achieve:

Fighting the Hospital Bill

Patient's portion	$ 20,000
Errors deleted	5,000
Charges forgiven	6,000
BIG SAVINGS =	**$11,000**

In the end, after months of back and forth, Michelle knocked about $11,000 off of that imposing hospital bill—more than half.

The Inside Track

I don't think it's worthwhile to fight a hospital bill without help. It's mind-numbing and soul-crushing. Michelle Katz did it, but she's a healthcare savings expert—and one of the most determined people I've ever met.

You can start the process by eliciting help from the patient advocate, a hospital employee whose job is to help you fight the hospital, if necessary. Remember, I told you you'd need this individual! The patient advocate may be willing to contact the doctors involved in your care and ask them for discounts on your behalf.

You can also formally appeal the *hospital* portion of your bill. Remember, 70 percent of patients who asked for a reduction in their bill were successful. Asking in advance is easier, but it's important to fight after the fact as well. With the help of the patient advocate, take your request to the hospital administrator—not the billing department. Billing departments are there to—you guessed it—collect bills. Some billing clerks may even be paid on commission, especially if the hospital outsources its billing.

If you do want to try to get your hospital bills reduced on your own—which I think is a rough road—the website http://BillAdvocates.com provides helpful resources. Click the "My Medical Bill" tab. For a membership fee of approximately $50, you will get access to a dictionary of medical billing terms, sample dispute letters, and other important links to educate yourself about the process. If all that is not enough, you can hire an advocate through the site. More on that option in a moment.

Pay Your Doctor to Explain Your Bill

This is a trick that has worked for Michelle Katz. I think it would work particularly well for a small-scale dispute. Try paying cash for an appointment with your doctor and asking him to explain your bill. Your doctor ought to be able to tell you what all the different codes and abbreviations mean. Sometimes doctors are so shocked at the total price that they offer to reduce their own portion on the spot!

Hiring Help

They go by many names—claims assistance professional, medical claims professional, healthcare claims advocate, medical billing advocate—but those who have hired one have another word: godsend. These pros know how to read a murky medical bill, spot the glaring errors, and negotiate on your behalf. Some charge an hourly fee, ranging from $25 to $150, for their work, but others work on contingency. You pay nothing unless they negotiate a lower payment for you! That means they are highly motivated to do just that. They then charge a percentage of the amount they saved you—15 to 35 percent is typical.

Cynthia K. of Florida thought being diagnosed with breast cancer was the worst thing that could happen to her. But then the hospital where she had her 40-minute lumpectomy overcharged her. Before the operation, the hospital told her it would cost $5,000. Instead she got a bill for $12,700—right in the middle of her devastating course of chemotherapy. To make matters worse, Cynthia, an artist, was uninsured.

Desperate for help, she hired a medical billing advocate. Her advocate found all sorts of classic errors. The hospital had billed Cynthia for two first hours in the operating room. How many first hours can there be? There were drugs listed on the medical *bill* even though they weren't in Cynthia's medical *record*. And the hospital had charged Cynthia $192 for a postoperative support bra that her advocate was able to find for just $19 on the Internet! Here's what this skillful, passionate advocate was able to do for Cynthia:

 How the Medical Billing Advocate Helped

Original hospital bill	$ 12,710
Negotiated hospital bill	5,852
BIG SAVINGS =	**$ 6,858**

With attention to detail—and a dose of determination—Cynthia's advocate cut her bill by $6,858—more than half.

Pay Your Hospital Bill or You Could Hear from Debt Collectors

The medical community used to benevolently write off unpaid bills. But times are tight and more and more hospitals are hiring debt collectors. The hospital is unlikely to report your unpaid bill to the credit bureaus, but you can bet a debt collector will. So, by all means, fight the errors on your bills to get them reduced, but then find a way to pay the remainder that you owe.

How to Find an Advocate

Because healthcare claims advocates go by so many names, (to repeat, they call themselves claims assistance professionals, medical claims professionals, healthcare claims advocates, medical billing advocates) it can be confusing to search for them on the Internet. When searching, keep in mind that auditing a medical bill is mostly paper and phone work, so your advocate doesn't have to be located in the same area as you.

Here are several sources of professionals who can help you:

- **Medical Billing Advocates of America**: http://BillAdvocates .com.
- **Alliance of Claims Assistance Professionals**: http://Claims.org.
- **Patient Advocate Foundation**: http://PatientAdvocate.org.
- **Healthcare Advocates, Inc.**: http://HealthcareAdvocates.com.
- **Health Proponent**: www.HealthProponent.com.
- **Care Counsel**: http://CareCounsel.com. (This service is only available through employers, so check with your HR department to see if your company participates.)

BIG TIPS

- If your doctor has privileges at multiple hospitals, find out which is the cheapest.
- Make sure the hospital—and every doctor treating you—accepts your insurance.
- Try to negotiate a flat fee or percentage discount in advance.
- Request your complete medical record and itemized medical bill and compare the two.
- Appeal your bill to the patient advocate, ombudsman, or hospital administrator—not the billing department.
- Hire a professional to fight your hospital bills for you.

Conclusion

As you have seen, if you set out to SAVE BIG (not small), you will save *more* money in *less* time.

I demonstrated $1,176,916 worth of BIG SAVINGS in this book by cutting our top five costs: houses, cars, credit, groceries, and healthcare. You would have to install low-flow showerheads in 200 houses for 65 years, adequately inflate the tires of five cars for 282 years, not go to other banks' ATMs 59,113 times, pack your lunch every workday for the next 12 years, and give up 1,783 magazine subscriptions to achieve that savings!

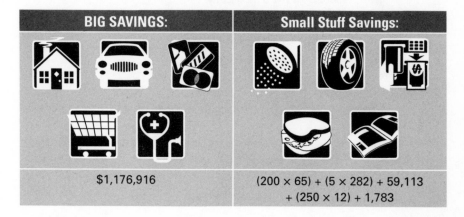

BIG SAVINGS:	Small Stuff Savings:
$1,176,916	$(200 \times 65) + (5 \times 282) + 59,113 + (250 \times 12) + 1,783$

Besides, those are the little pleasures that keep the big responsibilities from bumping into each other. What would life be without strong showers and hot coffee? Without long lunches and juicy magazines? I'm not saying you should go crazy indulging yourself with every single little expenditure; I'm just saying Small Stuff Savings are not the best road to riches.

And yet plenty of authors say they are. So, for one last time, let's do the math.

If you pursued the Small Stuff Savings we so often hear about—showerheads, tires, ATMs, lunches, magazines—your total savings per year would be $4,007 for a family of four. Let's say you managed to keep this up for 40 years and invested the money you saved, earning a 10 percent rate of return. After 40 years, you would have $1,950,815. That sounds pretty impressive.

But now watch what happens when you SAVE BIG on your top five costs—houses, cars, credit, groceries, and health care. Yes, I showed you $1,176,916 worth of savings in the pages of this book, but not every BIG SAVINGS technique is meant to be used every year. So since we're talking about a 40-year time period, let's be conservative and say you save one-fortieth of my total each year. That would be $29,423 a year.

If you invested that $29,423 each year, after 40 years—at that same 10 percent rate of return—you would have $14,324,641!

 ## BIG SAVINGS

- *Yes, $14,324,641!*
- I think I've proved my point.
- My work here is done.

Index